Lecture Notes in Computer Science 2382

Edited by G. Goos, J. Hartmanis, and J. van Leeuwen

Springer
Berlin
Heidelberg
New York
Barcelona
Hong Kong
London
Milan
Paris
Tokyo

Alon Halevy   Avigdor Gal (Eds.)

Next Generation Information Technologies and Systems

5th International Workshop, NGITS 2002
Caesarea, Israel, June 24-25, 2002
Proceedings

 Springer

Series Editors

Gerhard Goos, Karlsruhe University, Germany
Juris Hartmanis, Cornell University, NY, USA
Jan van Leeuwen, Utrecht University, The Netherlands

Volume Editors

Alon Halevy
University of Washington, Department of Computer Science and Engineering
Sieg Hall, Room 310, Mailstop 352350, Seattle, WA, 98195, USA
E-mail:alon@cs.washington.edu

Avigdor Gal
Technion – Israel Institute of Technology
William Davidson Faculty of Industrial Engineering and Management
Technion City 3200, Haifa, Israel
E-mail:avigal@ie.technion.ac.il

Cataloging-in-Publication Data applied for

Die Deutsche Bibliothek - CIP-Einheitsaufnahme

Next generation information technologies and systems : 5th international
workshop ; proceedings / NGITS 2002, Caesarea, Israel, June 24 - 25, 2002.
Alon Halevy ; Avigdor Gal (ed.). - Berlin ; Heidelberg ; New York ;
Barcelona ; Hong Kong ; London ; Milan ; Paris ; Tokyo : Springer, 2002
   (Lecture notes in computer science ; Vol. 2382)
   ISBN 3-540-43819-X

CR Subject Classification (1998): H.4, H.3, H.5, H.2, D.2.12, C.2.4

ISSN 0302-9743
ISBN 3-540-43819-X Springer-Verlag Berlin Heidelberg New York

Springer-Verlag Berlin Heidelberg New York
a member of BertelsmannSpringer Science+Business Media GmbH

http://www.springer.de

© Springer-Verlag Berlin Heidelberg 2002
Printed in Germany

Typesetting: Camera-ready by author, data conversion by PTP Berlin, Stefan Sossna e. K.
Printed on acid-free paper   SPIN 10870481   06/3142   5 4 3 2 1 0

Preface

NGITS 2002 was the fifth workshop of its kind, promoting papers that discuss new technologies in information systems. Following the success of the four previous workshops (1993, 1995, 1997, and 1999), the fifth NGITS Workshop took place on June 24–25, 2002, in the ancient city of Caesarea.

In response to the Call for Papers, 22 papers were submitted. Each paper was evaluated by three Program Committee members. We accepted 11 papers from 3 continents and 5 countries, Israel (5 papers), US (3 papers), Germany, Cyprus, and The Netherlands (1 paper from each).

The workshop program consisted of five paper sessions, two keynote lectures, and one panel discussion. The topics of the paper sessions are: Advanced Query Processing, Web Applications, Moving Objects, Advanced Information Models, and Advanced Software Engineering.

We would like to thank all the authors who submitted papers, the program committee members, the presenters, and everybody who assisted in making NGITS 2002 a reality.

June 2002   Alon Halevy, Avigdor Gal

NGITS 2002 Conference Organization

Program Committee Co-chairs: Alon Halevy (University of Washington, Washington, USA)
Avigdor Gal (Technion, Israel)
Local Arrangements Chair: Nilly Schnapp (Technion, Israel)
Steering Committee: Opher Etzion (IBM Haifa Research Lab, Israel)
Ami Motro (George Mason University, Virginia, USA)
Arie Segev (U.C. Berkeley, USA)
Ron Y. Pinter (Technion, Israel)
Avi Silberschatz (Bell Laboratories, New Jersey, USA)
Peretz Shoval (Ben-Gurion University, Israel)
Moshe Tennenholtz (Technion, Israel)
Shalom Tsur (BEA Systems Inc., California, USA)

NGITS 2002 Program Committee

Table of Contents

The Fifth Workshop on Next Generation Information Technologies and Systems (NGITS'2002)

Enabling Design-Centric eBusiness Applications

Arie Segev

Haas School of Business
University of California, Berkeley, CA 94720-1900
segev@haas.berkeley.edu

This talk discusses a research project on models for supporting of end-to-end eBusiness processes associated with design-centric applications. Design-centric applications are those where various business processes are initiated in the context of a design process. Our focus is on ad-hoc design environments that are characterized by collaborative processes among the initiators of the design and other players involved in moving the conceptual design to an actual implementation. This project is done in collaboration with the department of architecture, and the specific domain chosen for it is office design (either Business-to-Business or Business-to-Consumer). The conceptual results, however, apply to numerous other domains such as contract manufacturing, general construction projects, and designing and building one-of-a-kind complex products. The project examines next-generation eBusiness models and processes that best support collaborative office design, procurement of products and services, negotiations, and implementing (or building) the contacted solutions. A prototype system will be described and various implementation alternatives discussed.

A. Halevy and A. Gal (Eds.): NGITS 2002, LNCS 2382, p. 1, 2002.
© Springer-Verlag Berlin Heidelberg 2002

Select-Project Queries over XML Documents[*]

Sara Cohen, Yaron Kanza, and Yehoshua Sagiv

Dept. of Computer Science,
The Hebrew University,
Jerusalem 91904, Israel
{sarina, yarok, sagiv}@cs.huji.ac.il

Abstract. This paper discusses evaluation of select-project (SP) queries over an XML document. A SP query consists of two parts: (1) a conjunction of conditions on values of labels (called the *selection*) and (2) a series of labels whose values should be outputed (called the *projection*). Query evaluation involves finding tuples of nodes that have the labels mentioned in the query and are related to one another other in a meaningful fashion. Several different semantics for query evaluation are given in this paper. Some of these semantics also take into account the possible presence of incomplete information. The complexity of query evaluation is analyzed and evaluation algorithms are described.

1 Introduction

Increasingly large amounts of data are accessible to the general public in the form of XML documents. It is difficult for the naive user to query XML and thus, potentially useful information may not reach its audience. Search engines are currently the only efficient way to query the Web. These engines do not exploit the structure of documents and hence, are not well suited for querying XML.

As a long-term goal, we would like to allow a natural-language interface for querying XML. It has been noted that the universal relation [9,12,13] is a first step towards facilitating natural-language querying of relational databases. This is because of the inherent simplicity of formulating a query against the universal relation. Such queries usually consist of only selection and projection and are called *select-project* or *SP* queries. Evaluating queries over the universal relation was studied in [11,7].

Many languages, such as XQuery [3] and XML-QL [6] have been proposed for querying XML. However, these languages are not suitable for a naive user. They also require a rather extensive knowledge of document structure in order to formulate a query correctly. The language EquiX [4] has been proposed for querying XML by a naive user. However, EquiX queries can only be formulated against a document with a DTD. A query language for XML must also take into consideration incomplete information. This has been studied in [2,8].

---

[*] Supported by Grant 96/01-1 from the Israel Science Foundation

A. Halevy and A. Gal (Eds.): NGITS 2002, LNCS 2382, pp. 2–13, 2002.

In this paper we explore the problem of answering an SP query formulated against an XML document. In order to formulate a query, users only need to know the names of the tags appearing in the document being queried. Queries consist of two parts:

- **Select:** boolean conditions on tags of a document (e.g., title = 'Cat in the Hat');
- **Project:** names of tags whose values should appear in the result (e.g., price).

Answering an SP query requires finding elements in a document that are *related* to one another in a *meaningful fashion*. Intuitively, such sets of elements correspond to rows in a universal relation that could be defined over an XML document. However, there are several questions that arise in this context:

- How can we decide when elements are related in a meaningful fashion? This becomes especially difficult when one considers the fact that documents may have varied structure.
- How can we deal with incompleteness in documents? If a document may be missing information, then we may have to discover whether a particular element is meaningfully related to an element that does not even appear in the document.

This paper deals with these questions.

Section 2 presents some necessary definitions and Section 3 present query semantics. In Sections 4 and 5 we discuss the complexity of answering SP queries over XML documents and present algorithms for query evaluation. Section 6 concludes.

2   Definitions

In this section we present some necessary definitions. We specify our data model and describe the syntax of *select-project* or *SP* queries.

Trees. We assume that there is a set $\mathcal{L}$ of labels and a set $\mathcal{A}$ of constants. An XML document is a tree T in which each *interior node* is associated with a *label* from $\mathcal{L}$ and each *leaf node* is associated with *value* from $\mathcal{A}$. We denote the label of an interior node n by $lbl(n)$ and the value of a leaf node n' by $val(n')$. We extend the *val* function to interior nodes n by defining $val(n)$ to be the concatenation of the values of its leaf descendents. In Figure 1 there is an example of such a tree, describing information about books. The nodes are numbered to allow easy reference.

Let T be a tree and let $n_1, \ldots, n_k$ be nodes in T. We denote by $lca\{n_1, \ldots, n_k\}$ the *lowest common ancestor* of $n_1, \ldots, n_k$. Let T_{lca} be the subtree of T rooted at $lca\{n_1, \ldots, n_k\}$. We denote by $T_{n_1, \ldots, n_k}$ the tree obtained by pruning from T_{lca} all nodes that are not ancestors of any of the nodes $n_1, \ldots, n_k$. We call this tree the *relationship tree* of $n_1, \ldots, n_k$. For example, in Figure 1, $lca\{15, 19, 21\}$ is 13. The relationship tree of 15, 19, 21 contains the nodes 13, 14, 15, 19 and 21.

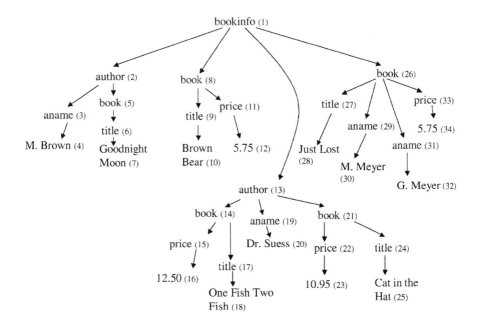

Fig. 1. An XML document describing books for sale

Relations. A *tuple* has the form $t = \{l_1 : a_1, \ldots, l_k : a_k\}$ where l_i and a_i are a *column name* and a *value*, respectively. We will use $l_i(t)$ to denote the value a_i. We call $\{l_1, \ldots, l_k\}$ the *signature* of t. A *relation* R is a set of tuples with the same signature, also called the signature of R.

Let N be a set of nodes in which no two nodes have the same label. Let L be the set of labels of nodes in N. The set N naturally gives rise to a tuple denoted t_N with signature L. Formally, if $n \in N$ and $lbl(n) = l$, then $l(t_N) = n$. Given a set of labels L' that contains L, the set N gives rise to a tuple with signature L', denoted $t_{L',N}$ by padding t_N with null values (denoted $\perp$), as necessary.

Select-Project Queries. A *condition* has the form $l \, \theta \, a$, $a \, \theta \, l$, or $l \, \theta \, l'$ where l, l' are labels, a in a constant, and θ is an operator (e.g., $<$, $=$, $\in$). A *query* has the form

$$q(l_1, \ldots, l_k) \leftarrow c_1 \wedge \cdots \wedge c_n \tag{1}$$

where l_i are labels and c_j are conditions. We do not allow a label to appear more than once among $l_1, \ldots, l_k$. We sometimes denote the above query by $q(l_1, \ldots, l_k)$ or simply by q. We call the conjunction $c_1 \wedge \cdots \wedge c_n$ the *selection* of q and we call the sequence $(l_1, \ldots, l_k)$ the *projection* of q. Note that we allow the selection to be an empty conjunction of conditions. We denote the empty conjunction by $\top$. We call queries with empty selections *project queries*. The set of labels appearing in either the selection or the projection of q is denoted $lbl(q)$. We will say that q is defined *over* the set $lbl(q)$.

Example 1. We present a few queries and their intuitive meaning.

- Pairs of titles and their respective prices:

$$q(\mathsf{title}, \mathsf{price}) \leftarrow \top$$

- Titles and prices of books written by Dr. Suess that cost less than \$12:

$$q(\mathsf{title}, \mathsf{price}) \leftarrow (\mathsf{aname} = \text{'Dr.Suess'}) \wedge (\mathsf{price} < 12)$$

- Title, author and price of books written by Meyer:

$$q(\mathsf{title}, \mathsf{aname}, \mathsf{price}) \leftarrow \text{'Meyer'} \in \mathsf{aname}$$

3   Query Semantics

Consider a query q and a tree T. Suppose that $lbl(q) = \{l_1, \ldots, l_k\}$. Intuitively, we can understand query evaluation as a two-step process. First, compute a relation R which contains tuples of nodes from T with labels $l_1, \ldots, l_k$ that are *related* in a *meaningful fashion*. We call this relation the *relational image* of T with respect to $l_1, \ldots, l_k$ and it is denoted $R(q, T)$. Next, evaluate the selection and projection given in q on $R(q, T)$ to derive the query result.

   In order to compute the relational image of a tree with respect to a set of nodes, we must be able to decide which nodes are related in a meaningful fashion in a given tree. We observe that nodes are not meaningfully related if their relationship tree contains two different nodes with the same label. Intuitively, two nodes in a tree that have the same label correspond to different entities in the world. Thus, in Figure 1, nodes 22 and 24 are related. However, nodes 22 and 27 are not since their relationship tree contains the label book twice. This reflects the intuition that 22 is the price of the book with title 24 and not the price of the book with title 27.

   We formalize this idea. Let $n_1, \ldots, n_k$ be nodes in T. We say that $n_1, \ldots, n_k$ are *interconnected*, denoted $\approx (n_1, \ldots, n_k)$, if the tree $T_{n_1, \ldots, n_k}$ does not contain any two nodes with the same label. We say that N is *maximally interconnected* with respect to a set of labels L if there is no strict superset N' of N with labels from L that is also interconnected. Now, given a query q over labels L, let $\mathcal{S}$ be the set of all sets of maximally interconnected nodes in T with labels from L. The relational image of T w.r.t. L is defined as follows

$$R(q, T) := \{t_{L,N} \mid N \in \mathcal{S}\}.$$

   The relational image of a tree contains nodes that are related to each other. However, some such relationships may be more significant than others. Nodes are more likely to be meaningfully related if their lowest common ancestor is relatively deep in the tree. If their lowest common ancestor is very high, then it is more likely that their relationship is coincidental. Thus, nodes 19 and 24 are more likely to be related then nodes 19 and 27. Note that in both these cases, the relationship trees do not have any repeated labels.

Let N be a set of interconnected nodes. We say that N' is an *improvement* on N, denoted $N \prec N'$ if

- $N \setminus N' = \{n_1\}$, $N' \setminus N = \{n_2\}$, $lbl(n_1) = lbl(n_2)$, i.e., N' is derived from N by replacing n_1 with n_2;
- For all nodes n in $N \cap N'$, the lowest common ancestor of $\{n_2, n\}$ is a descendent of the lowest common ancestor of $\{n_1, n\}$.

If N is maximal w.r.t. $\prec$, we say that N is $\prec$-*maximal*. We can remove some of the tuples in $R(q, T)$ that may be related in a less significant fashion, using the definition above. Let $\mathcal{S}^{\prec}$ be the set of all sets of maximally interconnected nodes in T that are also $\prec$-maximal. We define the $\prec$-*relational image* of T w.r.t. L as

$$R^{\prec}(q, T) := \{t_{L,N} \mid N \in \mathcal{S}^{\prec}\}.$$

Example 2. Consider the query

$$q(\text{title}, \text{price}) \leftarrow (\text{aname} = \text{'Dr. Suess'}) \wedge (\text{price} < 12).$$

The $\prec$-relational image of q over the tree presented in Figure 1 is

title	aname	price
Goodnight Moon	M. Brown	$\perp$
Brown Bear	$\perp$	5.75
One Fish Two Fish	Dr. Suess	12.50
Cat in the Hat	Dr. Suess	10.95
Just Lost	M. Meyer	5.75
Just Lost	G. Meyer	5.75

We extend the function *val* to sets of tuples of nodes in the natural fashion. Note that the tuple

$$(\text{'One Fish Two Fish'}, \text{'Dr. Suess'}, 10.95) = val(17, 19, 22)$$

is not in $R^{\prec}(q, T)$, since its relationship tree contains the same label twice. The tuple

$$(\text{'Just Lost'}, \text{'Dr. Suess'}, 5.75) = val(27, 19, 33)$$

is also not in $R^{\prec}(q, T)$ since $(27, 19, 33) \prec (27, 31, 33)$. However, ('Just Lost', 'Dr. Suess', 5.75) is in $R(q, T)$.

When computing the result of a query, we may be interested in tuples that are related in a less or more significant fashion. Thus, we consider evaluating queries over both the relational image and the $\prec$-relational image of a tree. Note that both $R(q,T)$ and $R^{\prec}(q,T)$ can contain null values. Let $R_s(q,T)$ be the tuples in $R(q,T)$ that do not contain null values. We define $R_s^{\prec}(q,T)$ similarly. We differentiate between *strong query results*, which are derived from tuples which do not contain null values, and *weak query results*, which may be derived from tuples with null values. We extend the function *val* to sets of tuples of nodes in the natural fashion.

The *strong* result of a query $q(l_1,\dots,l_k) \leftarrow c_1 \wedge \dots \wedge c_n$ evaluated over a tree T is defined as

$$q(T)_s := \pi_{l_1,\dots,l_k}(\sigma_{c_1 \wedge \dots \wedge c_n}(val(R_s(q,T)))).$$

We define the $\prec$-*strong* result of evaluating q over T, denoted $q(T)_s^{\prec}$ similarly by substituting $R_s^{\prec}(q,T)$ for $R_s(q,T)$ above. The *weak* result of evaluating q over T is

$$q(T)_w := \pi_{l_1,\dots,l_k}(\sigma_{c_1 \wedge \dots \wedge c_n}(val(R(q,T))))$$

where selection is applied over tuples with null values using standard three-valued logic. We define the $\prec$-*weak* result, denoted $q(T)_w^{\prec}$, similarly.

Example 3. Recall the query q from Example 2. Both the $\prec$-strong and $\prec$-weak query result over the tree in Figure 1 is $\{(\text{'Cat in the Hat'}, 10.95)\}$.

As an additional example, evaluating the query $q(title, aname, price) \leftarrow \top$ will yield the $\prec$-weak query result containing all rows in the relation from Figure 1. The $\prec$-strong query result will contain all rows but the first two.

4   Computing Strong and $\prec$-Strong Query Results

In this section we consider the problem of finding strong query results and $\prec$-strong query results. We show that given a query and a tree, it is NP-complete to determine whether $q(T)_s$ or $q(T)_s^{\prec}$ is non-empty. We then present several different algorithms to compute strong and $\prec$-strong query results.

4.1   Complexity

We show that checking for nodes that are interconnected is NP-complete.

Theorem 1 (NP-Completeness of Interconnectiveness). *Let T be a labeled tree and let $l_1,\dots,l_k$ be a set of labels. Determining whether there are nodes $n_1,\dots,n_k$ in T such that $lbl(n_i) = l_i$ and $\approx(n_1,\dots,n_k)$ is NP-complete.*

Proof. Membership in NP is easy. We show that the problem is NP-hard by a reduction from 3-SAT. Let U be a set of variables and let $F = C_1 \wedge \dots \wedge C_k$ be conjunction of clauses over U such that each C_i is of size 3. We create a tree T from the formula. To simplify, we do not specify values of leaf nodes, since they may be chosen arbitrarily.

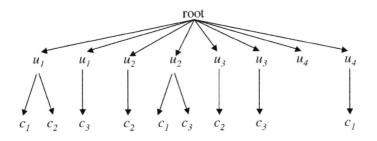

Fig. 2. A tree for an example formula

- The root of T is r and $lbl(r) = $ root.
- For each variable $u \in U$ there are two children of r, namely u_p and u_n. Both nodes have label u.
- For each clause C_i and for each variable u in C_i, if u appears positively in C_i, then node u_p has a child labeled C_i. If u appear negatively in C_i, then node u_n has a child labeled C_i.

As an example, Figure 2 depicts the tree corresponding to the formula $(u_1 \vee \neg u_2 \vee \neg u_4) \wedge (u_1 \vee u_2 \vee u_3) \wedge (\neg u_1 \vee \neg u_2 \vee \neg u_3)$.

Let L be the set of labels $\{C_1, \dots, C_k\}$. It is not difficult to see that F is satisfiable if and only if there are nodes $n_1, \dots, n_k$ such that $lbl(n_i) = C_i$ and $T_{n_1, \dots, n_k}$ does not contain the same label twice.   □

Corollary 1 (Strong Query Results). *Let q be a project query and let T be a tree. Checking whether $q(T)_s$ is nonempty is NP-complete.*

In order to show that checking whether $q(T)_s^{\prec}$ is nonempty is also NP-complete we need a lemma.

Lemma 1. *Let N be a set of interconnected nodes. It is possible to check in polynomial time if N is $\prec$-maximal.*

Proof. We can check if N is $\prec$-maximal in the following fashion. For each node $n_1 \in N$ and for each other node n_2 in T with $lbl(n_1) = lbl(n_2)$ check if the set $N \setminus \{n_1\} \cup \{n_2\}$ is an improvement on N. This can be checked in polynomial time.   □

Corollary 2 ($\prec$-Strong Query Results). *Let q be a project query and let T be a tree. Checking whether $q(T)_s^{\prec}$ is nonempty is NP-complete.*

4.2   Algorithms

In this section we present several different algorithms for computing strong query results. These algorithms can be used to compute $\prec$-strong results by adding a phase in the computation where sets of nodes that are not $\prec$-maximal are discarded. Throughout this discussion, we consider a query q with labels $l_1, \ldots, l_k$ and a selection condition $c_1 \wedge \cdots \wedge c_n$. We present a naive method of computation. We then present two improvements on this method.

Naive Method. We divide query evaluation into two phases. In the first phase, given a tree T, find all k-tuples of nodes in T that have labels from $l_1, \ldots, l_k$. For each such tuple, compute the corresponding relationship tree. Discard the tuple if the relationship tree contains a repeated label. In the second phase, compute the selection and projection from q to yield the query result. Note that it possible to push selection when computing strong query results, but not when computing $\prec$-strong query results.

Incremental Method. We attempt to improve on the first phase of query evaluation, by taking advantage of the following property:

> **The A Priori Property:** Suppose that $\approx (n_1, \ldots, n_k)$. For all subsets, $\{n_{i_1}, \ldots, n_{i_j}\}$ of $\{n_1, \ldots, n_k\}$, it holds that $\approx (n_{i_1}, \ldots, n_{i_j})$.

The Incremental Method builds sets of interconnected nodes with labels $l_1, \ldots, l_k$ incrementally. First, the set $\mathcal{S}_1$, defined below, is computed:

$$\mathcal{S}_1 = \{\{n\} \mid lbl(n) = l_1\}.$$

Then, we compute $\mathcal{S}_{i+1}$ from $\mathcal{S}_i$ in the following fashion

$$\mathcal{S}_{i+1} = \{N \cup \{n\} \mid N \in \mathcal{S}_i \text{ and } lbl(n) = l_{i+1} \text{ and } \approx (N \cup \{n\})\}.$$

Note that when extending $\mathcal{S}_i$ to $\mathcal{S}_{i+1}$, we try extending each set in $\mathcal{S}_i$ with each node labeled l_{i+1}. The set $\mathcal{S}_k$ contains exactly the same sets as those created in phase one of the Naive Method. This method tries fewer combinations of nodes than the Naive Method. However, it is guaranteed not to miss interconnected sets because of the a priori property.

Incremental Tree Walk Method. The Incremental Tree Walk Method improves upon the Incremental Method by not trying to extend each set of nodes in $\mathcal{S}_i$ with all nodes having label l_{i+1}. Instead, for each set N in $\mathcal{S}_i$, we find all nodes labeled l_{i+1} that are interconnected with N by *walking* around the tree surrounding N. Given a set N, these nodes are found as follows. Let L be the labels of the nodes in the relationship tree of N. Let n_0 be an arbitrary node in N. The nodes with label l_{i+1} that extend N to an interconnected set are derived by calling TreeWalk(n_0, l_{i+1}, N, L), presented in Figure 3. Intuitively, TreeWalk walks around the tree in all possible directions in an attempt to find nodes with label l_{i+1}. When a repeated label is found, the walk is terminated.

TreeWalk(n_0, l_{i+1}, N, L)

if $n_0 \notin N$ and $lbl(n_0) \in L$ **then return** $\emptyset$;
if $lbl(n_0) = l_{i+1}$ **then return** $\{n_0\}$;
$Res := \emptyset$;
for each neighbor n of n_0 **do**   /* children and parent of n_0 */
        $Res := Res \cup$ TreeWalk($n, l_{i+1}, N, L \cup \{lbl(n_0)\}$)
return Res

Fig. 3. Incremental step of the Incremental Tree Walk Method

5   Computing Weak Query Results

In this section we consider the problem of finding weak answers to queries. Surprisingly, for project queries, weak answers can be found in polynomial time in the size of the input (i.e., the query and the document tree) and the output. However, the complexity of finding $\prec$-weak answers in still unknown. We present some necessary definitions and then a polynomial algorithm for computing weak answers.

Let N be a set of nodes. If there are no two nodes in N with the same label, we say that N is *proper*. Let N and N' be sets of nodes. We define a special union operator $\uplus$,

$$N \uplus N' := N \cup N' \setminus \{n \in N \mid \exists n' \in N'(lbl(n) = lbl(n'))\}.$$

Note that $\uplus$ is not a symmetric operator and that $N \uplus N'$ is proper if N and N' are proper.

Given a project query q over labels $l_1, \ldots, l_k$, the weak result of applying to a tree T is derived directly from the set $\mathcal{S}$ of sets of maximally interconnected nodes. By calling the procedure ComputeWeakResults($\{l_1, \ldots, l_k\}, T$), presented in Figure 4, we can compute the set $\mathcal{S}$.

We prove that the algorithm is correct with a series of lemmas.

Lemma 2. *If* $N \in$ ComputeWeakResults($\{l_1, \ldots, l_k\}, T$) *then* N *is interconnected.*

Proof. We show that only interconnected sets of nodes are added to $\mathcal{S}$ in the procedure. The sets added in lines 1 and 6 are clearly interconnected since they contain a single node. The set N_4 is proper since N_3 is proper and $N_1 \cup N_2$ is proper. The set N_5 is proper, since it is a subset of N_4 and it is also connected. Therefore, N_5 is interconnected. Clearly, $n_0 \in N_5$. Therefore, $(N_5 \cap N) \cup \{n_0\} \subseteq N_5$, added in line 15, is interconnected. $\square$

Lemma 3. *Let N be a set of interconnected nodes and let $n_{lca} := lca\{N\}$. Suppose that $n \in N$ and N contains at least two nodes. Then, there is a node $n' \in N$ such that $n \neq n'$ and $n_{lca} = lca\{n, n'\}$.*

Proof. Suppose that $N = \{n_1, \dots, n_k, n\}$. We define $n_{lca}^i := lca\{n, n_i\}$ for $i \leq k$. Note that since n_{lca}^i is an ancestor of n for all i, all the nodes n_{lca}^i lay on a single path. Let n_j be a node such that n_{lca}^j is an ancestor of n_{lca}^i for all i. Clearly, n_{lca}^j is then the lowest common ancestor of N. □

Lemma 4. *If N_{max} is a maximally interconnected set in T w.r.t. the labels $\{l_1, \dots, l_k\}$, then $N_{max} \in$ ComputeWeakResults$(\{l_1, \dots, l_k\}, T)$.*

Proof. We prove this claim by induction on k, the number of labels. For $k = 1$ the claim obviously holds. We assume correctness for $k - 1$ and prove for k.

Suppose that N_{max} is a maximally interconnected w.r.t. labels $\{l_1, \dots, l_k\}$. If N_{max} does not contain any node with label l_k, then by the induction hypothesis, $N_{max} \in$ ComputeWeakResults$(\{l_1, \dots, l_{k-1}\}, T)$. Clearly, N_{max} is also in ComputeWeakResults$(\{l_1, \dots, l_k\}, T)$.

Otherwise, let n_0 be the node in N_{max} with label l_k. Then, $N_{max} \setminus \{n_0\}$ is interconnected. If $N_{max} \setminus \{n_0\}$ is empty, then $N_{max} = \{n_0\}$ is added to $\mathcal{S}'$ in line 6. Otherwise, by the induction hypothesis there is a set N, such that $N_{max} \setminus \{n_0\} \subseteq N$ and $N \in$ ComputeWeakResults$(\{l_1, \dots, l_{k-1}\}, T)$.

Let n be a node in N_{max} such that $lca\{n_0, n\} = lca\{N_{max}\}$ and $n \neq n_0$. Such a node exists, by Lemma 3. Clearly, $n \in N$. Given the values defined for n_0, N and n, the set $N_1 \cup N_2$ (line 11) is proper since $\{n_0, n\}$ is interconnected. The set N_5 contain nodes from T_N that are interconnected with $\{n_0, n\}$. This hold since N_5 is both proper and connected. It is not difficult to see that $N_{max} = (N_5 \cap N) \cup \{n_0\}$ which is added to $\mathcal{S}'$ as required. □

Theorem 2 (Correctness of ComputeWeakResults). *Let N be a set of nodes. Then, $N \in$ ComputeWeakResults$(\{l_1, \dots, l_k\}, T)$ if and only if N is maximally interconnected w.r.t. $\{l_1, \dots, l_k\}$. In addition, ComputeWeakResults runs in polynomial time relative to the input and output.*

Proof. By Lemma 4, every maximally interconnected set is returned by ComputeWeakResults. By Lemma 2, every set returned by ComputeWeakResults is interconnected. Since line 17 removes sets that are contained in other sets, every set returned must also be maximal.

To show that ComputeWeakResults runs in polynomial time, it is sufficient to show that line 17 does not remove too many sets, since the rest of the procedure is clearly polynomial. Observe that in each iteration of the loop in line 2, the set $\mathcal{S}$ can only grow. Intuitively, this holds since sets created can never be *merged*. Therefore, at most a polynomial number of sets are removed. □

6   Conclusion

The concept of formulating select-project queries against XML documents was introduced. We believe that such queries can be the foundation for user interfaces

---

ComputeWeakResults($\{l_1, \ldots, l_k\}, T$)

1. $\mathcal{S} := \{\{n\} \mid n \in T \text{ and } lbl(n) = l_1\}$
2. **for** i $= 2$ **to** k **do**   /* loop over labels */
3. $\mathcal{S}' := \emptyset$
4.   **for each** $N \in \mathcal{S}$ **do**   /* loop over all sets created so far */
5.   **for each** $n_0 \in T$ with $lbl(n_0) = l_i$ **do**   /* loop over all possible
                                                  extensions to N */
6. $\mathcal{S}' := \mathcal{S}' \cup \{\{n_0\}\}$
7.   **for each** $n \in N$ **do**   /* loop over elements of N */
8. $n_{lca} := lca(n_0, n)$
9. $N_1 := \{\text{nodes on the path between } n_0 \text{ and } n_{lca}\}$
10. $N_2 := \{\text{nodes on the path between } n \text{ and } n_{lca}\}$
11.   **if** $N_1 \cup N_2$ proper **then**
12. $N_3 := \{\text{nodes in } T_N\}$ /*nodes in relationship tree
                                                  of N */
13. $N_4 := N_3 \uplus (N_1 \cup N_2)$
14. $N_5 := \{\text{nodes in } N_4 \text{ that are connected by a path of}$
                           $\text{nodes in } N_4 \text{ to } n_0\}$
15. $\mathcal{S}' := \mathcal{S}' \cup \{(N_5 \cap N) \cup \{n_0\}\}$
16. $\mathcal{S} := \mathcal{S} \cup \mathcal{S}'$
17.   Remove from $\mathcal{S}$ sets that are strictly contained in a set in $\mathcal{S}$
18. **return** $\mathcal{S}$

Fig. 4. Polynomial algorithm to compute weak results of a query on a tree

that allow easy formulation of queries by a naive user. Select-project queries can also be used to allow naive users to retrieve interesting portions of a document that are naturally related. Several different semantics for query evaluation were described. These semantics take into consideration that documents may not contain complete information, a situation that arises frequently in the context of the Web. The complexity of query evaluation was analyzed and evaluation algorithms were presented.

There are several interesting directions in which this work can be extended. Presently, query results are tuples of data. Allowing query results to be in XML could be useful. Our language can be extended to compute joins by allowing a label to appear more than once in a query. We believe that it will not be difficult to extend our work to deal with such queries. By transforming XML documents to relations, it is possible to join these documents with other documents and to join them with relations, for example by using full-disjunction [10]. This allows integration of XML documents with relations and can be used as a complimentary method to the integration method suggested in [5]. It is also of interest to allow additional relational operators in a query.

References

1. S. Abiteboul. Querying semi-structured data. In *In Proc. of the 6th International Conference on Database Theory (ICDT)*, volume 1186 of *Lectures Notes in Computer Science*, pages 1–18. Springer-Verlag, January 1997.
2. S. Abiteboul, L. Segoufin, and V. Vianu. Representing and querying xml with incomplete information. In *Proc. of the 20th ACM Symp. on Principles of Databae Systems (PODS)*, Santa Barbara (California, USA), May 2001. ACM Press.
3. D. Chamberlin, J. Clark, D. Florescu, J. Robie, J. Siméon, and M. Stefanescu. XQuery 1.0: An XML query language, June 2001. Available at http://www.w3.org/TR/xquery.
4. S. Cohen, Y. Kanza, Y. A. Kogan, W. Nutt, Y. Sagiv, and A. Serebrenik. Combining the power of searching and querying. In *In Proc. of the 7th International Conference on Cooperative Information Systems (CoopIS)*, volume 1901 of *Lecture Notes in Computer Science*, pages 54–65, Eilat, (Israel), September 2000. Springer.
5. S. Cohen, Y. Kanza, and Y. Sagiv. SQL4X: A flexible query language for XML and relational databases. In *Informal Proc. of the 8th International Workshop on Database and Programming Languages (DBPL)*, Marino, (Rome, Italy), September 2001.
6. A. Deutsch, M. Fernandez, D. Florescu, A. Levy, and D. Suciu. XML-QL: A query language for XML, 1998. Available at http://www.w3.org/TR/NOTE-xml-ql.
7. R. Fagin, O. Mendelzon, and J. D. Ullman. A simplified universal relation assumption and its properties. *ACM Trans. on Database System (TODS)*, 7(3):343–360, 1982.
8. Y. Kanza, W. Nutt, and Y. Sagiv. Queries with incomplete answers over semi-structured data. In *Proc. of the 18th ACM SIGACT-SIGMOD-SIGART Symp. on Principles of Database Systems (PODS)*, pages 227–236, Philadelphia, (Pennsylvania), May 1999. ACM Press.
9. D. Maier, J. D. Ullman, and M. Y. Vardi. On the foundation of the universal relation model. *ACM Trans. on Database System (TODS)*, 9(2):283–308, 1984.
10. A. Rajaraman and J. D. Ullman. Integrating information by outerjoins and full disjunctions. In *Proc. of the 5th ACM SIGACT-SIGMOD-SIGART Symposium on Principles of Database Systems*, Montreal, (Canada), June 1996. ACM Press.
11. Y. Sagiv. Can we use the universal instance assumption without using nulls? In *Proc. of the ACM SIGMOD Symp. on on the Management of Data*, pages 108–120, 1981.
12. J. D. Ullman. The U. R. strikes back. In *Proc. of the ACM Symposium on Principles of Database Systems (PODS)*, pages 10–22, Los Angeles, (California), March 1982. ACM Press.
13. J. D. Ullman. *Principles of Database and Kowledge Base Systems*, volume II. Computer Science Press, 1989.

Answering Cooperative Recursive Queries in Web Federated Databases

Mira Balaban, Nikolai Berezansky, and Ehud Gudes

Information Systems Engineering and Dept. of Computer Science
Ben-Gurion University, Beer-Sheva, Israel
{mira,nicol,ehud}@cs.bgu.ac.il

Abstract. Evaluation of recursive queries and computing transitive closures require multiple accesses to the involved relations. In a federated database this leads to multiple accesses to the participants of the federation. Since the components are not uniform in terms of computation power, reliability, and communication delays, it might be desirable to minimize the number of accesses to the individual databases, and to maximize the size of the obtained answer with respect to time.
Based on this observation, we developed cooperative query planning methods, termed *Deep Federated Semi-Naive* (DFSN), for computing the strong partial transitive closure of a relation. We have implemented and tested these algorithms in a real database environment. The experimental results show better performance of the DFSN methods over the conservative semi-naive approaches in that they produce large answer sets in time that is considerably shorter than the time needed by the conservative approaches.

1   Introduction

Federated databases support the integration of multiple data sources into a database that functions as a single, uniform database [9]. The participants in a federation preserve their independent status and their characteristic features. Some data sources can be faster than others, and some can be more reliable than others, etc. The performance of the federation as a whole is improved if it utilizes the advantages of its members. In particular, it might be desirable to minimize the number of accesses to the individual databases, and maximize the size of the obtained answer with respect to time. The first criterion is based on the assumption that access to the data sources may be expensive, while the second results from possible malfunctioning of communication lines[1]. These performance measures are especially relevant for answering recursive queries, where multiple accesses to the data sources are necessary.

A recursive query is a query $? - r(x, Y)$ posed to a set of recursive logic rules that characterize an intensional relation r. A rule is recursive if its head

---

[1] The criteria of maximizing the size of the relevant answer over time, is related to the area of *Anytime* algorithms, in which one desires to get even approximate or non-full answer before the optimal or full answer is found, see e.g. [5]

A. Halevy and A. Gal (Eds.): NGITS 2002, LNCS 2382, pp. 14–28, 2002.

predicate appears in its body. A rule is linearly recursive if the head predicate appears only once in the body. A transitive closure rule is a linearly recursive rule of the form: $r(X,Z) : -A(X,Y), r(Y,Z)$, where A(X,Y) is an extensional (base) predicate, defined in one (or more) of the databases that participate in the federation. A *Strong Partial Transitive Closure* (SPTC) query is a query $? - r(\{c_1, \ldots, c_n\}, X)$ or $? - r(X, \{c_1, \ldots, c_n\})$ posed to the rules $r(X,Z) : -A(X,Y), r(Y,Z)$, and $r(X,Z) : -A(X,Y)$, where each c_i is a constant. The *Strong Partial Transitive Closure* problem involves the computation of a restriction of the transitive closure to the query values.

In this paper we deal with the problem of computing a *strong partial transitive closure* [10]), of a relation that is spread among the participants of the federation. Such a problem might arise, for example, in a federation of TRANSPORT databases shown in Figure 1, where each participant database includes data about a single kind of transport, e.g., flights, trains, buses, camels, etc. Although the example is artificial, it is typical of many Web applications, for example, a Web Agent which is traveling through the network to find the best deals possible on a multi-leg flight from one location to another. Such multi-leg flight may involve searching multiple databases of different airline companies.

In Figure 1, the information on the three types of transportation vehicles is distributed over three different sites. An SPTC problem is given in the query "Which places are accessible from a and b". Answering this query requires several accesses to each of the participants, yielding the answer:
$\{(a,c), (a,d), (a,e), (b,d), (b,e), (a,f), (b,h), (a,h), (a,i), (a,g), (a,j)\}$.
Clearly, minimizing the number of accesses to the data sources, and maximizing the size of the obtained answer in a given time can improve the performance of a query answering algorithm. A similar situation exists in a Web-based parts catalog, where parts are composed of sub-parts and the information on the sub-parts is contained in catalogs in different web sites. This paper deals with computing SPTC queries in a federated database.

2   Related Work

This paper is related to work in several areas. First there is work on query processing in federated databases, especially using the Internet [6, 7]. This type of federated databases are characterized by a global schema which is used to translate the input query into several sub-queries, each is sent to a local DBMS. The main tasks in such query processing are:

1. Select the database (site) most relevant to the user query.
2. Find the query fragment to be evaluated at each of the selected sites.
3. Merge the results in an "optimized" way.

Note that once the sub-queries are sent to the local DBMSs, the answer is returned, and the local sites are not contacted again. This is due to the *static* nature of the query plan (i.e. all decisions about what to retrieve and from where are

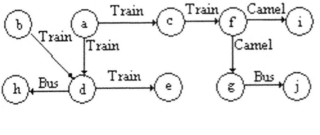

Trains	
source	destination
a	c
a	d
d	e
b	d
c	f

Buses	
source	destination
d	h
g	j

Camel	
source	destination
f	g
f	i

Fig. 1. Example 1 - A federated TRANSPORT database

determined by the optimizer, at query optimization time). In the Web environment there is further complexity that the data sources, may not be standard DBMS so Mediators are needed to access them [4].

The second related area is Web query languages. In these languages (and the related Web search engines) the query processing is not static anymore, since the sites information is not known in advance, as it resides within the Web documents. W3QL [8] is one of the best known web query languages. This language with its powerful syntax allows for the specification of complex *content-based* queries which navigate the web, fill out forms of search tools automatically, and use some termination criteria or path-length bound for termination. Although it is possible to limit the search to one or only few sites, no attempt is made in W3QL to optimize the search locality when multiple sites are searched. This is the emphasis of the current paper.

The third most related area is the evaluation of transitive closure queries. The semi-naive method [3] applies the recursive rules in a repetitive manner, starting from the base relations, until no new tuples are obtained. The search is focused to a given query, when the *magic-set* transformation is first applied to the recursive rules [2], and the semi-naive algorithm is applied to the transformed rules. The combination of the semi-naive algorithm with the magic-set transformation is termed the *optimized semi-naive* algorithm [10]. Other algorithms further improve the performance by using more depth-first search, using heuristics to direct the computation, and employing more conservative data structures [1, 10]. The emphasis of Toroslu's paper[10] and the previous paper by Jiang [1], is to avoid repeated scans of edges, however in these algorithms there is no consideration of site locality. Our algorithms are restricted to tree structures, but emphasize the inter-site vs. the intra-site accesses, and the adaptation to federated databases. In summary, our paper is the first, to our knowledge, to propose algorithms for evaluating transitive closure queries for Web federated databases.

3 Algorithms for Computing the Strong Partial Transitive Closure in a Federated Database

The optimized semi-naive algorithm for computing the strong partial transitive closure of a single *binary* extensional relation is given in Algorithm 1 below (as was presented in [10]). The algorithm conducts a breadth-first search in the base relation graph, starting from the values specified in the query. It uses two auxiliary binary relations *wave* and *closure*. *wave* keeps the results of the last iteration, and *closure* accumulates the partial transitive closure.

Algorithm 1 *The* **Optimized Semi-naive Algorithm** (SN)

Goal: *Computing the strong partial transitive closure of an extensional relation.*
Input*:   An extensional relation A, and a set of query values Q.*
Output*: Partial transitive closure for the query values, given in variable closure.*
Method :$wave = \{(q,q)|q \in Q\}$
$\qquad closure = \emptyset$
$\qquad$ **while** $wave \neq \emptyset$ **do**
$\qquad\qquad wave = \pi_{1,4}(wave \bowtie_{1.2=2.1} A)$
$\qquad\qquad wave = wave - closure$
$\qquad\qquad closure = wave \cup closure$

In the rest of this paper we refer to the while loop in the SN algorithm as a routine **PTC**$(A, wave, closure)$, for computing the partial transitive closure of a base relation A, starting with *wave* and *closure* as above. Therefore, the SN algorithm can be summarized by: $SN(A,Q) = \mathbf{PTC}(A, \{(q,q)|q \in Q\}, \emptyset)$

In a federated database the base relation can be split among several data sources. The transitive closure can be computed either, by copying all relation parts into a single source, or by conducting a simultaneous breadth first search over the data sources in the federation. The first approach is appropriate if the answer to a query involves large portions of the component relations, since it reduces communication traffic, in the cost of a single large data transfer. The second approach is more appropriate for answering a strong partial transitive closure query, since it might involve only a small portion of a relation. If we are interested in all locations which can be reached from Tel-Aviv using some friendly airlines, the cost of multiple communications is much less than transferring a huge flight database to a single component. Therefore, it is unrealistic to shift all parts of the base relation into a single component.

The transitive closure in the distributed case can be viewed as the combined transitive closure of several extensional relations, each provided with its own performance parameters. The *combined transitive closure* is the intensional relation, defined by the rules: $r(X, Z) : -A_i(X, Y), r(Y, Z),$ and $r(X, Z) : -A_i(X, Y),$ where A_i is the part of the A relation in the i-th participant. The strong partial combined transitive closure can be computed by a slight generalization of the optimized semi-naive algorithm, as specified in Algorithm 2. The idea is to let all components perform a single step in each cycle. Since in each step the current wave is changed, each component must keep its own private wave, so that it does not interfere with the other components.

Algorithm 2 *The* **Federated Optimized Semi-naive Algorithm** (FSN).

Goal: *Computes the strong partial combined transitive closure of an extensional relation that is spread among the data sources in a federated database FDB.*

Input: *Extensional relations A_i, each located in data source i in the federation. A set of query values Q.*

Output: *Partial transitive closure for the query values, given in variable closure.*

Method : $wave = \{(q, q) | q \in Q\}$

$closure = \emptyset$

while $wave \neq \emptyset$ **do**

    for every data source i:

        $wave_i = \pi_{1,4}(wave \bowtie_{1.2=2.1} A_i)$

        $wave_i = wave_i - closure$

        $closure = wave_i \cup closure$

    $wave = \bigcup_{i \in FDB} wave_i$

3.1   The Deep Federated Optimized Semi-naive Algorithms

Algorithm 2 treats all the participants in the federation equally. Adopting a graph based view of binary relations, where the values serve as nodes, and tuples serve as directed edges, then in each round every component extends the partial transitive closure by proceeding one step in its graph. In the TRANSPORT federated data base in Figure 1, in a single access to the TRAINS component with input values $\{a, b\}$ and an empty transitive closure, the algorithm computes only the pairs $\{(a, c), (a, d), (b, d)\}$. Clearly, the number of accesses to the components is reduced if the TRAINS component can return the whole partial transitive closure for $\{a, b\}$, which is $\{(a, c), (a, d), (b, d), (a, e), (a, f), (b, e)\}$. Moreover, the size of the computed answer is maximized with respect to the computation time.

Algorithm 3, below, is motivated by these observations. The components operate independently, using each, its own local wave ($wave_i$), and notifying the rest of the federation about new tuples that are found. The algorithm can be implemented in a synchronous or asynchronous manner. In the latter, which underlies the experiments that are described in the next section, the different computation power of the components plays a major role. (The difference in computation power derives not only from variable hardware, but also from the existence of different DBMSs, the existence of different indexes, etc) A fast component can apply its independent **PTC** routine several times while a slow component is busy with a single **PTC** application. A **PTC** application in a component is triggered by new findings in the other components, which are collected into the local wave of the component. The result of the application is sent to all other components. The parallel algorithm terminates when all components are blocked. Note, that the asynchronous computation may also be implemented using a coordinator which plays the role of transferring the messages between the various nodes, but does not wait for their synchronous completion

The connectivity factor: In general, it is expected that the performance of the FSN algorithm is improved if the independent components compute whole partial transitive closures at any round of the algorithm. However, during multiple experiments that we conducted, the results were, surprisingly, different. We tested federations where the data sources were graphs with depth greater than 1, and indeed the number of accesses to the components was reduced. Still, the size of the computed answer did not increase in time. The reason for this unexpected behavior is that each component spent much time on extending its last *wave*, with no increase in the size of the computed answer. In the FSN algorithm this stage occurs only in the last cycle of the loop. Consequently, on a time axis, the FSN algorithm still had a better performance than the new one. In order to avoid this problem, the **PTC** routine is modified to accept a fourth *connectivity* parameter, that provides an *estimation* on the depth of the partial transitive closure graph. The **PTCE** routine computes the partial transitive closure that is bounded by the connectivity parameter. Algorithm 3 uses the connectivity bounded **PTCE** routine in a parallel and asynchronous manner.

Algorithm 3 *The* **Deep Federated Optimized Semi-naive Algorithm** (DFSN).

Goal: *Same as in Algorithm 2.*
Input: *Extensional relations A_i, each located in data source i in the federation.*
          Estimated connectivity measures e_c^i for each of the A_i relations, respectively.
          A set of query values Q.
Output: *Partial transitive closure for the query values, given in variable closure.*
Method : *for every data source i: $wave_i = \{(q,q)|q \in Q\}$*
          $closure = \emptyset$
          for every data source i:
              do forever
                  export **PTCE**$(A_i, wave_i, closure, e_c^i)$
                  Wait for input from other sources

In this algorithm, each source waits for input from other sources, and as soon as such input is accepted, it begins a new computation. At the end of the computation it sends its new "wave" to the other sources. The computation stops when there is nothing new to report. Note that since sources execute independently of each other, there is an implementation issue here as to whether a source buffers several inputs before it starts an execution.

The experiments presented in the next section show that when the connectivity parameter is not greater than the actual minimal depth of the partial transitive closure graph, the DFSN algorithm improves the FSN algorithm with respect the the two criteria of minimizing the number of accesses to the components, and increasing the size of the computed answer with time.

4   Experiments

This section presents the results of the experimental performance evaluation for the algorithms FSN and DFSN. We use the following performance measures: (1) **T** – Run time. T is the clock time[2], that includes both the computation time and the communication time. (2) **N** – Size of the answer set found by the algorithm. The performance of the algorithms is described by a $T \times N$ graph that describes the size of the answer set along a time axis.

The experimental setup consists of a central computer (coordinator) that runs the algorithms DFSN and FSN and communicates with three data sources. The role of the coordinator in the DFSN algorithm is to facilitate the asynchronous computation as explained in the previous section, and to accumulate the experiments results. The parameters T and N are calculated by the coordinator. The database is divided between the three data sources (the coordinator has no data). Each data source runs the PTCE routine on its own data, which is stored in an MS-access relational database. A request for computing the next iteration is translated into several SQL queries from the Access-DB depending on the connectivity factor.

The coordinator and the sources are all Pentium II-133 computers with 128MB, connected via a fast Ethernet network (10MB/sec). That is, the data sources have an equal computation power, and all communication lines are the same. It follows then that the computation time for a PTCE of one data source is determined only by the size of the data. Since the communication network is relatively fast and all the sources have the same power, we also set up an experiment where artificial delays are inserted to messages or to sites. This way, slower and mixed communication networks can be simulated.

4.1   Evaluation of Experiments

The evaluation of the experiments uses several parameters for comparing the two algorithms. Consider the graphs shown in Figure 2 (see next section for a detailed description of the experiments). In the left graph, DFSN seems to

---

[2] In our implementation, the system run on dedicated PC computers, so the computation time is close to the CPU time, which is depended only on the database size

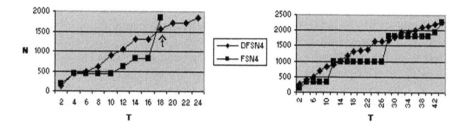

Fig. 2. Example of an intersection point

outperform FSN until point $\hat{t}$, while after that point FSN seems to be a better choice. In the right graph DFSN seems always to outperform FSN, although not with such a clear advantage.

Comment. Intuitively, DFSN should always beat FSN since it uses the same resources and only saves time since nobody waits for "its" companions to finish their cycles. However, the situation is more delicate since the performance depends also on the size of input for each source, and the exact timing of each source. A situation may exist where a source starts to work JUST BEFORE another source produces a large set of data. In that case, the "eager" source loses, by not waiting a bit longer for the slower source. In such situations, FSN (which is completely synchronous) seems to have a better performance, starting from that critical point in time. Usually, that would be an "intersection" point, where FSN becomes superior over DFSN.

These observations become clearer if we observe a new function: $ratio(t) = \frac{N_{DFSN}(t)}{N_{FSN}(t)}$. Figure 3 depicts the *ratio* comparison function for Figure 2. In the right-hand case, the recommendation is clearly to use DFSN. In the left-hand

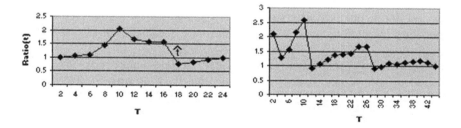

Fig. 3. Ratio function of the intersection point example

case, $ratio(t) \geq 1$, $\forall t \leq \hat{t}$ and $ratio(t) < 1$, $\forall t > \hat{t}$. Therefore DFSN is better before $\hat{t}$ while FSN is preferable later on. In that case, a combination of the two algorithms is recommended. A point $\hat{t}$, at which the algorithms behave as in the left case, is termed *intersection point*. Our recommendations are as follows: If $ratio(t) \geq 1$ for most time points, then DFSN is preferable, but if there exists an intersection point $\hat{t}$ then a combination of the two algorithms may be recommended. The experiments presented in the following sections aim at pointing to an estimation of the intersection point based on the properties of the database or of the computation/communication subsystems. There are two sets of experiments: (1) Real experiments that compare the performance of DFSN and FSN as affected by the database properties, using the Network setup described earlier. (2) Simulation experiments that simulate variety in computation power in the data sources, and take into account communication line delays.

4.2   Input Database Construction

The performance of the two algorithms is heavily dependent on the structure and topology of the databases in each site. In order to control this structure for our experimental evaluation, we developed an elaborate synthetic database generation procedure. The generated database is represented as a graph of the binary relations, where nodes correspond to values, and directed edges stand for tuples that contain the values represented by the nodes. The parameters that dictate the construction of the input databases are as follows: (1) $\mathbf{b_i}$ - Branching factor in the graph of component i (so far we assume a fixed branching factor). (2) $\mathbf{c_i}$ - Connectivity factor for component i, defined as the maximal path length in the local graph of the relation of component i . (3) $\mathbf{a}$ - alternation factor for the whole federated database. This factor specifies the number of possible alternations between the graphs of the individual relations.

Algorithm **create-database** generates a tree for the whole federated database. Assuming a set of sub-trees in each of the data sources, the algorithm scans each of these sub-trees, and for every leaf and every different data source, it generates a new sub-tree that is connected to it, and resides in the other data source. The width and depth of these new sub-trees are controlled by the Branching and Connectivity parameters respectively. This process continues until the desirable database size (alternating factor) is reached.

We can present the generated database by compressing every subtree for a component into a single edge, and connecting its root with its leaves. The database tree can be viewed as a depth a tree of sets of labeled nodes. Figure 4 displays an output database of algorithm **create-database**, with two components named src_0 and src_1, where $b_0 = 2$, $c_0 = 2$ and $b_1 = 3$, $c_1 = 1$, respectively. The database is represented as a compressed tree. As can be seen in Figure 4, since $a=1$, the database is composed of four parts, two parts in each source. The first part of source *src0* contains a sub-tree of height 2, with two sons per node, for total of four nodes (corresponding to $b_0 = 2$, $c_0 = 2$). The first part of *src1* contains a sub-tree of height 1, with three sons per node, (corresponding to $b_1 = 3$, $c_1 = 1$). The third and fourth parts are constructed similarly. Using these parameters, and the above procedure, large and complex structured databases can be generated.

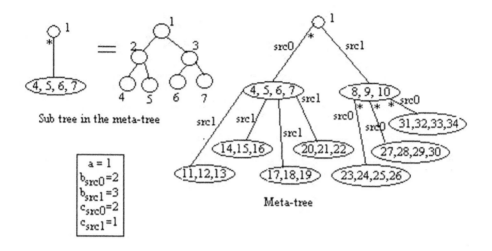

Fig. 4. A database generated by Algorithm **create-database**

4.3   Real Experiments

The experiments described in this section compare the performance of DFSN and FSN, as affected by the database properties, in the real network environment. Our expectation is that DFSN is better when the data sources compute answer sets with significantly unequal size, and when there is large interdependence among the data sources. Therefore we conducted experiments where for either small or large interdependence we test the algorithms with equal or unequal size for the answer set of the sources. The size of the answer set of the data sources is determined by the factors **b** and **c** described in Section 4.2 and the interdependence is captured by the parameter **a**. The database size ranges from 3000 tuples, up to 15000 tuples.

Experiments with small interdependence factor (a = 1). We performed three experiments presented in Figure 5. (The table at the lower right represents the different connectivity and branching factors in each of the three sites.) The graphs describe the average over several experiments, so to minimize the impact of different order of arrivals of answers to the coordinator. In each graph the size of the answer set is depicted vs. Time (in seconds). We see that in experiment 1.1 there is an intersection point $\hat{t} \sim 23$. DFSN is preferable up to $\hat{t}$ and then FSN takes over. In experiments 1.2 and 1.3 DFSN out-wins FSN.

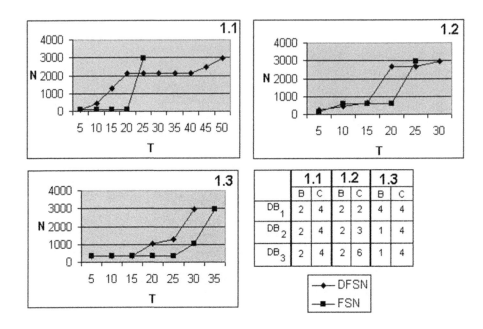

Fig. 5. Experiments with **a** = 1

As can be seen from the table in Figure 5, in experiments 1.2 and 1.3 (in contrast with 1.1), there are large differences between the sizes of the data sources (due to variability in **b** or **c**), and therefore their computation times are quite different, and indeed our assumption that DFSN will behave better in these cases is confirmed.

Note that at the beginning of the graphs (left side) the two algorithms are almost the same. The reason is that since the answer sets at this stage are small, the differences are not visible on the graph. Similar behavior is exhibited by the next set of experiments.

Experiments with large interdependence factor (a = 3). We performed three experiments described in Figure 6. In graphs 1.4 and 1.5, even though the two graphs intersect, this is not an intersection point since FSN is better for only a very short interval. The intersection point, if exists, happens towards the end of the operation. As can be seen from the graphs, the advantages of DFSN over FSN grow in direct correlation with the factor a.

Next we discuss the effects of delays in the communication network.

4.4   Delay Simulation Experiments

The simulation experiments in this section are based on the assumption that transmission time ($\mathbf{T_t}$) has a linear dependence on the size of the communication

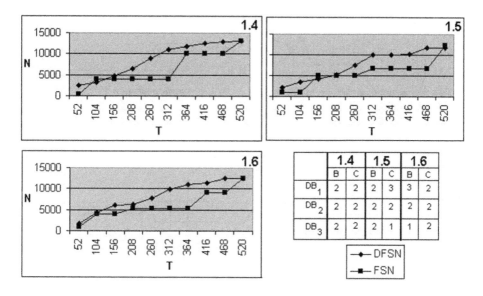

Fig. 6. Experiments with **a** = 3.

message (**S**). Therefore, transmission time may be calculated as: $\mathbf{T_t} = D + \alpha * \mathbf{S}$, where D represents a constant delay which reflects the distance of the data-source from the coordinator, and α represents a delay which depends only on the size of the message (answer-set).

To implement this, we added to each site, before sending the result a "sleep" of length: $\mathbf{T_t}$, which simulates the required delay. We performed two sets of experiments, both with constant factors of Connectivity, Branching and Alternation. Note, that the databases in this section are smaller (2000 tuples) since the system runs much slower.

Simulation Experiments with $D = 0$. In this set of experiments we examine the influence of the parameter α on the performance of the system ($\mathbf{D} = 0$). In our experiments, $\alpha = 1$ in transmission of 1000 tuples is equivalent to delay of 1000 msec (1 sec).

We can see in Figure 7 that as we increase α, the performance of DFSN improves. This can be expected since larger α means that the slower component (which produces larger answer set) becomes even more slow, and the differences between components larger.

Simulation Experiments with $\alpha = 0$. In this set of experiments we examine the influence of parameter $\mathbf{D}$ on the performance of the system ($\alpha = 0$). In our experiments, $\mathbf{D} = 1000$ is analog to a delay of 1000msec (1 sec). We consider the following cases:

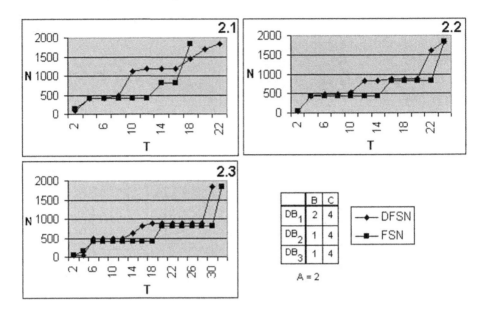

Fig. 7. Experiments with $D = 0$. In 2.1: $\alpha = 1$; In 2.2: $\alpha = 5$; In 2.3: $\alpha = 10$

- $D = 0$ for all sources (no artificial delay)
- $D = 10000$ for all sources (large delay, same for all sources)
- $D = 10000$ for one source and $D = 1000$ for other sources (unequal delays).

We can see in Figure 8 that the case of equal delays leads to worse results, worse than the case without delays. The reason is that if we add large equal delay to sources - the difference in reaction time become smaller, and so the performance of DFSN with respect to FSN gets worse. The advantage of DFSN is clearly visible in the non-equal delays case.

5   Conclusion

In this paper we demonstrated initial results of experiments in computing the strong partial transitive closure of a relation that is spread in different sites of a federated database. We introduced a method that exploits the fact that usually some components are faster than other components, and let such components work more intensively than others. Our experiments show that indeed, when the input databases of the components demonstrate a high level of connectivity (produce large transitive closures), our method yields large answer sets faster than the standard optimized semi-naive approach.

The experiments reported here are only in their initial stages. More work is necessary on characterizing the behavior of the DFSN algorithms on input databases with wilder structure. Furthermore, we did not experiment with true

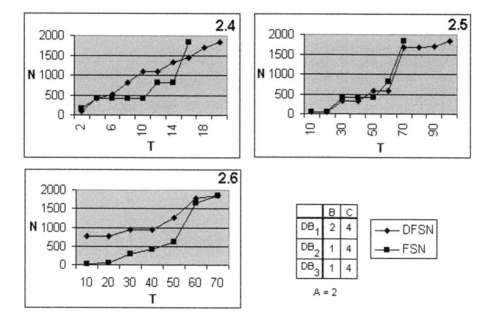

Fig. 8. Experiments with $\alpha = 0$. In 2.4: $\mathbf{D_{DB_1}} = \mathbf{D_{DB_2}} = \mathbf{D_{DB_3}} = 0$; In 2.5: $\mathbf{D_{DB_1}} = \mathbf{D_{DB_2}} = \mathbf{D_{DB_3}} = 10000$; In 2.6: $\mathbf{D_{DB_1}} = 10000$ and $\mathbf{D_{DB_2}} = \mathbf{D_{DB_3}} = 1000$

malfunctioning of sites. In the future we plan also to extend the experiments to federations of multiple clusters of sites, generalize the database structure to acyclic graphs, and investigate other parallel policies.

References

1. Jiang B. A suitable algorithm for computing transitive closure. In *Proc. 6th Int. conf. on data engineering*, pages 380–392, 1990.
2. F. Bancilhon, D. Maier, Y. Sagiv, and J. D. Ulman. Magic sets and other strange ways to implement logic programs. In *Proc. 5th ACM Symp. Principles of Database Systems*, pages 1–15, 1986.
3. F. Bancilhon and R. Ramakrishnan. An amateus's: Introduction to recursive query processing strategies. In *Proc. 5th ACM-SIGMOD Int'l Conf. Management Data*, pages 16–52, 1986.
4. Jacques Calmet, Sebastian Jekutsch, and Joachim Schü. A generic query-translation framework for a mediator architecture. In *Proc. 13 Int'l Conf. on Data Engineering*, pages 434–443, 1997.
5. Shlomo Zilberstein Eric A. Hansen. Monitoring the progress of anytime problem-solving. *National Conference on Artificial Intelligence (AAAI/IAAI)*, 2:1229–1234, 1996.
6. Luis Gravano and Yannis Papakonstantinou. Editing and metasearching on the internet. *Data Engineering Bulletin*, 21(2):28–36, 1998.

7. Laura M. Haas, Donald Kossmann, Edward L. Wimmers, and Jun Yang. Optimizing queries across diverse data sources. In *Proc. of 23rd Int'l Conf. on Very Large Data Bases*, pages 276–285, 1997.

8. David Konopnicki and Oded Shmueli. Information gathering in the world-wide web: The w3ql query language and the w3qs system. *ACM Transactions on Database Systems*, 23(4):369–410, 1998.

9. Amit P. Sheth and James A. Larson. Federated database systems for management distributed, heterogeneous, and autonomous databases. *ACM Computing Surveys*, 22(3):193–236, 1990.

10. I. H. Toroslu and G. Z. Qadah. The effective computation of strong partial transitive-closure. In *Proc. 9th Int'l Conf. Data Eng.*, pages 530–537, 1996.

Strongly Typed Server Pages

Dirk Draheim and Gerald Weber

Institute of Computer Science
Free University Berlin
Germany
{draheim,weber}@inf.fu-berlin.de

Abstract. We present NSP, a new, statically typed server pages technology. NSP supports arrays and user defined types within input forms. It is the result of designing server pages from scratch. It addresses the needs of server pages developers who want to build cleaner, better reusable, more stable systems.

1   Introduction

Next Server Pages (NSP) is a programming model for system dialogues based on dynamically generated pages, like today's web interfaces. In the following we summarize NSP's original contributions to server pages development.

- Strong type system
    - Parameterized pages. A web application is accessed through a set of single pages, which together comprise the system interface. NSP pages are remote methods that send HTML output back to the caller.
    - Static type checker. NSP defines a strong type system which incorporates NSP pages that are called across the net. A new widget set is supporting technology for it. At deployment time the system interface is statically checked as a whole against sophisticated rules for writing forms. The NSP rules guarantee that no type error occurs concerning the interplay between the pages of the system.
    - Complex types. Arrays and user defined types may be incorporated in writing forms by using special mechanisms.
    - Native typed form parameters in the scripting language. The scripts within the server page receive the values passed via a form in the native data types of the respective scripting language, and not only as string values.
    - No unresolved links. Since NSP uses its own syntax for links and forms to other pages within the same system interface, it is possible to check, whether these links and forms point to existing targets within the system dialogue.
- Reverse engineering. From a system written in NSP the developer can generate a specification in the high level specification language Angie.

A. Halevy and A. Gal (Eds.): NGITS 2002, LNCS 2382, pp. 29–44, 2002.

The NSP approach is oriented mainly towards building enterprise information systems [13] rather than building information architectures. NSP does not compete with content management systems or content management frameworks.

NSP is a paradigm for dynamically generated server pages that is independent from the chosen scripting language. However, for every language supported by NSP a nontrivial language mapping has to be provided. The current main development and therefore the presentation of NSP in this paper is oriented towards Java. The Java language mapping exemplifies the amalgamation of NSP with the scripting language.

The source code of an NSP page is an XML document. The language NSP is the result of changing and extending XHTML with respect to the new NSP features. A system developed with NSP runs with standard browsers as ultra-thin clients - no plug-ins are necessary.

In section 2 we motivate NSP by showing up the deficiencies of current server scripts and our theoretical model for the development of NSP. In section 3 we give a hands on introduction to NSP, afterwards an overview of the whole NSP language in section 4. Section 5 explains the use of NSP with respect to documentation and reverse engineering. Finally in section 6 we describe the relation of NSP to other approaches, which will turn out to be orthogonal to NSP.

NSP is a powerful problem oriented implementation method. It is fully integrated with a corresponding analysis method by the authors, which is called form oriented analysis [10][8][11]. This analysis method uses a conceptual model of web style applications. Such applications are called submit/response style applications. This allows further abstraction form web technology details. Form oriented analysis is strongly typed like NSP. Application models developed in form oriented analysis map perfectly to NSP technology. Moreover, the NSP dialogues derived from form oriented analysis have a clear separation of logic and presentation [9] similar, but more elaborate than Model 2 architectures.

2   Motivation

Today many web applications rely heavily on dynamically generated pages. They are often built from HTML pages with embedded server side scripts. Well known technologies in this domain are PHP, Active Server Pages (ASP), or Java Server Pages (JSP).

The interaction between browser and server is synchronous communication: the user of an HTTP dialogue causes the browser to send page requests to the server. These requests can be seen as remote method calls on the server. The HTML form standard offers a text based remote parameter passing mechanism for dynamic websites. The submitted parameters are called HTML form parameters in the following. The described parameter passing mechanism is untyped with respect to the parameter set, the single parameters, and finally with respect to the return value, namely the generated page. The same mechanism can be used in HTTP links as well: they can contain URLs following the syntax for HTML form parameter transmission. These links have to be created on the server side. NSP aims to bring the benefits of static type checking to the programming of such dialogues. For simplicity, wherever we want to reason about the system interface, we suppose that the system interface is based completely on pages generated by server scripts. Furthermore we will discuss in the following NSP in the concrete combination with Java, which also allows us to discuss the improvements to JSP achieved by NSP.

We want to recall that the JSP technology is a server side scripting technology in that it is a proposed standard technique to implement servlets [3][15][6]. JSP lets the programmer feel like programming a preprocessor for servlets, because many details of the Java Servlet API are visible.

The previously explained lack of typing in the HTTP form mechanism is not mitigated in any form by the server side scripting techniques like JSP. JSP offers the HTML form parameters to script code through an object oriented mechanism via the HTTPRequest parameter. The interesting parameters, namely the HTML form parameters provided by the forms or links calling the page, are neither typed, nor statically type checked. The static type checking is performed only on the technical level, e.g. concerning the HTTPRequest and HTTPResponse parameters. In the same way, JSP does not offer any support for creating correct calls to other JSP pages in forms and especially not in links. For links, the programmer must code the parameter passing to another server script within the result page by manually concatenating script output in the special HTML syntax.

The NSP approach does not restrict the potentials of JSP in any way, but has overcome the aforementioned problems, mainly because it is based on a clear model of page based dialogues. In the NSP model, a page has a fixed parameter list and is callable across the net. Therefore an NSP page is also named a dialogue method or method for short. The calls to this method are triggered by the user interaction with another page of the dialogue. Dialogue methods produce HTML pages as return values. The produced HTML document will be called the result page.

Each result page offers to the user the choice between different links or forms as the next step in the dialogue. These links and forms are calls to dialogue methods. Forms can be seen as editable method calls offered to the user. One of the main contributions of the NSP static type checker is to check the link and form syntax against the method declaration of the called dialogue method.

This introduces one of the most important observations in the NSP concept: from the viewpoint of the type system of NSP the generated result pages are the actual code, which has to be considered. Although the generated code is naturally not available at deployment time, NSP defines rules for writing the server script parts, the so called NSP coding rules, which are

- non prohibitive: all reasonable applications of scripting are still allowed,
- statically checkable: accordance with NSP coding rules can be checked at compile time,

- sufficient: if the NSP coding rules are followed, the question of whether the generated HTML code will be type-safe or not can be decided.

The NSP technique is independent from any particular server side scripting technology, it could even be abstracted from HTTP/HTML and could lead to a general standard for specifying page based dialogues. Such a generalization is prepared by the notion of submit/response style applications in form oriented analysis [10].

3   A First Example

The following example points up the most important NSP notion, i.e. the type-safe call of an NSP page across the net. This minimal example allows the registration of a webshop customer.

A standard HTML page may reference the NSP page "Shop" by a hyperlink. If this link is followed by the user, an HTML page is sent that contains a link to a registration page. Note that the hyperlink to the registration dialogue method is not realized by a standard <a href> tag, but by a new NSP tag structure for links. The reason for this will become obvious later.

Within the registration page a form is offered to the user. This form sends the user input to the dialogue method "NewCustomer". An NSP form targets a dialogue method that is specified via its callee attribute. The called method has a well-defined signature. Somewhat similar to the parameter mechanism in ADA, a targeted formal parameter of a called method is explicitly referenced by its name. For this purpose the <input> tag has a param attribute. A form must provide actual parameters exactly for the formal method parameters, either by user input or hidden parameters. In the present simple example this is fulfilled. In general the overall demand for type-safe calls of NSP methods causes sophisticated rules for writing forms and a new innovative widget set.

If the dialogue method "NewCustomer" is invoked, inline Java code is executed. This Java code calls a user defined imported business method.

```
<nsp name="Shop">
  <head><title>Shop</title></head>
  <body>
    <link callee="Registration">
      <linkbody>Customer Registration</linkbody>
    </link>
  </body>
</nsp>
<nsp name="Registration">
  <head><title>Registration</title></head>
  <body>
    <form callee="NewCustomer">
      <input widget="textfield" param="customer"></input>
      <input widget="intfield" param="age"></input>
```

```
      <submit></submit>
    </form>
  </body>
</nsp>

<nsp name="NewCustomer">
  <head><title>New Customer</title></head>
  <java>import myBusinessModel.CustomerBase;</java>
  <param name="customer" type="String"/>
  <param name="age" type="int"/>
  <body>
    <java>
      CustomerBase.createCustomer(customer,age);
    </java>
    <redirect callee="Shop"></redirect>
  </body>
</nsp>
```

4   Language Description

4.1   Top-Level Structure

An NSP page consists of a head and a body. The signature of the page is defined with appropriate <param> tags between the page's head and body. The <param> tags have attributes for specifying names and types of the parameters. Java code may be placed inside <java> tags. The dialogue method parameters are accessible in the inline Java code.

In addition to <java> tags it is possible to use <javaexp> tags as a controlled variant of direct, i.e. Java coded, writing to the output stream. In NSP no special non-XML syntax for expression scriptlets like the JSP <%= %> signs is available. Because of that it is not possible to generate NSP tag parts, especially attribute values may not be generated. Element properties that may have to be provided dynamically, are supported by elements rather than attributes in NSP. As a result an NSP page is a valid XML document. Therefore NSP will benefit immediately from all new techniques developed in the context of XML. In particular, NSP can be used in combination with style sheet technologies [20].

4.2   Type System

In a typed programming language the call to a method must fit exactly the method signature. This notion is picked up but elaborated further due to the special needs of programming a web interface. In order to understand the type system of NSP one has to realize that in NSP the static type rules apply to generated forms. In NSP the following form declaration has to be considered invalid, because three input fields target the same parameter, which is not an array parameter.

```
<nsp name="M">
  <head><title>M</title></head>
  <param name="i" type="int"/>
  <body></body>
</nsp>

<!-- form inside another page -->
<form callee="M">
  <java>
  for (int j=1;j<3;j++) {
    </java><input widget="intfield" param="i"></input><java>
  }
  </java>
  <submit></submit>
</form>
```

That is, in NSP all HTML code which is created dynamically by a form declaration is not just considered as a block for capturing actual parameters. Instead it is considered as a method call offered to the user as a whole. Precisely in this sense the form has to support the signature of the called method exactly. Altogether this leads to rules for writing NSP code. These rules pay tribute to the fact that server pages are essentially a mix of HTML and scripting code. The aim of the subsection 4.2 is to elaborate these so called NSP coding rules for writing type-safe forms, which are designed in a way that the resulting notion of type correctness may be checked statically. Correct NSP code is very natural and the NSP coding rules are easy to learn. Altogether NSP contributes the adaptation of typed programming discipline to the context of programming web interfaces.

The rules for writing type-safe forms are presented as a combination of declarative characterization and informal guidelines for coding through examples and counter-examples.

Input Capabilities. In NSP an actual form parameter may be provided by user input or by a hidden parameter. Note that we use the term "input capability" for input fields, input controls, and - a bit sloppy, though in accordance with usual HTML terminology - for hidden parameters, too. NSP offers at least the usual HTML form input capabilities but defines their usage with respect to type safety, i.e. a textfield may be used for String values for instance, radiobuttons for enumeration types, multiple select lists for array types. But NSP improves the HTML form controls in several ways, as will be outlined now.

Consider the following problems with HTML forms. In forms often so called required fields occur. These fields must be filled out by the user. With standard HTML the developer has to deal with required input fields explicitly. For example the submission of an invalid form may be prevented with client side scripting plus disabling the submit button as described in [12]. Alternatively a server side script may check if the actual required parameter is an empty string and must provide appropriate error messages and a new input capability if necessary. A similar problem arises with the entry of integer values. Usual scripts have to react on non-convertible values with extra dialogue.

In NSP these and similar problems are tackled from the outset. Consider the following examples.

```
1 <input widget="textfield" param="s" entry="required"></input>
2 <input widget="textfield" param="s" entry="optional"></input>
3 <input widget="integerfield" param="i" entry="required"></input>
4 <input widget="intfield" param="i"></input>
```

A textfield may be specified to be required (1). The encompassing form cannot be submitted, unless this field is filled out by the user. If a textfield is optional (2) and the field is not filled out, a null object becomes the actual parameter. For textfields, the entry attribute's default value is "optional". A textfield may target only a String value. For numbers extra widgets are provided. A Java Integer object may be gathered with an integerfield (3). Like a textfield the integerfield may be required or optional. Furthermore an entered value must be a number, otherwise it is not possible to submit the form. An intfield (4) is used to target parameters of type int. It behaves like an integerfield, but it is immutably required, because there exist no canonical mapping of an undefined value into a Java primitive type. The advanced developer can customize the default behavior of the NSP widgets. Further considerations led to a new innovative set of widgets in NSP.

The NSP widget set is realized both with client side and server side scripting technology. As an example consider the realization of an Integer input field with server side scripting technology. During the parsing of the transmitted parameter stream it is checked whether the parameter is convertible. If not, the calling form is redisplayed with the already entered values as default values. The client side realizations guarantee performance.

Forms and Links. Note that we use the term "basic type" for every Java primitive type, for every wrapper of a Java primitive type, for String, and for every JDBC API primitive SQL type throughout the paper. For a formal method parameter of basic type, there must be exactly one input capability in the generated HTML form in the result page. The generating NSP form code must ensure this for every possible execution path.

Therefore in NSP input capability tags may occur within conditional control structures, as long as all alternative branches produce exactly one input capability for the respective parameter. Furthermore in NSP input capabilities for basic type values must not occur within loops. With these rules, the type safety with respect to basic types may be statically checked.

For example the following form declaration is considered invalid.

```
<form callee="M">
  <java>
  if (x==3) {
    </java><input widget="intfield" param="i"></input><java>
  }
  </java>
  <submit></submit>
</form>
```

Instead the following form declaration is a correct alternative.

```
<form callee="M">
  <java>
  if (x==3) {
    </java><input widget="intfield" param="i"></input><java>
  } else {
    </java><hidden param="i">815</hidden><java>
  }
  </java>
  <submit></submit>
</form>
```

Note that a static type system like NSP's cannot prevent such dynamic type errors that result from using the output stream to send dynamically generated form fragments to the browser directly. Generally, using the output stream for sending HTML is considered bad style and may lead to dynamic errors. It is an NSP rule that the output stream must not be used in a way that corrupts the otherwise type-safe NSP system. A corrupted form that is caused by a prohibited use of the output stream may contain invalid input capabilities or a wrong number of input capabilities. This is just considered as a dynamic error, like division by zero. But even though such a dynamic type error should not occur, NSP provides sophisticated support for it. In the default case an appropriate exception is thrown. But beyond this a switch is offered by the tolerant attribute for every form. A tolerant form may have too many input capabilities for a parameter of basic type. Appropriate rules then guarantee that exactly one actual parameter is chosen. Note that it is not possible to switch off static type checking with the tolerant attribute. A form may only be tolerant with respect to provoked dynamic type errors.

In NSP the syntax for hyperlinks follows the form syntax. In NSP no tedious handling with special signs is needed in order to use hyperlinks with parameters. Links may only include hidden parameters as input capabilities. The value of a hidden parameter must be given by a Java expression.

```
<link callee="NewCustomer">
  <hidden param="customer">"John Q. Public"</hidden>
  <hidden param="age">32</hidden>
  <linkbody>underlined link name</linkbody>
</link>
```

Arrays. NSP offers sophisticated type-safe support for gathering arrays of values in forms. In the following form fragment, an Integer array parameter articleIds is targeted.

```
<form callee="N">
  <java>
  for (int i=0;i<8;i++) {
    </java>
    <input widget="integerfield" param="articleIds">
      <index>i</index>
    </input>
    <java>
  }
  </java>
  <input widget="integerfield" param="articleIds">
    <index>9</index>
  </input>
  <submit></submit>
</form>
```

All input capabilities that target the same array parameter together provide the submitted actual parameter. The index specifications must be unique. The greatest index determines the length of the array. In the example the invoked method receives an array of fixed length ten. Array elements which correspond to fields that were not filled out, are null objects. Furthermore, the ninth element is a null object, because no input capability exists for this index.

But NSP offers further features concerning arrays in forms. Consider for instance the following example.

```
<form callee="N">
  <input widget="integerfield" param="articleIds"></input>
  <input widget="integerfield" param="articleIds"></input>
  <input widget="integerfield" param="articleIds"></input>
  <submit></submit>
</form>
```

In this example the index tags are omitted. Now the invoked method just receives actually entered values. If an optional field is not filled out, no object at all will occur for it in the actual parameter array. This NSP feature frees the programmer from tedious work in many cases. All joint input capabilities of a targeted array parameter must either provide a unique index or otherwise omit the index.

In contrast to parameters of basic type no restriction on the occurrence of input capabilities is necessary, because both arrays of length zero and arrays containing null objects are considered correct.

User Defined Types. NSP allows the usage of user defined types in forms. One possibility to target a formal parameter of user defined type and its fields is the usage of path expressions. The following example demonstrates how a complete object tree concerning a user defined type structure may be gathered by a form this way. User defined types that should be used in NSP forms must follow the Java Beans naming convention. We use an obvious notation for user defined types in the following examples.

```
Customer {
  String name;
  Integer age;
  Address address;
}

Address {
  String street;
  int zip;
}

<nsp name="NewCustomer">
  <head><title>New Customer</title></head>
  <param name="customer" type="Customer"/>
  <body></body>
</nsp>

<nsp name="Registration">
  <head><title>Registration</title></head>
  <body>
    <form callee="NewCustomer">
      <input widget="textfield" param="customer.name></input>
      <input widget="integerfield" param="customer.age"></input>
      <input widget="textfield" param="customer.address.street"></input>
      <input widget="intfield" param="customer.address.zip"></input>
      <submit></submit>
    </form>
  </body>
</nsp>
```

Under all circumstances and for each type of a type structure, there must be either exactly one input capability for each of its fields of basic type or no input capabilities at all. Fields that have a user defined type must not have an input capability. Appropriate object references are generated automatically. Following a type structure path, the first time a type occurs that does not have any input capabilities, the generated object reference is the null object. Altogether these rules enable the usage of cyclic type structures in forms. This is exemplified in the following example.

```
A {
  A next;
  int i;
}
```

```
<nsp name="M">
  <head><title>M</title></head>
  <param name="anA" type="A"/>
  <body></body>
</nsp>

<nsp name="N">
  <head><title>M</title></head>
  <body>
    <form callee="M">
     <input widget="intfield" param="anA.i"></input>
     <input widget="intfield" param="anA.next.i"></input>
     <input widget="intfield" param="anA.next.next.i"></input>
     <submit></submit>
    </form>
  </body>
</nsp>
```

Beside path expressions, NSP offers a parenthesis mechanism for targeting parameters of user defined type, that is similar to the "with" construct of MODULA2.

```
<form callee="NewCustomer">
  <with param="customer">
    <input widget="textfield" param="name"></input>
    <input widget="integerfield" param="age"></input>
    <with param="address">
      <input widget="textfield" param="street"></input>
      <input widget="intfield" param="zip"></input>
    </with>
  </with>
  <submit></submit>
</form>
```

Beyond the usage for abbreviation, the "with" tag becomes an important construct if a formal array parameter of user defined type is targeted, because the input capabilities of fields that constitute a single array element must be grouped together. Not all layouts may be realized with this mechanism, because it is possible that a required layout structure contradicts the necessary structure of an XML document. Therefore NSP provides another low-level opportunity to group input capabilities together via tag keys.

4.3   Functional Decomposition

NSP provides tags for the usual redirect and include directives known from the Servlet API's RequestDispatcher, but this time in the method oriented NSP style.

```
<nsp name="HelloWorld">
  <head><title>Hello World</title></head>
  <body>
    <redirect callee="M">
      <hidden param="head">"Hello"</hidden>
    </redirect>
  </body>
</nsp>

<nsp name="M">
  <head><title>M</title></head>
  <param name="head" type="String"/>
  <body>
    <call callee="N">
      <hidden param="message"> head + "World !" </hidden>
    </call>
  </body>
</nsp>

<nsp name="N">
  <head><title>N</title></head>
  <param name="message" type="String"/>
  <body>
    <javaexp>message</javaexp>
  </body>
</nsp>
```

As demonstrated in the above example, in NSP an include directive is given consequentially by a server side call of a dialogue method. Again NSP gains from its solid conceptual basis: if the Servlet API is used it must be ensured that a servlet targeted by the include directive does not send a head. This problem is tackled in NSP from the outset. The method's head is pushed into the output stream if and only if a method is called across the net.

5   Reverse Engineering of User Dialogues with Angie

NSP also aims at improving the quality of documentation of the system interface. For this purpose, NSP allows reverse engineering, namely the automatic generation of a documentation of the whole system interface in the easy to read specification language Angie. An earlier version of Angie called Gently [7] was developed by the authors as a specification language for forward engineering of system dialogues. Angie extracts from a system interface all pages with their signatures together with the contained links and forms. A further very useful information generated in Angie is the list of callers for each method. The generated Angie document is the suitable place for comments, which are passed through from the NSP files, and therefore is amenable to proposed specification techniques like [14] or [18], too. The standard reverse engineering tool of Java, namely javadoc, is not suitable for documenting servlets. Applying javadoc to the customized server script classes leads only to the documentation of the technical parameters HTTPRequest and HTTPResponse. The interesting parameters, which are significant for the business logic, namely the HTML form parameters provided by the forms or links calling the page, cannot be documented automatically.

6   Related Work

6.1   Web Services contra HTML/HTTP User Dialogues

Web Services [16] are widely regarded as a major technological shift in the usage of the web. Web services are primarily discussed in the B2B domain. Web services can be used synchronously in a request/response style or they can be asynchronous, message oriented. Web services possess a type system, the Web service definition language [19].

At first glance, web services may seem inspired from and similar to user interfaces, using the same protocol, namely HTTP. With respect to the NSP static type checking we can identify a clear difference between web services and HTTP/HTML user interfaces: in web services, synchronous or asynchronous, there is no necessary type relation between different messages, although there may be a type system. The types of different messages can be chosen freely according to the needs of the business case.

In HTML dialogues however, if the user is supposed to send a form with data to the server, then a page containing this form must have been previously sent to the user. More generally speaking, we have a necessary relation between a typed user request and a systems response before that request. This relation is based in the mechanism itself.

In other words, in HTML dialogues, the type information is not transmitted once and used for all subsequent interactions, but it is transmitted before every typed request, and it is directly transformed into the displayed form, which the user actually fills out.

This is in our view not an accidental design mismatch between web services and HTML/HTTP dialogues, but a fundamental difference caused by the fact that web services are accessed automatically, and HTML dialogues are designed for end users. The end user can react to every input form offered to him immediately, the web service can only repeat those interaction sequences that have been in principle laid out and validated once manually beforehand. On the other hand it is clear that web service technologies are not able to address this unique feature of NSP.

6.2   Web Application Frameworks

NSP delivers genuinely new features, and is therefore not comparable to other approaches [2] [4] [5] [17]. However, NSP can be easily mistaken to be a variant of architectural approaches or approaches for separating logic and presentation. We therefore give an overview of current efforts in these two areas, which receive widespread attention. However one should note that not a single one of these projects deliver any of the unique selling points of NSP.

Server side scripting technologies, like ASP, JSP and PHP allow to embed script code into HTML, or more generally XML. None of these technologies offer NSP's static type checking. Another approach is chosen by the WebMacro [17] system, which allows the separation between Java and HTML. It uses the Java reflection mechanism to access Java Beans from HTML Templates. WebMacro is a first example for Sun's Model 2 Architecture. Again, WebMacro does not offer a specialized support for type-safe dialogues.

WebMacro leads over to the architectural frameworks for web interfaces, which allow to create presentation layers that follow a certain software architecture. An example is Struts [5], a Framework for User Interfaces, which results in a peculiar Model 2 Architecture. Another Model 2 architectural framework is Barracuda [2]. Both do not offer the type check facilities of NSP. Another framework, which lies explicitly the emphasis on separation of content and presentation, is the Cocoon [4] framework.

6.3   The "System Calls User" Approach

In the language Mawl [1] the control flow in the server script spans the whole user session. The server script is suspended whenever a page is presented to the user. The approach can be seen as a "system calls user" approach, since the process of presenting a page to the user and retrieving the input from her has the semantics of a function call from the viewpoint of the script: the data presented to the system are the parameters of the procedure, the data entered by the user are the return values. However, Mawl allows only for one form per page, hence it abandons the core paradigm of hypertext. Principally a workaround would be possible by emulating several forms and links as one single superform. This however would lead to a bad design of systems built with this technology, which would suffer from an "ask what kind" antipattern: for every form hard-wired case structures must be used to branch the session flow. This would imply high coupling and low cohesion.

7   Conclusion

The abstract notions developed in NSP are independent from the underlying scripting language. NSP does not impose a special architecture onto the system, it does not prescribe a server side technology, it does not appear on the network protocol, and therefore needs neither client side installations, nor does NSP reduce performance. In effect, NSP causes no burden for development, openness or availability. NSP has no necessary source code footprint, no network footprint, no architecture footprint, no footprint on the running system. NSP allows the use of complex types in input forms. System interfaces developed with NSP are automatically documented by the reverse engineering tool and language Angie. The NSP technology is fully integrated with form oriented analysis, a corresponding analysis method developed by the authors.

NSP is the only approach for HTML interfaces that allows static type checking of links and forms against called server scripts and delivers parameters to server scripts type-safely and in the native types of the language. NSP makes it possible for the first time during the evolution of web interface frameworks, that the whole uppermost layer for the direct conversational interaction between browser and server is freed of type and linkage errors. To that purpose, NSP has a unique feature: it can statically check, whether the dynamically generated code will be type-safe. This is made possible by the NSP coding rules.

References

1. Atkins, D., Ball, T., Bruns, G., Cox, K.: Mawl: a domain-specific language for form-based services. In IEEE Transactions on Software Engineering, June 1999.
2. Barracuda. http://barracuda.enhydra.org/.
3. Brown, S. et. al.: Professional JSP, 2nd edition. Wrox Press, April 2001.
4. Cocoon. http://xml.apache.org/cocoon/.
5. Davis, M.: Struts, an open-source MVC implementation. IBM developerWorks, February 2001.
6. Davidson, J.D., Coward, D.: Java Servlet Specification, v2.2. Sun Press, 1999.
7. Draheim, D., Weber, G.: Specification and Generation of JSP Dialogues with Gently. In: Proceedings of NetObjectDays 2001, tranSIT, ISBN 3-00-008419-3, September 2001.
8. Draheim, D., Weber, G.: An Introduction to Form Storyboarding. Technical Report B-02-06. Institute of Computer Science, Free University Berlin, March 2002. http://www.inf.fu-berlin.de/inst/pubs/tr-b-02-06.abstract.html
9. Draheim, D., Weber, G.: An Overview of state-of-the-art Architectures for Active Web Sites. Technical Report B-02-07. Institute of Computer Science, Free University Berlin, March 2002. http://www.inf.fu-berlin.de/inst/pubs/tr-b-02-07.abstract.html
10. Draheim, D., Weber, G.: Form Charts and Dialogue Constraints. Technical Report B-02-08. Institute of Computer Science, Free University Berlin, March 2002. http://www.inf.fu-berlin.de/inst/pubs/tr-b-02-08.abstract.html
11. Draheim, D., Weber, G.: An Introduction to State History Diagrams. Technical Report B-02-09, Institute of Computer Science, Free University Berlin, March 2002. http://www.inf.fu-berlin.de/inst/pubs/tr-b-02-09.abstract.html
12. HTML 4.01 Specification. W3C, 1999.
13. Kassem, N., and the Enterprise Team.: Designing Enterprise Applications with the Java 2 Platform, Enterprise Edition. Sun Microsystems, 2000.
14. Meyer, B. Applying "design by contract". IEEE Computer, 25(10):40-51, October 1992.
15. Pelegri-Llopart, E., Cable, L.: Java Server Pages Specification, v.1.1. Sun Press, 1999.
16. SOAP. http://www.w3.org/TR/SOAP/.
17. Webmacro. http://www.webmacro.org/, 2002.

18. Warmer, J.; and Kleppe, A.G. The Object Constraint Language. Addison-Wesley, 1999.
19. Web Services Description Language (WSDL) 1.1. http://www.w3.org/TR/wsdl.
20. The Extensible Stylesheet Language (XSL), http://www.w3.org/Style/XSL/.

A New Privacy Model for Web Surfing

Yuval Elovici, Bracha Shapira, and Adlai Maschiach

Department of Information Systems Engineering,
Ben-Gurion University, Beer-Sheva Israel
elovici@inter.net.il, {bshapira,meshiach}@bgumail.bgu.ac.il

Abstract. Privacy is becoming a serious challenge in computerized environments, especially the Web where many companies constantly attempt to violate the privacy of users. When a user requests a service on the Internet, an eavesdropper can reveal his identity, the WEB site he accesses (end server), the link between them, and infer private information about the user. The computer security community has concentrated on improving user privacy by hiding his identifiable tracks on the WEB, thus assuring his anonymity while surfing. However, users may want or need to identify themselves over the net but still retain their information needs and profile in private. The privacy model suggested in this paper is aimed at preserving users' privacy while allowing them to identify themselves to various services, and prevents eavesdroppers from using identifiable users' tracks to construct a user profile. The model is based on the generation of faked transactions in various fields of interest in order to prevent the eavesdropper from accurate derivation of the user profile. The basic idea underlying the model is to confuse the eavesdropper's automated programs with wrong data. A privacy measure is defined that reflects the degree of confusion a system can cause to the eavesdropper. A prototype system was developed to check the feasibility of the model and to conduct experiments to examine its effectiveness.

1. Introduction

Personal information privacy is an important issue facing the growth and prosperity of the Internet and protecting it has ignited a debate that pits privacy advocates against technology growth enthusiasts.

Many companies on the Web constantly violate the privacy for their own commercial benefits, and consequently users whose privacy is important forego important WEB services in order to prevent exposure. Normally, Web users leave identifiable tracks at every surfed Web site [1]. The tracks can be differentiated between information rooted in the communication infrastructure involved, and information rooted in the user's explicit or implicit information, such as his actions and behavior [5, 7]. In the current study only with information that comes implicitly or explicitly from the user is dealt.

When a user requests a service on the Internet an eavesdropper can reveal his identity, the Web site he accesses (end server), and the link between them. The eavesdropper might be the end server, the user's Internet Service Providers, or anyone

A. Halevy and A. Gal (Eds.): NGITS 2002, LNCS 2382, pp. 45-57, 2002.

else able to listen to the communication between the user and the end server. The eavesdropper can collect data about the content of pages the user visited, times he spent, and frequency, and duration of exchanges. This data can be used to derive the users' profiles and their personal information interests by employing various machine learning and user modeling techniques. A user profile might be used for personalization of various information-gathering services, but, on the negative side, it could also be used to target advertisements and other undesirable goals without the user's authorization or awareness. While a user might change his IP number, e-mail address and geographical location to preserve privacy, it is more difficult to change his user-profile as it is similar to a fingerprint.

The computer security community has concentrated on improving user anonymity on the Web by hiding the identifiable tracks originating from the communication infrastructure involved, and by creating an anonymous channel between the user and the accessed site. However, hiding the identifiable tracks is not an adequate solution when the user is requested to identify itself to the end server. The identification may be required for services provided to identified members or when payment is needed and involves credit cards.

In the current study, we present a new non-anonymous privacy model that can be applied for privacy preservation while accessing public information repositories. The suggested model allows identification of the user, but is aimed at preventing eavesdroppers from using identifiable users' tracks to construct a user profile. The model is based on continuous examination of the real user profile while surfing, and on continuous generation of faked transactions in various fields of interest. The faked transactions are generated in order to disrupt the eavesdroppers' process of profile derivation. The log of transactions that the eavesdroppers record consists of user real and faked transactions. The faked transaction simply confuses the eavesdropper's derivation algorithm by providing wrong data. The suggested model uses statistical methods to construct the real user profile and to generate confusing faked transactions.

In addition, a new privacy measure is defined that enables user to calibrate a desired degree of privacy. The measure is based on the distance between the real user profile and a profile based on the faked generated transactions. The remaining of the paper is organized as follows: section 2 reveals related background on Web anonymity and user profiling; section 3 introduces the model while portraying its objectives and goals. Section 4 presents the prototype system that was developed to implement the model and shows preliminary results. Section 5 includes conclusive remarks and future research.

2. Background

The background relates to the following topics relevant to this study:
• Web privacy and anonymity
• User profiling

2.1 Internet Privacy and Anonymity

A number of tools have been developed to help Internet users surf the Web anonymously. These tools focus on ensuring that requests to Web sites cannot be linked to an IP address identifying the user.

Some of the better-known tools are:

- *Anonymizer* - [3], (http://www.anonymizer.com), submits HTTP requests to the Internet on behalf of its users so that the only IP address revealed to the WEB sites is that of the *Anonymizer.* However, users have to trust the *Anonymizer* and their own ISPs who can still observe their activities.

- *Crowds* – an anonymity agent developed at AT&T labs [12, 13] based on the idea of "blending into a crowd", i.e., concealing one's actions among the actions of others. To execute web transactions using this approach, a user first joins a crowd of users. A user's request to a web server is passed to a random member of the crowd who can either submit the request directly to the end server or forward it to another randomly chosen member. Neither the end server nor any of the crowd members can determine where the requests originated. However, *Crowds* does not offer receiver anonymity. Any request includes the end server's address, which can be viewed by any crowd member, to enable submitting the request to the end server.

Other tools include *Onion-Router*   [6, 18], in which users submit layered encrypted data that specifies the cryptographic algorithms and keys. At each pass through each onion-router on the way to the recipient, one layer of encryption is removed.

All the above-mentioned tools assume that the users have no need or desire to be identified. The only type of solution that is suggested for private identified access is originated at the Web sites and attempt to build users trust in the Internet services. Some initiatives exist such as, *TRUSTe* [2], that are dedicated to building consumers' trust on the Internet by licensing Web sites to display a "trustmark" on their sites.

This solution depends on the good will of Web sites and limits the users access to the licensed sites when privacy is desired. Our privacy non-anonymous model originates at the user, and does not rely on a third party, nor limit access to specific sites.

2.2 User Profiling

While the user is browsing, an eavesdropper may acquire knowledge about the user. There exist various implicit acquisition methods, which are usually employed by different user modeling components in information retrieval (IR) and information filtering (IF) systems to form a user profile 8, 16, 11]. The user profile is used to represent the user's information needs and to predict relevancy of various data items for him, based on the similarity between the user profile and the data item.

During implicit user profile acquisition, no active user involvement is necessary. The user profile is inferred from his behavior and activities on information items that he reads. Such activities include time spent on reading a data item, whether the data item is kept it in his "favorites" list, and so on, [10, 9]. Eavesdroppers use implicit profile acquisition by logging Web pages that users browse in, and derive their profiles from the content of the pages. In this study, the model tackles the eavesdroppers' profile acquisition ability by deterioration of its data, i.e., changing its log of user activities by faking activities.

In our model we use the vector space model [14, 15], which is a common method to represent user profiles. The vector space model is based on the representation of documents and profiles by a vector of significant weighted terms. The terms weights reflects their importance in the document and their scarcity in the entire collection. A document d is represented by an n-dimensional vector space:

$$d = \left(w_1, w_2, ..., w_n \right)$$

(1)

where w_i represents the weight of terms i in document d. One common method for term weighting is TF*IDF [15]. The term weight computation is based on its frequency in the document (TF) – reflecting the importance of the term in the document -, and on the inverse of the term frequency in the collection - (IDF) – reflecting the extent of which this term differentiates between documents. A user profile consists of a vector of weighted terms representing the user areas of interests. The profile can be derived, (as done in our model), from a set of documents relevant to the user. A new document is considered relevant to a user if the vector representing the document is sufficiently similar to the user profile. The similarity between a candidate document and a profile, or between two profiles, is defined by vector distance measuring methods, such as Euclidian distance or cosine. We use the cosine measure, commonly used in information retrieval [4]. The cosine measure represents the cosine of the angle between two vectors in the vector space. The similarity between the two vectors is in the interval of [0,1] where lower angles are closer to 1, and denote higher similarity.

$$S(u_j, u_k) = \frac{\sum_{i=1}^{n} \left(tu_{ij} \cdot tu_{ik} \right)}{\sqrt{\sum_{i=1}^{n} tu_{ij}^2 \cdot \sum_{i=1}^{n} tu_{ik}^2}}$$

(2)

where

u_j, u_k = vectors

tu_{ij} = the ith term in the vector u_j .

tu_{ik} = the ith term in the vector u_k .

n = the number of unique terms in each vector.

3. New Privacy Model

The Model is designed for environments where users access pages on the Web requiring identification. The users wish to preserve their privacy from accessed Web sites and from any eavesdropper on the path between the user computer and the sites. A basic assumption underlying the model is that protecting the user privacy can be partially accomplished by concealing the user information interests, i.e. his profile. As explained in section 2, the user information interests can be represented in the form of a vector of weighted terms that represents the user profile.

In order to formulate the model the following definitions are used:

- A *User Transaction* is defined as an access to a web page from the user computer.
- *Internal user profile* (IUP) is defined as the user profile constructed inside the user's computer. The profile is based on the content of pages the user accesses using his browser.
- *External user profile* (EUP) is defined as the user profile based on the information that flows from the Web to the user's computer.

An eavesdropper is able to compute the EUP by eavesdropping the traffic between the user computer and the Web. We assume that eavesdroppers do not have any smart agents, such as a computer viruses, inserted in the user's computer, and are therefore not able to compute the IUP. However, the EUP and the IUP are usually identical, since the pages accessed by the user in his computer are the same pages flowing from the Web to the user's computer.

The suggested model includes a component that monitors the user transactions and accordingly generates faked transactions in various fields of interest. The faked transactions are aimed at preventing the eavesdropper from accurate derivation of the IUP by confusing its automated programs with wrong data. The faked transactions are mistakenly considered as user's transactions by eavesdroppers. Therefore, *the EUP, which is based on faked transactions, is different from the IUP, which is based on users' transactions.*

The model architecture is shown on Figure 1. It consists of three main components: Browser Monitor Transaction Generator, and Profile Meter. The following section portrays in detail each of the components.

3.1 Browser Monitor

Input-Output: The Browser Monitor receives as input the user transactions and produces as output a vector of weighted terms for each transaction result. The vector represents a page that a user visited. Each vector is sent to the Profile Meter. The Browser Monitor also sends a trigger to the Transaction Generator for each new user transaction.

Functionality: While the user is surfing the Web using a browser, the Browser Monitor analyzes the content of all the user's transactions result, i.e. the Web pages that are presented to the user. For each user's transaction, the Browser Monitor generates for each user's transaction results a vector of weighted terms to represent the transaction. $V_{t^U}^U$ denotes the vector of weighted terms for a transaction at time stamp t^U. The vector $V_{t^U}^U$ is sent to the Profile Meter as input for the process of the construction of $IUP(t^U)$. $IUP(t^U)$ stands for the Internal User Profile (IUP) at time stamp t^U. For each user's transaction the Browser Monitor sends a trigger to the Transaction Generator to indicate a completion of a user's transaction.

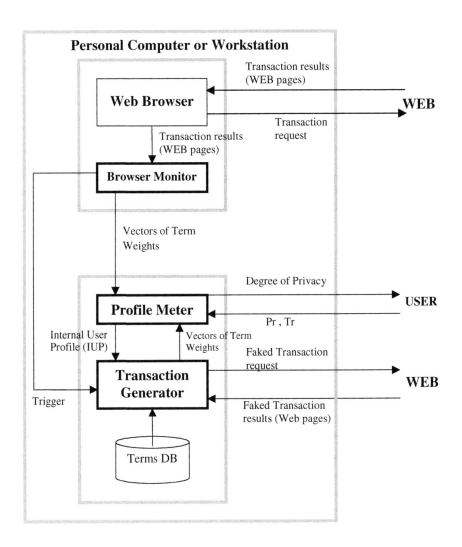

Fig. 1. Privacy Model Architecture

3.2 Transaction Generator

Input-Output: The Transaction-Generator receives a trigger from the Browser Monitor indicating a completion of a user transaction. Other inputs consist of a set of terms read from an internal Database of terms, and the Internal-User-Profile vector that is sent from the Profile-Meter. These sources of input are used by the Transaction-Generator to generate faked transactions sent to the Web. The Transaction Generator also sends the Profile Meter a vector of weighted terms for each faked transaction.

Functionality: The Transaction Generator generates faked transactions. The exact number of faked transactions generated for each user transaction is controlled by a system parameter that symbolizes the average number of faked transactions per user transaction. This parameter (denoted as Tr) can be calibrated by the user. The Transaction Generator does not generate *exactly* Tr transactions for each user transaction, but rather generates Tr transactions *in average* for each user's transaction. This is done to prevent eavesdroppers from discovering the regularity of faked transactions among user's transactions.

The faked transactions consist of Web pages in various fields of interests. In order to assure the confusion of eavesdroppers, most of the faked transactions should be composed of pages not related to the user interests. However, some faked transactions should include pages relating to the user interests in order to prevent eavesdroppers from distinguishing between faked and real transactions. If faked transactions relate only to areas of interests not relevant to the user, eavesdroppers may apply categorization techniques (such as clustering) on the set of users' transactions to categorize the transactions to "real" or "faked".

Sending a "faked transaction string" as a query to a search engine activates a faked transaction generation. The Transaction Generator randomly accesses selected pages from the set of results to the faked query. Each access to a page is a "faked transaction".

The mix of faked transaction relating to user interests, and faked transactions not relating to user interests, is obtained by constructing the "faked transaction query string" from a mix of terms originating from the Internal-User-Profile (IUP), along with random terms originating from an internal database of terms.

In addition, the Transaction-Generator builds a vector of term weights for each of the faked transactions results that he has generated. $V_{t^T}^T$ denotes the vector for a faked transaction result at time stamp t^T. The vectors are sent to the Profile Meter where they will be used to compute the EUP (External User Profile).

3.3 Profile Meter

Input-Output: The Profile Meter receives a vector of term weights $V_{t^U}^U$ from the Browser Monitor for each user transaction. Based on the vectors $V_{t^U}^U$ it computes the $IUP(t^U)$ which is the Internal User Profile at time stamp t^U. The $IUP(t^U)$ is sent to the Transaction Generator. The Profile Meter also receives a vector of term weights $V_{t^T}^T$ from the Transaction Generator for each faked transaction, and computes

the $FUP(t^T)$ which is the Faked User Profile at time stamp t^T.

Another Input-Output interaction of the Profile Meter is with the user. The Profile Meter sends the user information about his current degree of privacy (the privacy measure). and the user can set the Profile Meter parameters (Tr, Pr) in order to calibrate the desired degree of privacy.

Functionality: The following section describes in detail the four tasks that the Profile Meter is responsible for Figure 2 is a graphical illustration of the tasks:

3.3.1. Generation of the $IUP(t^U)$

In the event of receiving a user transaction vector $V_{t^U}^U$ of term weights from the Browser Monitor, the Profile Meter constructs $IUP(t^U)$ - the Internal User Profile at time stamp t^U. This is done by combining $V_{t^U}^U$ with former Pr-1 transaction vectors:

$$IUP(t^U) = \sum_{i=0}^{Pr-1} V_{t^U-i}^U \tag{3}$$

Pr is a system parameter that defines the number of previous transactions vectors to include in a construction of a profile. Pr can be calibrated by users.

3.3.2. Generation of the $FUP(t^T)$

In the event of receiving a faked transaction vector of term weights $V_{t^T}^T$ from the Transaction Generator, the Profile Meter constructs $FUP(t^T)$ - the Faked Transaction Profile at time stamp t^T. This is done by combining $V_{t^T}^T$ with former $Pr \times Tr - 1$ faked transactions vectors:

$$FUP(t^T) = \sum_{i=0}^{Pr \times Tr-1} V_{t^T-i}^T \tag{4}$$

Tr is a system parameter that defines the average number of faked transactions generated by the Transaction Generator for each user transaction. Tr can be calibrated by users:

3.3.3. Generation of the $EUP(t)$

In the event of receiving a transaction vector of terms weight, either a real user transaction vector, or a faked one, the Profile Meter constructs the $EUP(t)$. $EUP(t)$ denotes the External User Profile at time stamp t. To construct $EUP(t)$, the Profile Meter combines $IUP(t^U)$ and $FUP(t^T)$ into one vector:

$$EUP(t) = IUP(t^U) + FUP(t^T) \tag{5}$$

$EUP(t)$ is updated when either $IUP(t^U)$ or $FUP(t^T)$ changes . An eavesdroppers that observes the user activities, will derive $EUP(t)$ as the user profile, as $EUP(t)$ reflects all transactions that occurred in the user's environment. In fact, $EUP(t)$ is not the real user profile, rather, it is a blend of the user profile and faked transactions profile.

3.3.4. Computing the Privacy Measure

Whenever the $IUP(t^U)$, or the $EUP(t)$ changes, the Profile Meter computes the similarity between the profiles (IUP, EUP) by finding the cosine of the angle between the vectors:

$$S(IUP, EUP) = \frac{\sum_{i=1}^{n}(tiup_i \cdot teup_i)}{\sqrt{\sum_{i=1}^{n}tiup_i^2 \cdot \sum_{i=1}^{n}teup_i^2}} \tag{6}$$

where:

$tiup_i$ = the ith term in the vector IUP

$teup_i$ = the ith term in the vector EUP

n= the number of unique terms in each vector.

The similarity between the $IUP(t^U)$ and the $EUP(t)$ is used as a measure of privacy at time stamp t, and is sent to the user, which might in return calibrate Tr and

Pr in order to achieve his desired degree of privacy. The Profile Meter tasks are described in Figure 2.

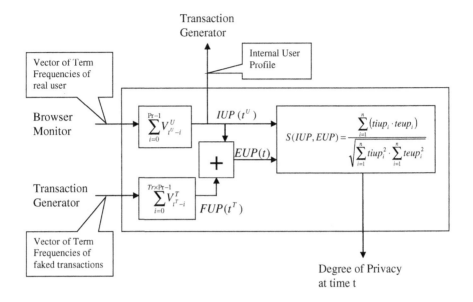

Fig. 2. *Profile Meter Internal Components*

4. Prototype System and Planned Experiments

An initial prototype system implementing the model was developed in order to examine the feasibility of the model and to conduct experiments. The system consists of a smart agent installed in the user computer. The system is built around the Microsoft Internet Explorer. The Browser Monitor component is written in C++ using MSDEV. The Transaction Generator and the Profile Meter are written using Borland C++ Builder.

Preliminary runs of the system were performed. One user generated about 550 transactions while browsing music related pages (looking for music albums, performers, songs, etc.) The system's parameters were set to Tr=5, Pr=30, thus, for each user's transaction, an average of five faked transactions were generated (Tr). The number of user's transaction vectors of terms that were combined to construct the $IUP(t^U)$ was set to 30 (Pr). The graph presented on Figure 3, shows the similarity $S(IUP, EUP)$ between $IUP(t^U)$ and $EUP(t)$ at each event of a new transaction, whether a user or a faked transaction. The values of $S(IUP, EUP)$ range from 0 to 1. Higher values of $S(IUP, EUP)$ suggest that $EUP(t)$ is similar to $IUP(t^U)$ while lower values suggests that $EUP(t)$ is less similar. Actually, the similarity reflects the degree of accuracy of the real user profile derivation that an eavesdropper could achieve and could be used as a privacy measure.

The very preliminary runs presented in Figure 3 show that the similarity seems low (ranges between 0-0.22). One can notice that the very first results (on the left side of the graph), when only few faked transactions where sent from the user computer, the similarity is high, starting from 1 when EUP and IUP are the same.. As the number of transactions increases, the similarity lessens. Similarity starts to stable to the degree of about 0.22 at $t>(Tr * Pr)$ (i.e. at $t>150$) transactions, when the IUP is generated including Tr a transactions, and the EUP is generated including Tr*Pr transactions (Tr faked transactions for each of the Pr user transactions). Further runs, experiments and analysis have to be done to infer any significant results.

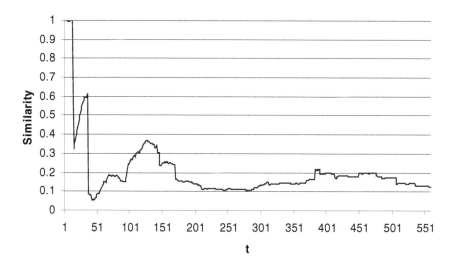

Fig. 3. Results of Preliminary Runs

5. Conclusions and Future Research

The new privacy model presented in this paper poses some important theoretical and practical significance.

- Non-anonymous privacy - The main advantage of the suggested model is the idea of privacy preservation. It enables the user to identify himself while preserving his privacy is essential in the current international situation where new laws aimed at fighting international terrorism are planned to force users to identify themselves while accessing public information such as the Web. In addition, the urgency of our solution stems from the fact that the Internet is transforming into a non-free service; more identifiable transactions will be required. Thus, anonymity cannot be a solution for privacy, and our model seems to be a suitable solution.

• Privacy measure – A new privacy measure is suggested based on the similarity between the Internal User Profile and the External User Profile. This idea of quantifying privacy is significant as it can be used to evaluate the degree of privacy guaranteed by systems, sites, or any software to access a public information repository, and allows users to define the degree of privacy that they want to achieve while using a system.

To evaluate the effectiveness of the model experiments are planned to test the system with a range of users, a range of profiles of the same users, and a range of profile domains. We will also examine:

1. The effect of different values of Pr on similarity. It is obvious that lower values of the parameter Pr will increase the frequency of the profile update, which is useful in the case where the user has several distinct user profiles, while higher values will decrease the frequency of profile update, which is useful in the case where the user does not change his profile frequently. We plan to empirically examine the effect of the frequency of profile adaptation on similarity results, and to try to define an optimum.

2. The effect of different values of Tr on system performance. It is obvious that higher values of Tr will increase the communication bandwidth towards the Internet. We want to define the relation between bandwidth and similarity, and thus define the additional bandwidth that is needed in order to confuse the eavesdropper to a certain degree.

References

1. Brier, S. : How to keep your privacy: Battle lines get clearer. The New York Times, January 13, (1997)
2. Benassi, P.: TRUSTe: An online privacy seal program. Communication of the ACM, 42(2) (1999) 56-59
3. Claessens, J., Preneel, B., Vandewalle, J.: Solutions for anonymous communication on the Internet. Proceedings of the 1999 IEEE International Carnahan Conference on Security Technology 487 (1999) 298-303
4. Frakes, W. B., Baeza-Yates, R. (ed.): Information Retrieval, Data Structures and Algorithms, Pentice Hall, NJ, USA (1992)
5. Goldschlag, D. M., Reed, M. G., Syverson, P. F.: Hiding Routing Information, Information Hiding, R. Anderson (editor), Springer-Verlag LLNCS 1174 (1996) 137-150
6. Goldschlag, D. M., Reed, M. G., Syverson, P. F.: Onion Routing for Anonymous and Private Internet Connections, Communications of the ACM 42 (2) (1999) 39-41
7. Grabber, E., Gibbons, P.B., Matias, Y., Mayer, A.: How to Make Personalized Web Browsing Simple, Secure, and Anonymous. Proceedings of Financial Cryptography (1997)
8. Hanani, U., Shapira, B., Shoval, P.: Information Filtering: Overview of Issues, Research and Systems, User Modeling and User-Adapted Interaction 11 (2001) 203-259

9. Konstan, A., Bradley, N. M., Malts, D., Herlocker, J. L., Gordon, L. R. and Riedl, J.: GroupLens:., Applying collaborative filtering to usenet news. Communications of the ACM 40(3) (1997) 77-87
10. Morita, M., Shinoda, Y.: Information filtering based on user behavior analysis and best match retrieval. Proceedings of the 17th Annual Intl. ACM SIGIR Conference on Research and Development (1994) 272-281
11. Oard, D.: The State of the Art in Text Filtering, *User Modeling and User Adapted Interaction*, 7(3) (1997) 141-178
12. Reiter, M.K., Rubin, A.D.: Crowds: Anonymity for Web Transactions, ACM Transactions on Information and System Security, 1(1) (1998) 66-92
13. Reiter, M.K., Rubin, A.D.: Anonymous Web Transactions with Crowds, Communications of the ACM 42(2) (1999) 66-92
14. Salton, G., Buckley, C.: Term-Weighting Approaches in Automatic Text Retrieval, Information Processing and Management, 24(5) (1998) 513-523
15. Salton, G., McGill, W.J.(ed.): Introduction to Modern Information Retrieval. McGraw-Hill. New-York (1983)
16. Shapira, B, Shoval, P., Hanani,U.: Experimentation with an Information Filtering System that Combines Cognitive and Sociological Filtering Integrated with User Stereotypes, Journal: Decision Support Systems 27 (1999) 5-24
17. Shapira B., Hanani U., Raveh A., Shoval P.: Information Filtering: A New Two-Phase Model Using Stereotypic User-Profiling. Journal of Intelligent Information Systems 8 (1997) 155-165
18. Syverson, P. F., Goldschlag, D. M., Reed, M. G.: Anonymous Connections and Onion Routing, Proceedings of the 18th Annual Symposium on Security and Privacy, IEEE CS Press, Oakland, CA, (1997) 44-54

Design and Implementation of a Distributed Crawler and Filtering Processor*

Demetrios Zeinalipour-Yazti[1] and Marios Dikaiakos[2]

[1] Dept. of Computer Science and Engineering
University of California, Riverside CA 92507, USA,
csyiazti@cs.ucr.edu
[2] Dept. of Computer Science
University of Cyprus, PO Box 20537, Nicosia, Cyprus,
mdd@ucy.ac.cy

Abstract. Web crawlers are the key component of services running on Internet and providing searching and indexing support for the entire Web, for corporate Intranets and large portal sites. More recently, crawlers have also been used as tools to conduct focused Web searches and to gather data about the characteristics of the WWW. In this paper, we study the employment of crawlers as a programmable, scalable, and distributed component in future Internet middleware infrastructures and proxy services. In particular, we present the architecture and implementation of, and experimentation with WebRACE, a high-performance, distributed Web crawler, filtering server and object cache. We address the challenge of designing and implementing modular, open, distributed, and scalable crawlers, using Java. We describe our design and implementation decisions, and various optimizations. We discuss the advantages and disadvantages of using Java to implement the WebRACE-crawler, and present an evaluation of its performance. WebRACE is designed in the context of eRACE, an extensible Retrieval Annotation Caching Engine, which collects, annotates and disseminates information from heterogeneous Internet sources and protocols, according to XML-encoded user profiles that determine the urgency and relevance of collected information.

1 Introduction

In this paper we present the design, implementation, and empirical analysis of WebRACE,, a distributed crawler, filtering processor and object cache. WebRACE is part of a more generic system, called *eRACE* (extensible Retrieval, Annotation and Caching Engine), which is a distributed middleware infrastructure that enables the development and deployment of content-delivery and mobile services on Internet [13]. eRACE collects information from heterogeneous

---

* This work was supported in part by the Research Promotion Foundation of Cyprus under grant PENEK-No 23/2000.

A. Halevy and A. Gal (Eds.): NGITS 2002, LNCS 2382, pp. 58–74, 2002.

Internet sources according to pre-registered, XML-encoded user and service profiles. These profiles drive the collection of information and determine the relevance and the urgency of collected information. eRACE offers a functionality that goes beyond the capabilities of traditional Web servers and proxies, providing support for intelligent personalization, customization and transcoding of content, to match the interests and priorities of individual end-users connected through fixed and mobile terminals. Its goal is to enable the development of new services and the easy re-targeting of existing services to new terminal devices.

WebRACE is the Web-specific proxy of eRACE. It crawls the Web to retrieve documents according to user profiles. The system subsequently caches and processes retrieved documents. Processing is guided by pre-defined user queries and consists of keywords-searches, title-extraction, summarizing, classification based on relevance with respect to user-queries, estimation of priority, urgency, etc. WebRACE processing results are encoded in a WebRACE-XML grammar and fed into a dissemination server, which is designed to select dynamically among a suite of available choices for information dissemination, such as "push" vs. "pull," the formatting and transcoding of data (HTML, WML, XML), the connection modality (wireless vs. wire-based), the communication protocol employed (HTTP, GSM/WAP, SMS), etc.

In the following sections we describe our design effort, and implementation experience with using Java to develop the high-performance Crawler, Annotation Engine and Object Cache of WebRACE. We also describe a number of techniques employed to achieve high-performance, such as distributed design to enable the execution of crawler modules to different machines, support for multithreading, caching of crawling state, customized memory management, employment of persistent data structures with disk-caching support, optimizations of the Java core libraries for TCP/IP and HTTP communication, etc. Finally, we provide performance measurements from typical executions of WebRACE.

The remaining of the paper is organized as follows: Section 2 presents an overview of the WebRACE system architecture and the challenges addressed in our work. Sections 3 and 4 describe the design and implementation of a Crawler and Object Cache, used to retrieve and store content from the Web. Section 5 presents the Filtering Processor that analyzes the collected information, according to user-profiles. Finally, Section 7 summarizes our conclusions.

2   WebRACE Design and Implementation Challenges

WebRACE is comprised of two basic components, the *Mini-crawler* and the *Annotation Engine*, which operate independently and asynchronously (see Figure 1). Both components can be distributed to different computing nodes, execute in different Java heap spaces, and communicate through a permanent socket link; through this socket, the Mini-crawler notifies the Annotation Engine every time it fetches and caches a new page in the Object Cache. The Annotation Engine can then process the fetched page asynchronously, according to pre-registered user profiles or other criteria.

In the development of WebRACE we address a number of challenges: First, is the design and implementation of a user-driven crawler. Typical crawlers employed by major search engines such as Google [3], start their crawls from a carefully chosen fixed set of "seed" URL's. In contrast, the Mini-crawler of WebRACE receives continuously crawling directives which emanate from a queue of standing eRACE requests (see Figure 1). These requests change with shifting eRACE-user interests, updates in the base of registered users, changes in the set of monitored resources, etc.

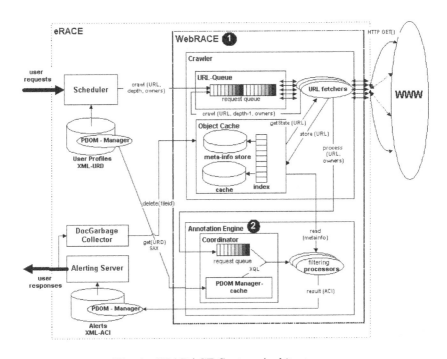

Fig. 1. WebRACE System Architecture.

Second, is the design of a crawler that monitors Web-sites exhibiting frequent updates of their content. WebRACE should follow and capture these updates so that interested users are notified by eRACE accordingly. Consequently, WebRACE is expected to crawl and index parts of the Web under short-term time constraints and maintain multiple versions of the same Web-page in its store, until all interested users receive the corresponding alerts.

Similarly to personal and site-specific crawlers like SPHINX [16] and NetAttache Pro [11], WebRACE is customized and targets specific Web-sites. These features, however, must be sustained in the presence of a large and increasing user base, with varying interests and different service-level requirements. In this context, WebRACE must be scalable, sustaining high-performance and short turn-around times when serving many users and crawling a large portion of the Web. To this end, it should avoid duplication of effort and combine similar requests when serving similar user profiles. Furthermore, it should provide built-in support for QoS policies involving multiple service-levels and service-level guarantees. Consequently, the scheduling and performance requirements of WebRACE crawling and filtering face very different constraints than systems like Google [3], Mercator [9], SPHINX [16] or NetAttache Pro [11].

Finally, WebRACE is implemented entirely in Java. Its implementation consists of approximately 5500 lines of code, 2649 of which correspond to the Mini-crawler implementation, 1184 to the Annotation Engine, 367 to the SafeQueue data structure, and 1300 to common I/O libraries. Java was chosen for a variety of reasons. Its object-oriented design enhances the software development process, supports rapid prototyping and enables the re-use and easy integration of existing components. Java class libraries provide support for key features of WebRACE: platform independence, multithreading, network programming, high-level programming of distributed applications, string processing, code mobility, compression, etc. Other Java features, such as automatic garbage collection, persistence and exception handling, are crucial in making our system more tolerant to run-time faults.

The choice of Java, however, comes with a certain risk-factor that arises from known performance problems of this programming language and its run-time environment. Notably, performance and robustness are issues of critical importance for a system like WebRACE, which is expected to function as a server, to run continuously and to sustain high-loads at short periods of time. In our experiments, we found the performance of Java SDK 1.3 satisfactory when used in combination with the Java HotSpot Server VM [15,14]. Furthermore, the Garbage Collector, which seemed to be a problem with earlier Java versions, has a substantially improved performance and effectiveness under Java v.1.3.

Numerous experiments with earlier versions of WebRACE, however, showed that memory management cannot rely entirely on Java's garbage collection. During long crawls, memory allocation increased with crawl size and duration, leading to over-allocation of heap space, heap-space overflow exceptions, and system crashes. Extensive performance and memory debugging with the OptimizeIt profiler [20] identified a number of Java core classes that allocated new objects excessively and caused heap-space overflows and performance degradation. Consequently, we had to develop our own data-structures that use a bounded amount of heap-space regardless of the crawl size, and maintain part of their data on disk. Furthermore, we re-wrote some of the mission-critical Java classes, streamlining very frequent operations. More details are given in the sections that follow.

3   The Mini-Crawler of WebRACE

A crawler is a program that traverses the hypertext structure of the Web automatically, starting from an initial hyper-document and recursively retrieving all documents accessible from that document. Web crawlers are also referred to as robots, wanderers, or spiders. Typically, a crawler executes a basic algorithm that takes a list of "seed" URL's as its input, and repeatedly executes the following steps [1]: It initializes the crawling engine with the list of seed URL's and pops a URL out of the URL list. Then, it determines the IP address of the chosen URL's host name, opens a socket connection to the corresponding server, asks for the particular document, parses the HTTP response header and decides if this particular document should be downloaded. If this is so, the crawler downloads the corresponding document and extracts the links contained in it; otherwise, it proceeds to the next URL. The crawler ensures that each extracted link corresponds to a valid and absolute URL, invoking a URL-normalizer to "de-relativize" it, if necessary. Then, the normalized URL is appended to the list of URL's scheduled for download, provided this URL has not been fetched earlier.

In contrast to typical crawlers [16,9], WebRACE refreshes frequently its URL-seed list from requests posted by the eRACE *Request Scheduler*. These requests have the following format:

$$[Link, \ ParentLink, \ Depth, \ \{owners\}]$$

Link is the URL address of the Web resource sought, *ParentLink* is the URL of the page that contained Link, *Depth* defines how deep the crawler should "dig" starting from the page defined by Link, and {*owners*} contains the list of eRACE users whose profile designates an interest for the pages that will be downloaded.

Making the Mini-crawler configurable through these configuration files renders it adaptable to specific crawl tasks and benchmarks. The crawling algorithm described in the previous section requires a number of components, which are listed and described in detail below:

- The *URLQueue* for storing links that remain to be downloaded.
- The *URLFetcher* that uses HTTP to download documents from the Web. The URLFetcher contains also a *URL extractor and normalizer* that extracts links from a document and ensures that the extracted links are valid and absolute URL's.
- The *Object Cache*, which stores and indexes downloaded documents, and ensures that no duplicate documents are maintained in cache. The Object Cache, however, can maintain multiple versions of the same URL, if its contents have changed with time.

The Mini-crawler is configurable through three files: a) `/conf/webrace.conf`, which contains general settings of the engine, such as the crawling start page, the depth of crawling, intervals between system-state save, the size of key data-structures maintained in main memory, etc.; b) `/conf/mime.types`, which controls what Internet media types should be gathered by the crawler; c) `/conf/ignore.types`, which controls what file extensions should be blocked by the engine; URL resources with a suffix listed in `ignore.types` will not be downloaded regardless of the actual mime-type of that file's content.

3.1   The URLQueue

The *URLQueue* is an implementation of our onw *SafeQueue* class. We designed and implemented SafeQueue to guarantee the efficient and robust operation of

WebRACE and to overcome problems of the `java.util.LinkList` component of Java [6]. We implemented SafeQueue as a circular array of *QueueNode* objects with its own memory-management mechanism, which enables the re-use of objects and minimizes garbage-collection overhead. Moreover, SafeQueue incorporates support for persistence, overflow control, disk caching, multi-threaded access, and fast indexing to avoid the insertion of duplicate QueueNode entries. More details on the design and implementation of SafeQueue can be found in [24].

URLQueue is a SafeQueue comprised of *URLQueueNode*, i.e., Java objects that capture requests coming from the Request Scheduler of eRACE. During the server's initialization, WebRACE allocates the full size of the URLQueue on the heap. The length of the URLQueue is determined during the server's initialization from WebRACE configuration files. At that time, our program allocates the heap-space required to store all the nodes of the queue. We chose this approach instead of allocating Queue Nodes on demand for memory efficiency and performance. In our experiments, we configured the URLQueue size to two million nodes, i.e., two million URL's. This number corresponds to approximately 27 MB of heap space. A larger URLQueue can be employed, however, at the expense of heap size available for other components of WebRACE.

3.2   The URLFetcher

The *URLFetcher* is a WebRACE module that fetches a document from the Web when provided with a corresponding URL. The URLFetcher is implemented as a simple Java-thread, supporting both HTTP/1.0 and HTTP/1.1. Similarly to crawlers like Mercator [9], WebRACE supports multiple URLFetcher threads running concurrently, grabbing pending requests from the URLQueue, conducting synchronous I/O to download WWW content, and overlapping I/O with computation. In the current version of WebRACE, resource management and thread scheduling is left to Java's runtime system and the underlying operating system. The number of available URLFetcher threads, however, can be configured during the initialization of the WebRACE-server. It should be noted that a very large number of URLFetcher threads can lead to serious performance degradation of our system, due to excessive synchronization and context-switching overhead.

The URLFetcher supports the Robots Exclusion Protocol (REP) that allows Web masters to declare parts of their sites off-limits to crawlers. In addition to supporting the standard Robots Exclusion Protocol, WebRACE supports the exclusion of particular domains and URL's. To implement the exclusion protocol, WebRACE provides a *BlockDomain* hash table, which contains all domains and URL's that should be blocked. In addition to handling HTTP connections, the URLFetcher processes the documents it downloads from the Web. To this end, it invokes methods of its *URLExtractor and normalizer* sub-component. The URLExtractor extracts links (URL's) out of a page, disregards URL's pointing to uninteresting resources, normalizes the URL's so that they are valid and absolute and, finally, adds these links to the URLQueue.

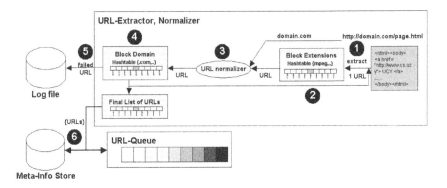

Fig. 2. URL Extractor Architecture.

As shown in Figure 2, the URLExtractor and normalizer works as a 6-step pipe within the URLFetcher. Extraction and normalization of URL's works as follows: in step 1, a `fastfind()` method identifies candidate URL's in the web-page at hand, removes internal links (starting from "#"), mailto links ("`mailto:`"), etc, and extracts the first URL that is candidate for processing. The efficient implementation of fastfind is challenging due to the abundance of badly formed HTML code on the Web. As an alternative solution we could reuse components such as Tidy [18] or its Java port, JTidy [12], to transform the downloaded Web page into well-formed HTML, and then extract all links using a generic XML parser. This solution proved to be too slow, in contrast to our `fastfind()` method which extracts links from a 70 KB web page in approximately 80ms.

In step 2, a *Proactive Link Filtering* (PLF) method is invoked to disregard links to resources that are of no interest to the particular crawl. PLF uses the `/conf/ignore.types` configuration file of WebRACE to determine the file extensions that should be blocked during the URL extraction phase. Deciding if a link should be dropped takes less than 1 ms and saves WebRACE of the unnecessary effort to normalize a URL, add it to the URLQueue, and open an HTTP connection, just to see that this document has a media type that is not collected by the crawler.

Step 3 deals with the normalization of the URL at hand. To this end, we wrote a *URL-normalizer* method, which alters links that do not comply to the scheme-specific syntax of HTTP URL's, as defined in the HTTP RFCs. The URL-normalizer applies a set of heuristic corrections, which give on the average a 95% of valid and normalized URL's. If a link cannot be normalized, it is logged for debugging purposes. The URL-normalizer has been tested succesfully on a test case of 150 problematic URL strings which did not conform to the scheme-specific syntax of HTTP URL's. We are continously upgrading the URL-normalizer as new problematic HTTP URL's appear in our log files.

For each Web page processed, the URL-normalizer makes extensive use of the `java.net.URL` library while checking the syntactic validity of the normalized

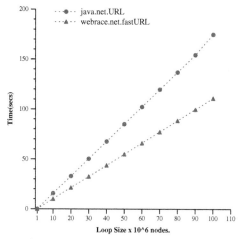

Total Times:[java.net.URL .vs webrace.net.fastURL] Benchmark

Fig. 3. webrace.net.URL Performance.

URL. This library, however, creates numerous objects that cannot be reused, resulting to excessive heap-memory consumption, an increased activity of the garbage collector, and significant performance degradation. To cope with these problems we implemented `webrace.net.fastURL`, a streamlined URL class that enables the reuse of URL objects via its `reparse(url)` method. `reparse(url)` allows the `webrace.net.fastURL()` class to disregard previously assigned string values of its private elements `host`,`protocol`,`port` and `file`, and replace them by new values that need to be validated for conformance to the syntax of HTTP URLs.

This optimization achieves twofold and threefold improvements of the normalization performance under Solaris and Windows NT respectively. Figure 3, presents the results of a `java.net.URL` vs. `webrace.net.fastURL` performance benchmark. In this benchmark, we evaluated `webrace.net.URL` by instantiating up to 10^8 new URL objects. The benchmark ran on a Sun Enterprise E250 Server with 2 UltraSPARC-II processors at $400MHz$, with $512MB$ memory, running the Solaris 5.7 operating system. The URL-normalizer took on the average $200ms$ for 100 URL's.

Step 4 filters out links that belong to domains that are blocked or excluded by the Robot Exclusion Protocols. Steps 1 through 4 are executed repeatedly until all links of the document at hand have been processed. Step 5 logs the URL's that failed the normalization process for debugging purposes. Finally, at step 6, all extracted and normalized URL's are collectively added to the URL-Queue, dropping all duplicate URL's and URL's that have been visited by the crawler already. The list of normalized URL's is also stored in the Meta-Info Store, so that during re-crawls the Mini-Crawler can avoid URL-extraction of unmodified pages.

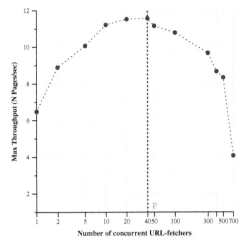

Number of Concurrent URL-fetchers executing in WebRACE (normal-log scale)

Fig. 4. URL-fetcher throughput degradation.

The URL extraction and normalization pipe requires an average of 300 ms to extract the links from a 70 KB HTML page and to normalize them appropriately, when executed on our Sun Enterprise E250 Server. To evaluate the overall performance of the URLFetcher, we ran a number of experiments, launching many concurrent fetchers that try to establish TCP connections and fetch documents from Web servers located on our 10/100Mbits LAN. Each URLFetcher pre-allocates all of its required resources before the benchmark start-up. The benchmarks ran on a 360MHz UltraSPARC-IIi, with 128MB RAM and Solaris 5.7. As we can see from Figure 4, the throughput increases with the number of concurrent URLFetchers, until a peak P is reached. After that point, throughput drops substantially. This crawling process took a very short time (3 minutes with only one thread), which is actually the reason why the peak value P is 40. In this case, URLQueue empties very fast, limiting the utilization of URLFetcher's near the benchmark's end. Running the same benchmark for a lengthy crawl we observed that 100 concurrent URLFetcher's achieve optimal crawling throughput.

Since the optimal crawling throughput can only be determined at runtime we have implemented a Performance Monitoring mechanism which maintains various statistics such as the *Connection, Processing and I/O delays* which allow us to approximate the optimal number of URLfetcher's running in the system. URLfetchers are consequently either dropped, by a pre-specified percentage (*drop_pct%*), or increased slowly (*increase_pct%*) on intervals were the system seems to sustain the current load.

4   The Object Cache

The *Object Cache* is the component responsible for managing documents cached in secondary storage. It is used for storing downloaded documents that will be retrieved later for processing, annotation and subsequent dissemination to eRACE users. The Object Cache, moreover, caches the crawling state in order to coalesce similar crawling requests and to accelerate the re-crawling of WWW resources that have not changed since their last crawl.

The Object Cache is comprised of an *Index*, a *Meta-Info Store* and an *Object Store* (see Figure 1). Although the Index resides in main memory at runtime for increased performance, it is serialized to secondary storage on regular intervals. The documents indexed by the Object Cache are stored on disk allowing us in that way to scale to many billion of documents. The Index of the Object Cache is implemented as a `java.util.HashTable`, which contains URL's that have been fetched and stored in WebRACE. That way, during re-crawls, *URLFetcher*'s can check if a page has been re-fetched, before deciding whether to download its contents from the Web. The Meta-Info Store collects and maintains meta-information for cached documents. Finally, the Object Store is a directory in secondary storage that contains a compressed version of downloaded resources.

4.1   Meta-info Store

The Meta-Info Store maintains a meta-information file for each Web document stored in the Object Cache. Furthermore, a key for each meta-info file is kept with the Index of the Object Cache to allow for fast look-ups. The contents of a meta-info file are encoded in XML and include:

- The URL address of the corresponding document;
- The IP address of its origin Web server;
- The document size in KB;
- The Last-Modified field returned by the HTTP protocol during download;
- The HTTP response header;
- All extracted and normalized links contained in this document;
- Information about the different document versions kept in the Object Cache.

An excerpt from a meta-info file is given in Table 1. Normally, a *URLFetcher* executes the following algorithm to download a Web page:

1. Retrieve a QueueNode from the URLQueue and extract its URL.
2. Make the HTTP connection, retrieve the URL and analyze the HTTP-header of the response message. If the host server contains the message "200 Ok," proceed to the next step. Otherwise, continue with the next QueueNode.
3. Download the body of the document and store it in main memory.
4. Extract and normalize all links contained in the downloaded document.
5. Compress and save the document in the Object Cache.
6. Save a generated meta-info file in the Meta-Info Store.

Table 1. Example of meta-information file.

```
< webrace:url>http://www.cs.ucy.ac.cy/~epl121/< /webrace:url>
< webrace:ip>194.42.7.2< /webrace:ip>
< webrace:kbytes>1< /webrace:kbytes>
< webrace:ifmodifiedsince>989814504121< /webrace:ifmodifiedsince>
<webrace:header>
  HTTP/1.0 200 OK
  Server: Netscape-FastTrack/2.01
  Date: Fri, 11 May 2001 13:50:10 GMT
  Accept-ranges: bytes
  Last-modified: Fri, 26 Jan 2001 21:46:08 GMT
  Content-length: 1800
  Content-type: text/html
< /webrace:header>
<webrace:links>
  http://www.cs.ucy.ac.cy/Computing/labs.html
  http://www.cs.ucy.ac.cy/
  http://www.cs.ucy.ac.cy/helpdeskF
< /webrace:links>
```

7. Add the key (hashCode) of the fetched URL to the Index of the Object Cache.
8. Notify the Annotation Engine that a new document has been fetched and stored in the Object Cache.
9. Add all extracted URL's to the URLQueue. The URLQueue disregards duplicate URL's in order to avoid leading the crawler into cycles.

To avoid the overhead of the repeated downloading and analysis of documents that have not changed, we alter the above algorithm and use the Meta-Info Store to decide whether to download a document that is already cached in WebRACE. More specifically, we change the second and third steps of the above crawling algorithm as follows:

2. Access the Index of the Object Cache and check if the URL retrieved from the URLQueue corresponds to a document fetched earlier and cached in WebRACE.
3. If the document is not in the Cache, download it and proceed to step 4. Otherwise:
    − Load its meta-info file and extract the HTTP Last-Modified time-stamp assigned by the origin server. Open a socket connection to the origin server and request the document using a conditional *HTTP GET* command (if-modified-then), with the extracted time-stamp as its parameter.
    − If the origin server returns a "304 (not modified)" response and no message-body, terminate the fetching of this particular resource, extract the document links from its meta-info file, and proceed to step 8.

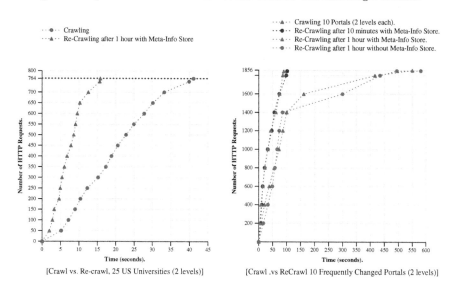

Fig. 5. Crawling vs. Re-Crawling in WebRACE in two different settings.

- Otherwise, download the body of the document, store it in main memory and proceed to step 4.

If a cached document has not been changed during a re-crawl, the URLFetcher proceeds with crawling the document's outgoing links, which are stored in the Meta-Info Store, and which may have changed.

To assess the performance improvement provided by the use of the Meta-Info Store, we conducted an experiment with crawling two classes of Web sites. The first class includes servers that provide content which does not change very frequently (University sites). The second class consists of popular news-sites, search-engine sites and portals (cnn.com, yahoo.com, msn.com, etc.). For these experiments we configured WebRACE to use 150 concurrent URLFetchers and ran it on our Sun Enterprise E250 Server, with the Annotation Processor running concurrently on a Sparc 5.

The diagram of Figure 5a presents the progress of the crawl and re-crawl operations for the first class of sites. The time interval between the crawl and the subsequent re-crawl was one hour; within that hour the crawled documents had not changed at all. The delay observed for the re-crawl operation is attributed to the HTTP "if-modified-since" validation messages and the overhead of the Object Cache. As we can see from this diagram, the employment of the Meta-Info Store results to an almost three-fold improvement in the crawling performance. Moreover, it reduces substantially the network traffic and the Web-servers' load generated because of the crawl.

The diagram of Figure 5b presents our measurements from the crawl and re-crawl operations for the second class of sites. Here, almost 10% of the 993

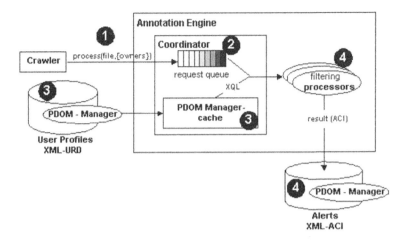

Fig. 6. WebRACE Annotation Engine.

downloaded documents change between subsequent re-crawls. From this diagram we can easily see the performance advantage gained by using the Meta-Info Store to cache crawling meta-information. It should be noted, however, that within the first $100msecs$ of all crawl operations, crawling and re-crawling exhibit practically the same performance behavior. This is attributed to the fact that most of the crawled portals reply to our HTTP `GET` requests with "301 (`Moved Permanently`)'' responses, and re-direct our crawler to other URL's. In these cases, the crawler terminates the connection and schedules immediately a new HTTP `GET` operation to fetch the requested documents from the re-directed address.

5   The Annotation Engine (AE)

The Annotation Engine processes documents that have been downloaded and cached in the *Object Cache* of WebRACE. Its purpose is to "classify" collected content according to user-interests described in eRACE profiles. The meta-information produced by the processing of the Annotation Engine is stored in WebRACE as annotation linked to the cached content. Pages that are not relevant to any user-profile are dropped from the cache.

Personalized annotation engines are not used in typical Search Engines [1], which employ general-purpose indices instead. To avoid the overhead of incorporating a generic look-up index in WebRACE that will be updated dynamically as resources are downloaded from the Web, we designed the AE so that it processes downloaded pages "on the fly.". Therefore, each time the Annotation Engine receives a ''`process(file,{users})`'' request through the established socket connection with the Mini-crawler, it inserts the request in the *Coordinator*, which is a SafeQueue data structure (see Figure 6). Multiple *Filtering*

Processors remove requests from the Coordinator and process them according to the *Unified Resource Descriptions (URD's)* of eRACE users contained in the request. Currently, the annotation engine implements a simple pattern-matching algorithm looking for weighted keywords that are included in the user-profiles, similar to that of [22].

Table 2. A typical URD.

```
<urd>
    <uri timing= "600000" lastcheck = "97876750000" port= "80"
        http://www.cs.ucy.ac.cy/default.html< /uri>
    <type protocol= "http" method= "pull" processtype= "filter"/ >
        <keywords>
                <keyword key= "ibm" weight= "1" / >
                <keyword key= "research" weight= "3" / >
                <keyword key= "java" weight= "4" / >
                <keyword key= "xmlp4j" weight= "5" / >
        < /keywords>
    <depth level= "4"/ >
    <urgency urgent= "1"/ >
< /urd>
```

URD is an XML-encoded data structure that encapsulates, within an eR-ACE user-profile, source information, processing directives and urgency information for Web services monitored by eRACE [23]. A typical URD request is shown in Table 2. URD's are stored in a single XML-encoded document, which is managed by a persistent DOM data manager (*PDOM*) [10]. The Annotation Engine fetches the necessary URD's from the *PDOM* data manager issuing XQL queries (eXtensible Query Language) to a GMD-IPSI XQL engine [10,17]. The GMD-IPSI XQL engine is a Java-based storage and query application developed by Darmstadt GMD for handling large XML documents. This engine is based on two key mechanisms: a) a persistent implementation of W3C-DOM Document objects [21]; b) a full implementation of the XQL query language. GMD-IPSI provides an efficient and reliable way to handle large XML documents through PDOM, which is a thread-safe and persistent XML-DOM implementation. PDOM supports main-memory caching of XML nodes, enabling fast searches in the DOM tree. A PDOM file is organized in pages, each containing 128 DOM nodes of variable length. When a PDOM node is accessed by a W3C-DOM method, its page is loaded into a main memory cache. The default cache size is 100 pages (12800 DOM nodes). Documents are parsed once and stored in Java serialized binary form on secondary storage. The generated document is accessible to DOM operations directly, without re-parsing. The XQL processor is used to query PDOM files.

The output of a filtering process in the Annotation Engine is encoded in XML and called an *ACI* (Annotated Cache Information) [23]; ACI's are stored

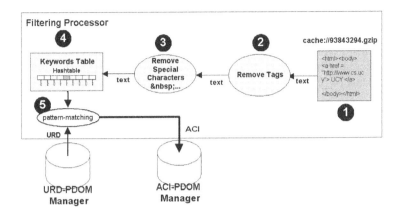

Fig. 7. The Filtering Processor.

in an XML-ACI PDOM database. ACI is an extensible data structure that encapsulates information about the Web source that corresponds to the ACI, the potential user-recipient(s) of the "alert" that will be generated by eRACE's Content Distribution Agents according to the ACI, a pointer to the cached content, a description of the content (format, file size, extension), a classification of this content according to its urgency and/or expiration time, and a classification of the document's relevance with respect to the semantic interests of its potential recipient(s). The XML description of the ACI's is extendible and therefore we can easily include additional information in it without having to change the architecture of WebRACE.

Filtering Processor (FP) is the component responsible for evaluating if a document matches the interests of a particular eRACE-user, and for generating an ACI out of a crawled page (see Figure 7). The Filtering Processor works as a pipe of filters: At step 1, FP loads and decompresses the appropriate file from the Object Cache of WebRACE. At step 2, it removes all links contained in the document and proceeds to step 3, where all special HTML characters are also removed. At step 4, any remaining text is added to a Keyword HashTable. Finally, at step 5, a pattern-matching mechanism loads sequentially all the required URD elements from the URD-PDOM and generates ACI meta-information, which is stored in the ACI-PDOM (step 6). This pipe requires an average of 200 msecs to calculate the ACI for a $70KB$ Web page, with 3 potential recipients.

In our experiments, we have configured the SafeQueue size of the Annotation Engine to 1000 nodes, which is more than enough, since it is almost every time clear if the AE operates with 10 Filtering Processors and the Mini-crawler with 100 URL-fetchers. We have also observed that the number of pending requests in the AE SafeQueue has reached a peak of 55 pending requests at a particular run of our system.

6   Conclusions

Although a number of papers have been published on Web crawlers [16,9,5, 4,19], proxy services and Internet middleware [2,8], the issue of incorporating flexible, scalable and user-driven crawlers in middleware infrastructures remains open. Furthermore, the adoption of Java as the language of choice in the design of Internet middleware and servers raises many doubts, primarily because of performance and scalability questions. There is no question, however, that Web crawlers written in Java will be an important component of such systems, along with modules that process collected content.

In our work, we addressed the challenge of designing and implementing a user-driven, distributed, and scalable crawler and filtering processor, in the context of the eRACE middleware. We described our design and implementation decisions, and various optimizations. Furthermore, we discussed the advantages and disadvantages of using Java to implement the crawler, and presented an evaluation of its performance. To assess WebRACE's performance and robustness we ran numerous experiments and crawls; several of our crawls lasted for days. Our system worked efficiently and with no failures when crawling local Webs in our LAN and University WAN, and the global Internet. Our experiments showed that our implementation is robust and reliable. Furthermore, that caching meta-information about the crawling state can result to significant improvements in crawling performance. Further optimizations will be included in the near future, such as the employment of distributed data structures [7] to make the Mini-crawler itself distributed.

References

1. A. Arasu, J. Cho, H. Garcia-Molina, A. Paepcke, and S. Raghavan. Searching the Web. *ACM Transactions on Internet Technology*, 2001. To appear.
2. C. M. Bowman, P. B. Danzig, D. R. Hardy, U. Manber, and M. F. Schwartz. The Harvest Information Discovery and Access System. In *Proceedings of the Second International WWW Conference*, 1995.
3. S. Brin and L. Page. The Anatomy of a Large-Scale Hypertextual (Web) Search Engine. *Computer Networks and ISDN Systems*, 30(1–7):107–117, 1998.
4. S. Chakrabarti, M. van den Berg, and B. Dom. Focused Crawling: A New Approach to Topic-Specific Web Resource Discovery. In *8th World Wide Web Conference*, Toronto, May 1999.
5. J. Cho, H. Garcia-Molina, and L. Page. Efficient crawling through URL ordering. In *Proceedings of the Seventh International WWW Conference*, pages 161–172, April 1998.
6. J. Gosling, B. Joy, and G. Steele. *The Java Language Specification*. Addison-Wesley, 1996.
7. S. Gribble, E. Brewer, J. Hellerstein, and D. Culler. Scalable, Distributed Data Structures for Internet Service Construction. In *Proceedings of the Fourth Symposium on Operating Systems Design and Implementation (OSDI 2000)*, 2000.

8. S. Gribble, M. Welsh, R. von Behren, E. Brewer, D. Culler, N. Borisov, S. Czerwinski, R. Gummadi, J. Hill, A. Joseph, R.H. Katz, Z.M. Mao, S. Ross, and B. Zhao. The Ninja Architecture for Robust Internet-scale Systems and Services. *Computer Networks*, 35:473–497, 2001.

9. A. Heydon and M. Najork. Mercator: A Scalable, Extensible Web Crawler. *World Wide Web*, 2(4):219–229, December 1999.

10. G. Huck, I. Macherius, and P. Fankhauser. PDOM: Lightweight Persistency Support for the Document Object Model. In *Proceedings of the 1999 OOPSLA Workshop Java and Databases: Persistence Options. Held on the 14th Annual ACM SIGPLAN Conference on Object-Oriented Programming Systems, Languages, and Applications (OOPSLA '99)*. ACM, SIGPLAN, November 1999.

11. Tympani Development Inc. NetAttache Pro. http://www.tympani.com/products/NAPro.html, 2000.

12. S. Lempinen. *Jtidy*. http://lempinen.net/sami/jtidy.

13. M.DIkaiakos and D.Zeinalipour. eRACE Project. http://www.cs.ucy.ac.cy/Projects/eRACE/, 2001.

14. Steve Meloan. The Java HotSpotTM Performance Engine: An In-Depth Look. Technical report, Sun Microsystems, June 1999. http://developer.java.sun.com/developer/technicalArticles/Networking/HotSpot/.

15. Sun Microsystems. The Java HotSpot TM Server VM. http://java.sun.com/products/hotspot/, 1999.

16. R. Miller and K. Bharat. SPHINX: A Framework for Creating Personal, Site-specific Web Crawlers. In *Proceedings of the Seventh International WWW Conference*, pages 161–172, April 1998.

17. GMD-IPSI XQL Engine. http://xml.darmstadt.gmd.de/xql/.

18. D. Raggett. *Clean up your Web pages with HTML TIDY*. http://www.w3.org/People/Raggett/tidy/.

19. S. Raghavan and H. Garcia-Molina. Crawling the Hidden Web. In *VLDB 2001: 27th International Conference on Very Large Data Bases*, September 2001. To appear.

20. VMGEAR. OptimizeIt!: The Java Ultimate Performance Profiler. http://www.vmgear.com/.

21. W3C. Document Object Model (DOM) Level 1 Specification. W3C Recommendation 1, October 1998. http://www.w3.org/TR/REC-DOM-Level-1/.

22. T. W. Yan and H. Garcia-Molina. SIFT - A Tool for Wide-Area Information Dissemination. In *Proceedings of the 1995 USENIX Technical Conference*, pages 177–186, 1995.

23. D. Zeinalipour-Yazti. eRACE: an eXtensible Retrieval, Annotation and Caching Engine, June 2000. B.Sc. Thesis. In Greek.

24. D. Zeinalipour-Yazti and M. Dikaiakos. High-Performance Crawling and Filtering in Java. Technical Report TR-01-3, Department of Computer Science, University of Cyprus, June 2001.

Moving Objects Information Management: The Database Challenge

(Vision Paper)

Ouri Wolfson

Department of Computer Science, University of Illinois, Chicago, IL, 60607

and Mobitrac Inc., Chicago, IL 60610

wolfson@cs.uic.edu

Abstract. Miniaturization of computing devices, and advances in wireless communication and sensor technology are some of the forces that are propagating computing from the stationary desktop to the mobile outdoors. Some important classes of new applications that will be enabled by this revolutionary development include location-based services, tourist services, mobile electronic commerce, and digital battlefield. Some existing application classes that will benefit from the development include transportation and air traffic control, weather forecasting, emergency response, mobile resource management, and mobile workforce. Location management, i.e. the management of transient location information, is an enabling technology for all these applications. Location management is also a fundamental component of other technologies such as fly-through visualization, context awareness, augmented reality, cellular communication, and dynamic resource discovery.

In this paper we present our view of the important research issues in location management. These include modeling of location information, uncertainty management, spatio-temporal data access languages, indexing and scalability issues, data mining (including traffic and location prediction), location dissemination, privacy and security, location fusion and synchronization.

1. Introduction

In 1996, the Federal Communications Commission (FCC) mandated that all wireless carriers offer a 911 service with the ability to pinpoint the location of callers making emergency requests. This requirement is forcing wireless operators to roll out costly new infrastructure that provides location data about mobile devices. In part to facilitate the rollout of these services, in May 2000, the U.S. government stopped jamming the signals from global positioning system (GPS) satellites for use in civilian applications, dramatically improving the accuracy of GPS-based location data to 5-50 meters.

As prices of basic enabling equipment like smart cell phones, hand helds, wireless modems, and GPS devices and services continue to drop rapidly, International Data Corp (IDC) predicts that the number of wireless subscribers worldwide will soar to

A. Halevy and A. Gal (Eds.): NGITS 2002, LNCS 2382, pp. 75–89, 2002.

1.1 billion in 2003. Spurred by the combination of expensive new location-based infrastructure and an enormous market of mobile users, companies will roll out new wireless applications to re-coop their technology investments and increase customer loyalty and switching costs. These applications are collectively called location-based services.

Emerging commercial location-based services fall into one of the following two categories. First, Mobile Resource Management (MRM) applications that include systems for mobile workforce management, automatic vehicle location, fleet management, logistics, transportation management and support (including air traffic control). These systems use location data combined with route schedules to track and manage service personnel or transportation systems. Call centers and dispatch operators can use these applications to notify customers of accurate arrival times, optimize personnel utilization, handle emergency requests, and adjust for external conditions like weather and traffic. Second, Location-aware Content Delivery services that use location data to tailor the information delivered to the mobile user in order to increase relevancy, for example delivering accurate driving directions, instant coupons to customers nearing a store, or nearest resource information like local restaurants, hospitals, ATM machines, or gas stations. Analyses Ltd. estimates that location based services will generate $18.5B in sales by 2006.

In addition to commercial systems, management of moving objects in location based systems arises in the military (see [6, 7]), in the context of the digital battlefield. In a military application one would like to ask queries such as "retrieve the helicopters that are scheduled to enter region R within the next 10 minutes".

Location management, i.e. the management of transient location information, is an enabling technology for all these applications. Location management is also a fundamental component of other technologies such as fly-through visualization (the visualized terrain changes continuously with the location of the user), context awareness (location of the user determines the content, format, or timing of information delivered), augmented reality (location of both the viewer and the viewed object determines the type of information delivered to viewer), and cellular communication.

Location management has been studied extensively in the cellular architecture context. The problem is as follows. In order to complete the connection to a cellular user u, the network has to know the cell id of u. Thus the network maintains a database of location records (key, cell-id), and it needs to support two types of operations: (1) Point query when a cellular user needs to be located in order to complete a call or send a message, e.g., find the current location (cell) of moving object with key 707-476-2276, and (2) Point update when a cellular user moves beyond the boundary of its current cell, e.g., update the current location (cell) of moving object with key 707-476-2276. The question addressed in the literature is how to distribute, replicate, and cache the database of location records, such that the two type of operations are executed as efficiently as possible. Related questions are how frequently to update, and how to search the database. Many papers have addressed this question, and two good surveys of the subject are [4, 14].

However, the location management problem is much broader. The main limitations of the cellular work are that the only relevant operations are point queries and updates that pertain to the current time, and they are only concerned with cell-resolution locations. For the applications we discussed, queries are often set oriented, location of a finer resolution is necessary, queries may pertain to the future or the past, and triggers are often more important than queries. Some examples of queries/triggers are: during the past year, how many times was bus#5 late by more than 10 minutes at some station (past query); send me message when a helicopter is in a given geographic area (trigger); retrieve the trucks that will reach their destination within the next 20 minutes (set oriented future query).

In terms of MRM software development, the current approach is to build a separate, independent location management component for each application. However, this results in significant complexity and duplication of efforts, in the same sense that that data management functionality was duplicated before the development of Database Management Systems. To continue the analogy, we need to develop location management technology that addresses the common requirements, and serves as a development platform in the same sense that DBMS technology extracted concurrency control, recovery, query language and query processing, and serves as a platform for inventory and personnel application development. And this is the objective of our DOMINO project (see [20]), and our venture-funded startup company called Mobitrac (www.mobitrac.com). In this paper we describe the main research challenges in building a general purpose location management system.

The rest of the paper is organized as follows. In section 2, we discuss modeling and spatio-temporal operators. In section 3, we discuss uncertainty in location management, and in section 4, we discuss location management in a distributed/mobile environment. In section 5, we discuss location and traffic prediction by data mining, and in section 6 we discuss indexing. In section 7 we discuss other issues, particularly privacy and location fusion. In section 8 we conclude the paper.

2. Location Modeling and Linguistic Issues

In this section we first outline a naïve solution and outline its drawbacks (subsection 2.1), then we describe a more sophisticated model that we proposed (subsection 2.2) and explain how it addresses some of the drawbacks. In subsection 2.3 we present a possible set of spatio-temporal operators that capture uncertainty, and can be used for querying location information.

2.1 A Naïve Solution and Its Drawbacks

A fundamental capability of location management is modeling of transient location information, particularly the location of mobile devices such as cell phones, personal digital assistants, laptops, etc. These devices are carried by people, or mounted on moving objects such as vehicles, aircraft, or vessels. The location information is updated by positioning technologies. Examples of such technologies include 1) GPS (that is transmitted from the device to the location server via a wireless network), 2) network based positioning that computes the location by triangulation of transmission towers, 3) fixed sensors in the environment (e.g. at a toll booth) that identify the moving object, and 4) cell-id that identifies the cell in which the moving object is located (a low resolution method).

A straightforward approach that is used by existing industrial applications such as fleet management and Automatic Vehicle Location (AVL), is to model the location as follows. For each moving object, a location-time point of the form (l, t) is generated periodically, indicating that the object is at location l at time t. l may be a coordinate pair (x,y), or a cell-id. The point is stored in a database managed by a Database Management System (DBMS), and SQL is used to retrieve the location information.

This method is called point-location management, and it has several critical drawbacks. First, the method does not enable interpolation or extrapolation. For example, assume that a user needs to know which police officers were within one mile from the location of an emergency that occurred at 3pm. This information can only be retrieved for the moving objects that happened to generate a location update at 3pm. If an object did not generate an update at 3pm, then its whereabouts at that time are unknown. The problem is even more severe for extrapolation, i.e. if a future location is requested; for example, which field service employees will be closest to a customer location at 5pm? This query cannot be answered by the point-location method, even though the future location of service personnel can be estimated based on current work schedules.

The second problem of the point-location method is that it leads to a critical precision/resource trade-off. An accurate picture of the precise location of moving objects would require frequent location updates that consume precious resources such as bandwidth and processing power.

Finally, a third problem of this method is that it leads to cumbersome and inefficient software development. Specifically, location based services will require the development of a vast array of new software applications. Doing so on top of existing DBMS technology has several drawbacks. First, existing DBMS's are not well equipped to handle continuously changing data, such as the location of moving objects. The reason for this is that in databases, data is assumed to be constant unless it is explicitly modified. For example, if the salary field is 60K, then this salary is assumed to hold (i.e. $60K is returned in response to queries) until explicitly updated. This constant-until-modified assumption does not hold for the location of moving objects which changes continuously. The second drawback is that location based services applications need to manage space and time information, whereas SQL is not designed and optimized for this type of queries and triggers. For example, the query "retrieve the vehicles that are inside region R always between 4pm and 5pm" would be very difficult to express in SQL. Finally, the location of a moving object is inherently imprecise because the database location of the object (i.e. the object-location stored in the database) cannot always be identical to the actual location of the object. This inherent uncertainty has various implications for database modeling, querying, and indexing. For example, there can be two different kinds of answers to queries, i.e. the set of objects that "may" satisfy the query, and the set that "must" satisfy the query. SQL semantics cannot account for this difference.

An interesting observation is that the point location management is used for two different cases. One in which the route of the moving object is known a priori (e.g. trucking fleet management, municipal transit), and the other in which such information is not available. For example, in location-aware advertising consumers usually cannot be assumed to provide their destination, and this is also the case for the enemy in digital battlefield applications. In other words, the information available a priori is not utilized for tracking, and it is not updated as a result of tracking.

2.2 Trajectory Location Management

In this section we outline our proposed model of a trajectory, explain how to construct it, and explain how it solves the problems associated with point location management. Let us observe that there are alternatives to the approach proposed here (see for example [9, 17]). If possible, our model makes use of a priori or inferred information about the destination of an object. For example, the destination can be inferred based on a motion pattern (e.g. the person travels to the office between 8am and 9am), or access to auxiliary information (e.g. a calendar may indicate a meeting at given time and address).

The method proposed is called trajectory location management. In this method we first obtain or estimate the source and destination of the moving object. For example, the object starts in New York City at 57th street at 8th Ave. at 7am and heads for Chicago at the intersection of Oak and State streets. Then, by using an electronic map geocoded with distance and travel-time information for every road section, a trajectory is constructed.

Before defining the trajectory, let us define the format of an electronic map. An electronic map is a relation. Each tuple in the relation represents a city block, i.e. the road section in between two intersections, with the following attributes:

- *Polyline*: the block polyline given by a sequence of 2D x,y coordinates: $(x_1,y_1),(x_2,y_2),...,(x_n,y_n)$. Usually the block is a straight line segment, i.e. given by two (x,y) coordinates.
- *Fid*: The block id number

The following attributes are used for geocoding, i.e. translating between an (x,y) coordinate and an address such as "1030 North State St.":

- *L_f_add*: Left side from street number
- *L_t_add*: Left side to street number
- *R_f_add*: Right side from street number
- *R_t_add*: Right side to street number

- *Name*: street name

- *Type*: ST or AVE

- *Zipl*: Left side Zip code

- *Zipr*: Right side Zip code

- *Speed*: speed limit on this city block

- *One way*: a Boolean One way flag.

The following attributes are used for computing travel-time and travel-distance.

- *Meters*: length of the block in meters

- *Drive Time*: typical drive time from one end of the block to the other, in minutes

Such maps are provided by, among others, Geographic Data Technology Co. (www.geographic.com) An intersection of two streets is the endpoint of the four block-polylines. Thus each map is an undirected graph, with the tuples representing edges of the graph.

The route of a moving object O is specified by giving the starting address or (x,y) coordinate (start_point), the starting time, and the ending address or (x,y) coordinate (end_point). An external routine available in most existing Geographic Information Systems, and which we assume is given a priori, computes the shortest cost (distance or travel-time) path in the map graph. This path denoted P(O) is given as a sequence of blocks (edges), i.e. tuples of the map. Since P(O) is a path in the map graph, the endpoint of one block polyline is the beginning point of the next block polyline. Thus the whole route represented by P(O) is a polyline denoted L(O). For the purpose of processing spatiotemporal range queries, the only relevant attributes of the tuples in P(O) are Polyline and Drive-Time.

Given that the trip has a starting time, for each straight line segment on L(O), we can compute the time at which the object O will arrive to the point at the beginning of the segment (using the Drive-Time attribute). This is the certain-trajectory, or c-trajectory. Intuitively, the c-trajectory gives the route of a moving object, along with the time at which the object will be at each point on the route. More formally, a c-trajectory is a sequence of straight-line $(x_1, y_1, t_1), (x_2, y_2, t_2), \ldots ,(x_n, y_n, t_n)$ in 3-dimensional space. The c-trajectory means that when the object starts at a location having coordinates (x_1, y_1) at time t_1, it will move on a straight line at constant speed and will reach location (x_2, y_2) at time t_2, and then it will move on a straight line at constant speed and will reach location (x_3, y_3) at time t_3, etc. The c-trajectory is an approximation of the expected motion of the object in space and time. The reason it is only an approximation is that the object does not move in straight lines at constant speed. However, given enough straight lines, the approximation can be accurate up to an arbitrary precision. The number of line segments on the trajectory has an important implication on the performance and precision of queries and triggers. Specifically, the performance increases and the precision decrease as the number of line segments decreases. We adjust and fine-tune the number of line segments on each trajectory by using a method that has been studied in computer graphics, namely line simplification (see [2, 8]).

The c-trajectory is stored in the server database and in a computer on board the moving object. At any point in time t between t_i and t_{i+1} the server can compute the expected location of the moving object at time t. Observe that this technique solves the first problem associated with point location management. Namely, trajectory location management enables both, location interpolation and extrapolation. The server can compute the expected location of the moving object at any point in time between the start and end times of the trip. For example, if it is known that the object is at location (x_5, y_5) at 5pm and at location (x_6, y_6) at 6pm, and it moves in a straight line at constant speed between the two locations, then the location at 5:16pm can be computed at anytime, i.e. before 5:16 (extrapolation) or after (interpolation).

Finally, the trajectory (or the uncertain trajectory) is obtained by associating an uncertainty threshold u_i with the i'th line segment on the c-trajectory. The line segment together with the uncertainty threshold constitute an "agreement" between the moving object and the server. The agreement specifies the following. The moving object will update the server if and only if it deviates from its expected location according to the trajectory by u_i or more. How does the moving object compute the deviation at any point in time? Its computer receives a GPS update every two seconds, so it knows its actual location at any point in time. It has the trajectory, so by interpolation it can compute its expected location at any point in time. The deviation is simply the distance between the actual and the expected location. More formally, a trajectory is polyline $(x_1, y_1, t_1, u_1), (x_2, y_2, t_2, u_2), ..., (x_n, y_n, t_n, u_n)$ in 4-dimensional space.

At the server, the trajectory is maintained by revising it according to location-updates from the moving object, and according to real-time traffic conditions obtained from traffic web sites. We have developed a traffic incident model, and a method of identifying the trajectories affected by a traffic incident. Observe that determining whether or not a trajectory is affected by a traffic incident is not a simple matter, and it requires prediction capabilities. For example, suppose that according to the current information Joe's van is scheduled to pass through highway section x twenty minutes from now, and suppose that a web site currently reports a traffic jam on highway section x. Will Joe's expected arrival time at his destination be affected by this? Clearly it depends on whether or not the jam will clear by the time Joe arrives at highway section x. We use historical information and a novel traffic model to make this prediction.

Observe that the agreement (namely the trajectory plus the uncertainty threshold) between the moving object and the server solves the second problem of point location management. Namely, the tradeoff between resource/bandwidth consumption and precision has been broken. In trajectory location management the location of a moving object can be computed with a high degree of precision, using a small number of location updates, or no updates at all. In particular, if the moving object is "on schedule", i.e., it does not deviate from its prescribed trajectory by more than the uncertainty threshold, then no resources are consumed for updates.

Finally, let us observe that a trajectory can be constructed based on past motion in which an object used the point location management. Namely, the trajectory can be constructed from a set of 3D points (x_1, y_1, t_1), (x_2, y_2, t_2), ... ,(x_n, y_n, t_n) that were transmitted by a moving object using the point location management method. One can simply connect the points along the shortest path on the map, and then associate an uncertainty u_i with line segment i. The uncertainty u_i can be bounded given the maximum speed of the object and the known times of the two GPS points immediately preceding and succeeding the i'th line segment (see [15]).

2.3 Data Access Operators

Finally, we propose to solve the third problem associated with point location management using a novel set of operators by which the database is accessed. The operators are used to query the database, and also to set triggers (or alerts) that are fired when interesting conditions are satisfied by the database (e.g. an object is expected to be late by more than one hour). The operators are designed to express when/where questions in an uncertain environment. They can be incorporated into the traditional SQL query language that has been widely adopted by commercial database systems. This means that one can ask queries and set triggers that combine the traditional database conditions with the new operators. This means, for example, that a dispatcher can ask a query such as: retrieve the service-personnel who have Qualification="dsl", and will be within 1 mile of 851 S. Morgan St. at 5pm. This also means that the operators can be combined using boolean operators such as and and or. An additional implication is that these operators/queries can be entered by a user on a client computer, and the same set of operators can be invoked from a program. The latter option enables development of complex spatial and temporal applications. Obviously the proposed set of operators is not exhaustive, but each operator in the set can on one hand be implemented efficiently, and on the other hand we believe that it is useful in a large class of applications. Although the operators are given here in textual form, but they can be implemented in point-and-click, drag-and-drop, graphical and visual form.

The new operators are divided into three classes, operators that pertain to a single trajectory, operators that pertain to the relationship of trajectories to fixed-location facilities or regions, and the relationship among multiple trajectories. These loosely correspond to point queries, range queries, and join queries, respectively, in traditional databases (see [10]). Each one of the immediately following subsections discusses one of these classes.

2.3.1 Some Operators That Analyze a Single Trajectory

- *WHEN object o CLOSEST TO address x*. The operator returns a list of times at which the object passes by or stops at address *x*. Observe that there may be a list of times, since the object may visit or pass by the same location more than once. If the object never passes by or visits *x*, then the operator returns the time when the object passes by the closest location to *x* on its trajectory. This operator is used, for example, when the customer at *x* needs to know when the technician will arrive at her location according to the current schedule.

- *VCR object o.* The operator "replays" the trajectory of object *o*. The replay can be done on a certain time-scale (e.g. a minute per second), and it can fast forward/rewind to a certain point in time.

2.3.2 Some Operators for Retrieving Trajectories That Stand in Certain Relationships to a Region or a Facility

- Each one of the operators in this class is a condition. The condition is satisfied by the objects that stand in a certain relationship (e.g. within distance *x*) to a fixed facility (i.e. a point on a map) or a region *R*, during *T*. Thus the conditions correspond to a spatio-temporal range query. Why then is there more than a single operator? The answer is threefold. First, since the expected location of an object changes continuously, one may ask for the objects that satisfy the condition *always* within *T*, or the objects that satisfy it *sometime* during *T*; similarly one can ask for the objects that satisfy the condition *somewhere* in R or *everywhere* in R. Second, there is an uncertainty associated with the location, and thus one can ask for the objects that *possibly* satisfy the condition, or the ones that *definitely* do so. Third, it turns out that the order in which the temporal quantifier is combined with the certainty quantifier important.

2.3.3 Some Operators for Identifying Relationships between Trajectories

Each one of the relationship-to-facilities operators can be applied as a relationship-between-trajectories operator. These are called join operators. For example:

- *Possibly-Within [distance d | travel-time t], Sometime in the time interval T.* The condition is satisfied by the pairs of trajectories which are within distance d or travel time t from each other, sometime in the time interval T. This operator is used, for example, in an air-traffic-control system that stores the trajectories of planes. We assume that, in contrast to the existing system in which planes fly on "highways in the sky", the new free-flight system has been implemented (see www.faa.gov/freeflight). The air traffic controller needs to know which planes are expected to be within distance *d* from each other, thus representing a safety hazard.

The opposite operator also applies. Specifically:

- *Possibly-Fartherthan [distance d | travel-time t], Sometime in the time interval T.*

3. Uncertainty Management

The location of a moving object is inherently imprecise because, due to continuous motion and due to the fact that the location cannot be reliably obtained at any point in time, the database location (i.e. the object-location stored in the database) cannot always be identical to the actual location of the object. Systems that do not manage this uncertainty delegate to the user the responsibility of understanding and taking into consideration its implications. Furthermore, even if the database is precise, applications that access this database may need query-imprecision support. For example, a user may ask if there is a traffic jam on highway I90, where the notion of a traffic jam is imprecise.

The objective of uncertainty management is to assist the user in accounting for uncertainty, and in expressing imprecise queries/triggers. This objective has various implications for database modeling (in our model the uncertainty is part of the trajectory), querying (possibly and definitely operators), indexing, and resource consumption.

Assuming that one can control the amount of uncertainty in the system, how should it be determined? Obviously, lowering the uncertainty would come at a cost. For example, if a moving object transmits its location to a location-database every x minutes or every x miles, then lowering x would decrease the uncertainty in the system, but increase bandwidth consumption and location-update processing cost; and vice versa, increasing x would reduce the uncertainty, but increase resource consumption. Similarly, adjusting the uncertainty thresholds u_j in our trajectory model has the same tradeoffs concerning resource consumption.

Next we outline our cost based approach to quantify this tradeoff as a demonstration of a possible formalization of the problem (see [21]). The information cost of a trip has the following three components: deviation cost, uncertainty cost, and communication cost. Using these costs we define a function that represents the overall information cost of a trip, and define the optimal uncertainty threshold as the value that minimizes this function.

We believe that the method of defining an uncertainty threshold and communicating only values that exceed the threshold is an important paradigm that has applications beyond location management. Indeed the uncertainty threshold paradigm was used in the context of data warehousing (see [19]) and general sensors (see [12]).

4. Location Dissemination in a Distributed Environment

It is often impractical or impossible to store the location database in a centralized location. This is the case, for example, in the cellular database discussed in the introduction, where a centralized architecture would create an intolerable performance problem. So the question is how to allocate, update and query trajectories in a geographically distributed environment. Another complication arises when the location database is not only distributed but also mobile. This is the case, for example, in a Mobile Ad-hoc Network (MANET). This is a system of mobile computers (or nodes) equipped with wireless broadcast transmitters and receivers which are used for communicating within the system. Such networks provide an attractive and inexpensive alternative to the cellular infrastructures when this infrastructure is unavailable (e.g. in remote and disaster areas), or inefficient, or too expensive to use (see [11]). Mobile Ad-hoc Networks are used to communicate among the nodes of a military unit, in rescue and disaster relief operations, in collaborative mobile data exchange (e.g. the set of attendees at a conference), and other "micro-networking" technologies (see [3]). In this case, the natural data allocation is for each moving object to store and maintain its own trajectory, and the problem is processing the queries discussed in section 2 with an acceptable delay, overhead and accuracy.

5. Location and Traffic Mining/Prediction

In many mobile commerce applications the system does not have a priori information about the future motion of a customer. In other words, in contrast to the single enterprise systems we discussed so far, a customer does not provide her location to potential merchants that match her profile. For example, if at 8 A.M. it is known that at 9 A.M. the customer will be close to a store that has a sale on merchandise that matches her profile, the system could transmit a coupon at 8 A.M.. This would allow the customer to plan a purchase stop. Location prediction is important in other applications such as wireless bandwidth allocation (in a cellular architecture, location prediction enables optimizing allocation of bandwidth to cells).

We have developed methods of motion prediction based on historical trajectories of moving objects. In other words, we are able to predict the location of a moving object at a certain future time. Our prediction methodology is based on the fact that often moving objects have some degree of regularity in their motion. That is, motion has a random part and a regular part, and the regular part has a periodic pattern (hourly, weekly, etc.). A typical example is the home-office-home pattern. If we are able to detect this pattern, then location prediction is relatively easy for rush hour. Therefore we decompose the motion prediction problem into two sub-problems: periodicity detection, and location prediction based on detected periodicity.

Periodicity detection seeks motion patterns. Assuming that we are given time-stamped sets of GPS points, the following are features of the patterns. First, patterns are partially periodic, i.e. sometimes only part of the motion repeats. For example, a person may usually travel from home to work along a fixed route between 7 A.M. and 8 A.M. every workday and back home between 5 P.M. and 6 P.M.. S/he may do other things and go other places during the rest of the day, and this constitutes the random part of the motion.

Second, the patterns are not necessarily repeated perfectly. For example, the home-to-work trajectory on one day may be different than on another day, due to different traffic conditions. Or, the person may decide to stay at home some workdays and thus miss certain periods.

Finally, the motion can have multiple periodic cycles. For example, the person may go fishing every Saturday and every other Sunday. In summary, our goal is to detect motion patterns that can be partially periodic, not perfectly repeated, and have multiple periodic cycles.

Location prediction in other environments and assuming other circumstances is also important. The ultimate challenge is to predict future location of a hostile moving object that is attempting to hide and deceive about its future location and destination. Location prediction is strongly related to another prediction problem, namely traffic prediction. In order to be able to predict the future location of a moving object, particularly the time of arrival at the destination, one has to be able to predict the traffic conditions that will be encountered en route. Work on traffic-conditions mining and prediction has begun (e.g. [22]), but much more remains to be done.

6. Indexing

Most of the database work in the area of Moving Objects was focused on indexing. In particular, the issue addressed is how to index a large number of 3-dimensional trajectories in order to perform efficient querying and updating of trajectories. Each one of the prevalent approaches is classified as primal (where each trajectory segment is represented as a line) or dual (where the trajectory segment is represented as a point). For example, references [16, 18] take the primal approach, and [1, 5, 13] take the dual approach.

Most existing works use synthetic data to verify performance. Much more research work is necessary in order to verify the performance of existing and new indexing methods in realistic moving objects scenarios; for example, objects moving with realistic speeds and speed variations on road networks given in existing electronic maps. Furthermore, in seems that the dual methods are not suitable to road networks in which moving objects switch from one road to another, particularly if the trajectory is known a priori. More research is required to adapt the dual method for road networks. Another issue is to analyze in-memory indexing and compare them with brute force methods. For many applications trajectories are several tens of miles, and the number of moving objects are in the hundreds or thousands, which implies that the trajectories can be maintained in main memory, but frequent trajectory-updates and queries may still create a severe performance problem. Finally, most existing work propose and evaluate a particular indexing method, but much more work is required in comparing various methods.

7. Other Issues

Privacy is an issue that immediately arises as a major concern when people are presented with location based applications. This makes systems in which clients learn their location without centralized tracking (e.g. [23]) particularly appealing. In our (controversial) opinion, the privacy problem will be solved by a trusted third party approach, similarly to the way the approach solved the privacy problem in financial credit card transactions and telephone communication. In other words, we feel that financial transactions and telephone communication that are at least as privacy-sensitive as tracking, have been satisfactorily solved by trust of credit card and telephone companies.

An important research problem is the fusion and synchronization of location-information obtained from multiple sources (e.g. GPS, dead-reckoning, proximity sensors, scene analysis). Such fusion is important in order to increase the accuracy of location information and its availability in variable terrain conditions. One particular approach to the problem is introduced in [24], but much more work is necessary in this area.

8. Conclusion

We believe that the pervasive, wireless, mobile computing is a revolutionary development, and location based services and mobile resource management are some of the initial manifestations of this revolution. In this paper we focused on location management, which is an enabling technology for a variety of applications and technologies related to this revolution. We discussed the research issues that need to be addressed in order to make location management a plug-in component in these applications and technologies. The first of these issues are location modeling. We discussed the drawbacks of existing approaches, and we proposed the trajectory as a four dimensional piece-wise linear function that captures the essential aspects of the moving object location. These aspects are two-dimensional space, time, and uncertainty. We also proposed a set of operators to access a database of trajectories.

Another research issue is uncertainty and imprecision management and control. We also discussed location management in a distributed and/or mobile environment, and issues of data mining, particularly prediction of location and traffic patterns. Finally, we briefly discussed the existing and necessary work in the areas of indexing and location fusion.

References

1. A.K. Agarwal, L. Arge, J. Ericskon: "Indexing moving points". Proc. of ACMPODS 2000 conference.
2. P.K. Agarwal and K. R. Varadarajan. Efficient Algorithms for Approximating Polygonal Chains. Discrete Comput. Geom., 23:273-291(2000)
3. F. Bennett, D. Clarke, J. Evans, A. Hopper, A. Jones, and D. Leask, Piconet: Embedded Mobile Networking, IEEE Personal Communications, 4(5), October 1997.

4. A. Bhattacharya, S. K. Das, Lezi-Update: An Information-Theoretic Approcah to Track Mobile Users in PCS Networks, *Proceedings of the fifth ACM/IEEE International Conference on MobileComputing and Networking (MOBICOM99)*, Seattle, WA, August, 1999.
5. H.D. Chon, D. Agrawal, A. El Abbadi: "Storage and Retrieval of moving objects" *in Proc. of Mobile Data Management 2001 conference, Springer Verlag Lecture Notes in Computer Science* No. 1987.
6. S. Chamberlain. Automated information distribution in bandwidth-constrained environments. *MILCON-94 conference*, 1994
7. S. Chamberlain. Model-based battle command: A paradigm whose time has come. *1995 Symposium on C2 Research & Technology, NDU*, June 1995
8. D.H. Douglas and T. K Peucker Algorithms for the reduction of the number of points required to represent a digitized line or its caricature. *Canad, Cartog.* 10(2):112-122, Dec. 1973
9. Ralf Hartmut Guting, Michael H. Bohlen, Martin Erwig, Christian S. Jensen, Nikos A. Lorentzos. Markus Schneider, and Michalis Vazirgiannis.: A Foundation for Representing and Querying Moving Objects, in *ACM-Transactions on Database Systems Journal* (2000), 25(1), 1-42
10. H. Garcia-Molina, J. D. Ullman, J. Widom. *Database System Implementation*, Prentice Hall, Upper Saddle River, NJ.
11. Z. J. Has, Panel Report on Ad Hoc Networks - MILCOM'97, *Mobile Computing and Communications Review*, Vol. 2, No. 1, January 1998.
12. Y. Huang, R. Sloan, O. Wolfson, "Divergence Caching in Client-Server Architectures", *Proceedings of the third International Conference on Parallel and Distributed Information Systems (PDIS)*, Austin, TX, Sept. 1994, pp. 131-139.]).
13. G. Kollios, D. Gunopulos, V.J. Tsotras: "On indexing moving objects". *ACM PODS 1999 conference*. ACM Press.
14. E. Pitoura, G. Samaras: "Locating Objects in Mobile Computing". *IEEE Transactions on Knowledge and Data Engineering*, Vol. 13, No. 4, July/August 2001
15. D. Pfoser, C.S. Jensen: "Capturing the uncertainty of moving objects representations". *Proc. of the 12 Intl. Conf. on Scientific and Statistical Database Management*, 2000. IEEE Computer Society.
16. S. Saltenis, C.S. Jensen, S.T. Leutenegger, M.A. Lopez: "Indexing the Positions of Continuously Moving Objects. *ACM SIGMOD Conference 2000*.
17. A. P. Sistla, O. Wolfson, S Chamberlain, and S. Dao: Modeling and Querying Moving Objects, In *Proc. of the International Conference on Data Engineering* (1997) pp. 422-432.
18. J. Tayeb, O. Ulusoy, and O Wolfson. A Quadtree-based dynamic attribute indexing method. *The computer Journal*, (41(3), 1998
19. C. Olston, J. Widom, Offering a Precision-Performance Tradeoff for Aggregation Queries over Replicated Data, *Twenty-Sixty International Conference on Very Large Data Bases (VLDB 2000)*, Cairo, Egypt, September 2000.
20. O. Wolfson, P. Sistla, B. Xu, J. Zhou, S. Chamberlain, N. Rishe,Y. Yesha, Tracking Moving Objects Using Database Technology in DOMINO, *Springer-Verlag Lecture Notes in Computer Science, number 1649, Proceedings of NGITS'99, The Fourth Workshop on Next Generation Information Technologies and Systems*, Zikhron-Yaakov, Israel, July 1999, pp. 112-119.
21. O. Wolfson, A. P. Sistla, S. Chamberlain, Yelena Yesha. Updating and Querying Databases that Track Mobile Units. *Distributed and Parallel Databases*, 7, 257-287, 1999

22. S. Handley, P. Langley, F. Rauscher, Learning to Predict the Duration of an Automobile Trip. *Proc. of the 4th International Conference on Knowledge Discovery and Data Mining (1998).*

23. N. Priyantha, A. Chakraborty, H. Balakrishnan, The Cricket Location-Support System, *Proc. of the 6th ACM Int. Conf. on Mobile Computing and Networking (MOBICOM),* Boston, MA, Aug. 2000.

24. J. Myllymaki, S. Edlund, Location Aggregation from Multiple Sources, *Proc. of the 3rd Int. Conference on Mobile Data Management (MDM),* Singapore, Jan. 02.

Specifying Local Ontologies in Support of Semantic Interoperability of Distributed Inter-organizational Applications

Michel Benaroch

School of Management, Syracuse University
Syracuse, NY 13244
mbenaroc@syr.edu

Abstract. Semantic interoperability through shared ontologies aims to ensure the semantic soundness of exchanges of services and data among distributed information systems (ISs). Collaboration via shared ontologies, however, requires that the *local ontology* of every co-operating IS be explicit. Unfortunately, common IS requirements specification methods are not geared towards producing the local ontology of an IS; they usually translate requirements into procedural notations that make a local ontology largely implicit in the software code. This paper presents a method for eliciting IS requirements and specifying them declaratively, in a way that makes explicit the local ontology. The resulting declarative requirements constitute explicit metadata that can be used to support semantic interoperability as well as enterprise modeling and knowledge management. We have already successfully applied our method to knowledge-based systems (KBSs). Since KBSs are also ISs, albeit more complex ones, our method offers a solid basis for creating ISs whose local ontologies are explicit.

1. Introduction

Interoperability among components of distributed information systems (ISs) is the ability to exchange services and data with one another. *Syntactic interoperability* ensures the correct passing of exchanges, based on agreements about the mechanisms carrying the exchanges (message passing protocols, object names, argument types, etc.). *Semantic interoperability* ensures that the exchanges make sense, based on agreements on the meanings of requested services and data (business rules, data entities, algorithms for computing requested values, etc.).

Ontologies are widely considered the ultimate solution to semantic interoperability [10]. When participating agents (persons, software components, ISs, etc.) share parts of the same domain as the basis for their co-operation, an ontology of the domain could facilitate their communications and collaboration. Generally, an *ontology* of a domain is a (partial) conceptualization of the domain in terms of the domain objects, their properties and distinctions, their relationships, (business) rules governing their behaviors, etc. [6]. Although there is no agreement on the exact constituents of an

A. Halevy and A. Gal (Eds.): NGITS 2002, LNCS 2382, pp. 90–106, 2002.

ontology [7], much research identifies two elements that every ontology must include: a hierarchy of domain entities (concepts) and their relations, and a set of domain constraints (also called axioms). More precisely, as seen in Fig. 1, an ontology forms a specialization hierarchy of domain concepts and their definition, with lower level concepts having close links with data-level terms in ER models and implementation-specific database schemas. Additionally, an ontology includes domain-level constraints over abstract concepts. Some of these are operational constraints of the kind specified at the level of a database schema. However, many other constraints necessary for meta-level (or knowledge-level) reasoning are not explicitly represented at the data level.

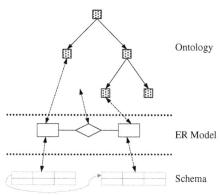

Fig. 1. Relationships between ontology, ER model and schema

There are two fundamental approaches to semantic interoperability using ontologies [11]. The first approach requires the availability of a shared ontology. Ontologies can form a specialization hierarchy like the one shown in Fig. 2a. A parent ontology (of a domain) is inherited by child ontologies (of sub-domains), but child ontologies may modify parts of a parent ontology. Thus, a parent ontology is a minimal shared understanding of its child ontologies. Ontologies closer in the hierarchy share more knowledge than distant ontologies. Under this view, semantic interoperability requires that applications interacting over a shared (sub)domain should have similar ontologies or at least share a common parent ontology. The second approach does not assume that availability of a shared ontology and therefore requires the availability of mappings between different ontologies, as seen in Fig. 2b. Note that that a hybrid of both approaches is also possible. Regardless of which one of these approaches one follows, it is clear that every software application must have its own local ontology explicit.

Our primary concern in this paper is with building the local ontology of a software application. Broadly speaking, the local ontology of an application is *explicit meta-data* embodying semantic information about procedures, their governing business rules, data entities they manipulate, etc. Unfortunately, applications developed using common process-, data- and object-oriented IS specification methods do not make their local ontology explicit, because their underlying semantic information is usually implicit in the software. Only a small part of this information is typically captured within CASE tools, and even this part is not integrated with the run-time environment.

Extracting such semantic information from an implemented application and documenting it as usable metadata may involve: (1) interviewing users and system developers so as to reveal their intuition about the meaning of data entities, their relationships, their roles in business processes, etc.; (2) reading source code and database schemas so as to uncover assumptions that data administrators and programmers made about the application design; and (3) analyzing run-time environments so as to identify functional dependencies and other constraints that are not explicitly modeled but may be enforced by the application. Clearly, this endeavor requires much human intelligence and judgment. An ideal alternative would be to create applications based on an IS specification method that make their local ontologies explicit in the first place.

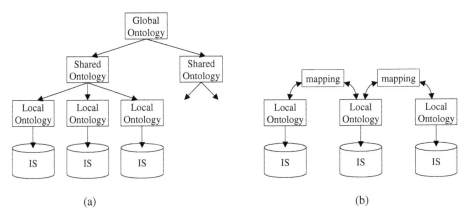

(a)   (b)

Fig. 2. Alternatives ways to use ontologies for semantic interoperability

This paper proposes a method for eliciting IS requirements and specifying them declaratively, in a way that makes explicit the local ontology of an application. More specifically, we present an IS requirements specification method that makes explicit much of the semantic information underlying the requirements and captures this information as usable metadata. We have already applied successfully an earlier version of our method to knowledge-based systems (KBSs) [2,3], and demonstrated how the method can be used to re-represent the procedurally coded knowledge of several conventional KBSs so that their local ontologies become explicit [1]. Since *KBSs are also ISs*, albeit more complex ones (because they deal with unstructured problems involving heuristic domain knowledge and/or heuristic control knowledge), our IS requirements specification method is a good basis for creating ISs whose local ontologies are explicit. Not only does our method permits creating local ontologies that facilitate semantic interoperability, it is also supportive of enterprise modeling and knowledge management. When system requirements are expressed declaratively, in terms of business rules, they contribute to the creation of explicit enterprise models that reflect the business "speak" directing how an enterprise "does business." Our requirements specification method could offer other potential benefits relative to the systems development process itself (i.e., development effort, development time, cost, etc.), but these benefits are outside the scope of this paper. Additionally, like with every new method, there are several open questions concerning the use of our method in practice (e.g., generaliziability to different types of ISs), however, these too are outside the scope of this paper.

The rest of this paper proceeds as follows. Section 2 highlights key drawbacks of common IS requirements specification methods relative to the notion of explicit local ontology. Sections 3 and 4 present our IS requirements specification method and why it can avoid these drawbacks. Section 3 explains how it is possible to conceptualize the function of any IS as problem-space search, just like with KBSs. Building on this conceptualization, Section 4 presents a fully declarative formalism for specifying IS requirements explicitly, in terms pertaining to business processes an IS aims to support. Section 5 offers concluding remarks and directions for future research.

2. Problems with Traditional Requirement Specification Methods

Software engineering research identifies three broad methods of system requirements specification [4].

- *Process-oriented methods* concentrate on describing the function of a system in terms of the steps taken to perform some procedure. They focus on processes that transform application data flowing into and out of those processes, where some flows terminate in (persistent) data stores identifying the data requirements of an application. Business processes are semi-formally described using hierarchical data flow diagrams (DFD), all the way to their most primitive subprocesses (see Fig. 3). Likewise, entity-relationship (ER) models are used to describe semi-formally the nature of data stores and their relationships (see Fig. 4).
- *Data-oriented methods* focus on specifying the data requirements of an application, on the premise that data are less changing than processes. By knowing allowable business relationships between data entities, the kind of data processing that can be applied to the individual attributes of entities is constrained by business rules. Data entities and their relationships are described using ER models. These ER models are then augmented using functional decomposition diagrams identifying business processes where data participates, procedural process dependency diagrams describing links between processes, and process DFDs reflecting events that trigger each process. Clearly, data-oriented methods are dual to process-oriented methods: the former focus on data that requires processing, and the latter on processes that change data.
- *Object-oriented methods* think in terms of objects that encapsulate both data and the processes (procedures) acting on that data. Here, the major analysis activities focus on defining objects, classes, and processes. Object-oriented methods use their own graphical diagrams and notations. These include object class diagrams depicting inheritance relationships between object classes, state-transition diagrams and process diagrams showing allowable changes for data objects as a result of messages that can flow between objects, and time-event diagrams showing the order in which state transitions can occur, among others.

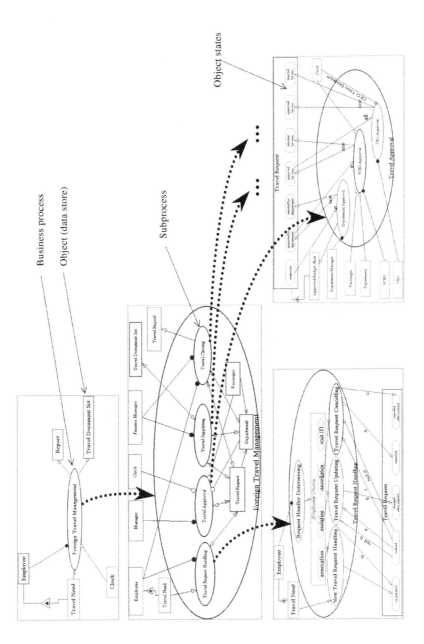

Fig. 3. Data flow diagram (DFD) reflecting business processes and the objects/data they effect (in a Travel Request Processing application)

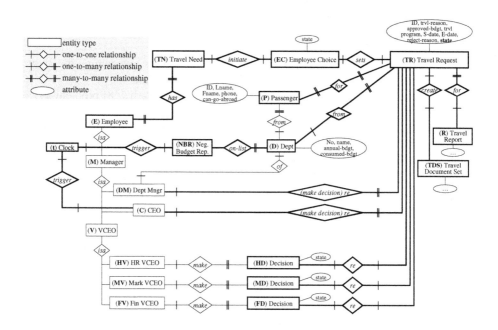

Fig. 4. Entity-relationship (ER) model depicting business data as entities and their relationships (in a Travel Request Processing application)

All these methods *specify and implement IS requirements procedurally* using DFDs, program flowcharts, procedural programming languages, etc. This practice leads to the three significant drawbacks whose importance is growing with the rapid rate at which inter-organizational ISs must be developed in the e-commerce context.

1. *No local ontological knowledge.* These methods are not geared towards capturing semantic information about the business rules underlying target business processes and the data entities they involve. And, the business rules themselves are implicit, as they are hardwired into procedural representations of system requirements.

2. *Loss of rules' identity.* The original representation of an application's business "speak" is lost since the identity of many business rules is lost. For example, given the rules "if A & B then C" and "if A & D then E", programmers are often tempted to optimize flowcharts by combining the rules into "If A Then (if B then C else, if D then E)".

3. *No support of enterprise modeling and knowledge management.* Since the business rules underlying an application are implicit and the exact location of their translation is disparate throughout the program code, the application cannot be modified easily to reflect dynamic business changes. Ideally, since business rules direct how an enterprise "does business", they must be treated as an explicitly managed knowledge asset.

3. Alternative IS Requirements Specification Method – Conceptual Underpinning

To see how our IS requirements specification method permits overcoming the above drawbacks, we must first understand the logic behind this method.

A way to conceptualize the function of an IS is using Newell's [8] problem-space paradigm (see Fig. 5). This paradigm assumes an initial state t_i describing what is known at the start of problem solving, a goal state t_g describing what is needed at the end of problem solving, and a set of state operators P for generating new states in the problem space. Starting from the current state, $t_c=t_i$, a new state t_c' is generated by applying one operator in P. Then, state t_c' is subjected to a goal test to see if it matches t_g. If not, additional states are generated, one at a time. This problem-solving process continues to use operators in P to generate new states until it forms a path from t_i to t_g.

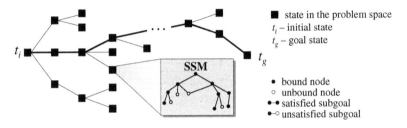

Fig. 5. Problem solving as problem-space search

Every IS processing (solving) a given case (problem situation) performs problem-space search. Starting from initial state t_i (e.g., an employee has a travel need), the IS gradually addresses subgoals as it moves towards a well-defined terminal state t_g (e.g., travel request rejected, or approved and fulfilled). In this sense, an IS can be said to embody business knowledge corresponding to two types of *rules* that govern the problem-space search.

- *Subgoaling rules* prescribe the subgoals to be dynamically posted during problem-space search. For example, two of the subgoals associated with a generated travel request is that it be "reviewed by the department manager to become *approved-by-department*" and "reviewed by the CEO to become *approved-by-CEO*". Each sub-goal is addressed by a specific action (state operator) that moves the problem-space search from one state to another. Each subgoal-action pair corresponds to a step in a business process that has a well-defined goal.

- *Goal-sequencing rules* specify the order by which subgoals are dynamically ad-dressed during problem-space search, that is, the order in which the search moves from one problem-space state to another. For example, a travel request must first be reviewed by the department manager and only then reviewed by the CEO. These rules can be seen as reflecting the order by which steps are performed within a business process.

These two types of rules permit describing any business process an IS may seek to support. For ISs that address well-structured (business) processes, both types of rules are deterministic, and problem-space search would involve a backtracking-free path traversal from t_i to t_g,[1] analogous to a deterministic execution of a specific path in a DFD.[2]

The structure permitting the dynamic posting and sequencing of subgoals is called a *situation-specific model* (SSM). To understand the notion of SSM, consider a hierarchical DFD describing some business process all the way to its primitive steps. Apparent from the DFD notation (Fig. 3), the primitive steps create, modify or destroy new or existing data entities (or objects). If we record every elementary action that these steps perform during problem-space search (see Footnote 2), the result is an SSM. This is why Fig. 5 depicts a problem-space state as an SSM. In effect, however, during search only one SSM is created, but it evolves as the search moves from one state to the next. Thus, at every moment during problem-space search, the SSM being created reflects all that has happened during the processing (solution) of a specific case scenario (problem situation).

Formally, an *SSM* is a graph, $\langle N, L \rangle$, where N is a set of nodes and L is a set of links between nodes in N. A *node* $n \in N$ is a tuple ($e\ i\ [a]$), where e denotes an entity's ontological identity (i.e., entity type), i is an instance of e, and $[a]$ is one or more optional attributes of i. For example, (*TR* tr-12 state="approved-by-dept") is a node representing a travel request instance called tr-12 whose state is "approved-by-dept". The ontological identity of entities is needed to distinguish between types of SSM nodes. A *terminal node* (leaf) $n \in N$ is an unbound node, denoted (e ?), whose i-value and/or a-value are "unbound". A *link* $l \in E$ connects two nodes, creating a *node-chain*; e.g., (*TR* tr-12)→(*P* {Sam, David}), which means that travel request instance tr-12 is associated with the list of passengers {Sam, David}. A link with a terminal unbound node is termed an *unsatisfied node-chain* or *subgoal*; e.g., (*TR* tr-12 state="requested")→(*P* ?), which means that travel request instance tr-12 is in state requested and currently associated with an unbound list of passengers.

Fig. 6 illustrates how an SSM evolves during the problem-space search for a Travel Request processing application. The initial SSM contains a Travel Need (TN) object. In state 1, this object is linked to an unbound Employee Choice (EC) object, corresponding to subgoal $TN{\rightarrow}?EC$, which becomes satisfied when the employee (user) sets object EC to state "generate". Similarly, in each of the following states, one or more new subgoals are posted to the SSM, and only one of the unsatisfied subgoals in the SSM gets to be addressed. It is subgoaling (business) rules that are responsible for the posting of new subgoals. For instance, in state 3, the subgoal $TR_{[requested]}{\rightarrow}?CeoD$ is posted as a result of applying the subgoaling rule: "every travel request in state 'requested' must be approved by the CEO". In state 3, as multiple unsatisfied subgoals

---

[1] For ISs that address unstructured processes (e.g., KBSs), the problem-space search could be less efficient because subgoaling rules may have an uncertain outcome and/or goal-sequencing rules could be heuristic.

[2] If we explode a DFD describing some business process all the way to primitive subprocesses, each primitive subprocess could be said to carry out an elementary action that is aimed at addressing one specific subgoal. In this sense, these subprocesses are actually the state operators responsible for moving the problem-space search across states.

are posted to the SSM, we can see the effect of goal-sequencing (business) rules on the order of pursuing these subgoals. Specifically, the decision to address subgoal $TR_{[requested]} \rightarrow ?P$ before subgoal $TR_{[requested]} \rightarrow ?DeptD$ is the result of applying the goal-sequencing rule: "every travel request must have a passengers lists before it can be approved or rejected by the departmental manager". Based on our problem-space conceptualization, this rule can be formally written as the declarative order relation: $\{TR_{[requested]} \rightarrow ?P > TR_{[requested]} \rightarrow ?DeptD\}$. As we emphasized earlier, ISs built based on the existing requirements specification methods hardwire subgoaling and goal-sequencing rules into procedural code.

During processing the initial SSM, SSM_i, undergoes changes as the problem-space search moves from one state to another. These changes correspond either to the insertion of new nodes to the SSM (e.g., node TR is added in state 2, Fig. 6) or to a change in attribute values of nodes already in the SSM (e.g., node DeptD changes state from "undetermined" to "approved" in state 4, Fig. 6). The reasoning process governing the iterative changes an SSM undergoes during its construction readily maps to the problem-space paradigm. Starting with SSM_i reflecting what is known in the initial problem-space state, evolving SSM_i into SSM_g follows the next iterative construction process.

(1) Let the current state be $SSM_c = SSM_i$.
(2) Generate a new state by expanding SSM_c:
    a. use subgoaling rules to identify gaps between SSM_c and SSM_g and post into SSM_c an unsatisfied subgoal for each identified gap;
    b. use goal-sequencing rules to choose which of all the unsatisfied subgoals posted to SSM_c to pursue next;
    c. generate SSM_c' by applying a state operator suitable for satisfying the chosen subgoal;
    d. let $SSM_c = SSM_c'$.
(3) Test SSM_c against SSM_g (i.e., termination conditions), and if $SSM_c \neq SSM_g$, go to step (2).

An architecture implementing this SSM construction process – called *ACE-SSM* – has already been applied to KBSs [1,2,3]. ACE-SSM accepts as input four explicit elements: a set of subgoaling rules (*G*), a set of goal-sequencing rules (*C*), a set of state operators (*S-op*), and a set of data entity types (*D*) whose instances are used to populate SSMs. Of these, *G* deserves attention because it is implicit in conventional ISs (and most KBSs). *G* constitutes metadata reflecting a meta-level goal structure of a target problem, or a template describing the structure that the SSMs constructed for a given problem (or by a target application) must posses. During problem-space search, *G* determines the subgoals that must be addressed in order to solve (process) a particular problem situation (case scenario), thus constraining the way the goal structure of that specific problem situation is evolved during problem-space search. Respectively, we can also say that *G* implicitly describes the goal problem-space state, SSM_g, whereas the evolving SSM_c being created explicitly describes the current problem-space state.

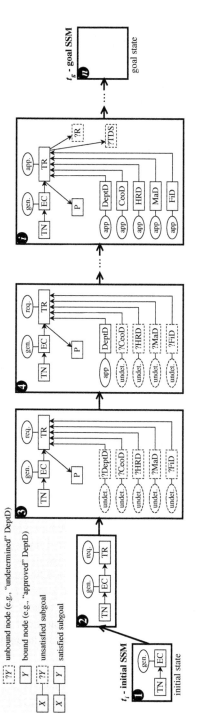

Fig. 6. Sample problem-space and the corresponding SSM evolution (for a Travel Request Processing application).

Entity (object) Types

EC	Employee-Choice (with states "generate", "update", or "cancel")
TR	Travel-Request (with states "requested", "approved", "ordered", or "canceled")
DeptD	Department-Decision (with states "undetermined", "approve", or "reject")
CeoD	CEO-Decision (----- " -----)
HRD	Human-Resource-VCEO-Decision (----- " -----)
MaD	Marketing-VCEO-Decision (----- " -----)
FiD	Finance-VCEO-Decision (----- " -----)
P	Passengers list
TN	Travel-Need
TDS	Travel-Document-set
R	Travel-Report

4. Declarative IS Requirements Specification Formalism

Following the above discussion, our method defines the *information requirements of an IS application* as a four-place tuple $\langle G, S\text{-}Op, C, D \rangle$, whose elements are defined above. Fig. 7 shows the order by which IS requirements are specified in relation to these four elements. Like in data-oriented specification methods, our method starts the IS requirements specification process with the creation of a standard ER model of the data requirements for a target business process (e.g., Fig. 2). An ER model is a three-place tuple $\langle E, A_j, R \rangle$. $E = \{e_j\}$ is a finite set of entity sets (object types). $A_j = \{a_{kj}\}$ is a finite set of attributes of $e_j \in E$, $\|A_j\| \geq 0$, with the k-th attribute of e_j denoted $a_k(e_j)$. And, $R \subseteq \{E \times E\}$ is a non-empty set of binary relationships between elements in E, with the ij-th relationship denoted $r_{ij}(e_i, e_j)$.[3] The specified ER model is the basis for specifying D as well as subgoaling rules in G, which, in turn, is the basis for specifying S-operators in $S\text{-}op$ and goal-sequencing rules in C. The rest of this section explains how this ER model drives the specification of the four other elements.

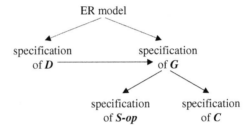

Fig. 7. Order of specifying the four elements of system requirements

Specifying Data Types (D). D is knowledge defining the domain concepts referenced by terms in the ER model, i.e., the domain concepts corresponding to the entity sets (object types) in E. This knowledge embodies two kinds of properties describing every abstract data-oriented concept in the ER model. To understand what do we mean by 'properties', it is useful to remember a simple fact: depending on the intended use of a target IS, each concept is assumed to serve a special function and, as such, it possess special properties necessary for that function [9]. Some of these properties are captured explicitly by all IS requirements specification methods, in the form of operational constraints of the kind specified at the level of a database schema (e.g., "*travel-request* entity has the admissible values {*requested, approved, ordered, canceled*}"). Other properties of each domain concept are not captured by typical IS requirements specification methods, because there is a silent agreement that those properties always holds. These properties include assumptions concerning each domain

---

[3] R is assumed to contain only binary relationships because any n-ary relationship, $r(e_1, e_2, \ldots, e_n)$, can be transformed into the series of binary relationships: $r_{1,2}(e_1, e_2), r_{1,3}(e_1, e_3), \ldots, r_{n-1,n}(e_{n-1}, e_n)$.

concept, necessary and sufficient conditions for an entity instance to belong to a certain class (concept), and assertions and axioms necessary for meta-level (or knowledge-level) reasoning about each concept (e.g., "*CEO* entity is a *person*"). These latter properties must be captured explicit as part of the local ontology of a target IS. Note that many of these traits do not necessarily need to be specified from scratch, but rather could be "imported" from existing higher-level ontologies [9].

Specifying Subgoaling Rules (*G*). Every relationship, $r_{ij}(e_i,e_j) \in R$, in the ER model is associated with one or more subgoaling rules that constrain the kind of changes that can occur to instances of e_i and/or e_j during processing. We therefore refer to subgoaling rules also as *goal constraints*. A *goal constraint* provides the semantics of a direct relation between entity types that must hold true in every SSM created for the target business process. We write goal constraints as quantified first-order predicate formulae. While these formulae can have several forms, their left-hand-side (LHS) always states pre-conditions to the posting of a subgoal implied by their right-hand-side (RHS). One form of goal constraints is:

$$\forall e_1,...,e_m [...] \Rightarrow \exists e_j \ r_{ij}(e_i,e_j) \qquad e_j \in S \subset E, \ e_i \in (E-S), \ r_{ij} \in R$$

When violated, the RHS of such a goal constraint posts to the SSM $e_i \rightarrow ?e_j$ as a new unsatisfied subgoal, where $?e_j$ is a new unbound SSM object that later must be bound to an instance of object e_i.

Example 1:
$\forall TR$ state(TR)="req" $\Rightarrow \exists P$ for(P,TR) – "every travel request in state requested must have an associated passengers list". When a travel request instance, say tr-12, is in state requested, this constraint posts the new unsatisfied subgoal (TR tr-12 state="req")→(P ?), based on the relation for(P,TR)∈ R.

Another form of goal constraints is:

$$\forall e_1,...,e_m [...] \wedge a_k(e_i)=v_1 \Rightarrow a_k(e_i)=? \qquad e_i \in E, \ a_k \in A_i, \ a_i \in \square$$

In form of goal constraints, ? means "undetermined".

When violated, such a constraint posts a new subgoal entailing a numeric manipulation of attribute a_k of object e_i.

Example 2:
$\forall TR \ \forall Dept \ \forall CeoD$ re($TR,CeoD$) $\wedge$ of($Dept,TR$) $\wedge$ state(TR)="ordered" $\Rightarrow$ travel-budget($Dept$)=? – "if a travel request was ordered, the department's yearly travel budget is no longer current". This constraint posts the subgoal (TR tr-12 state="ordered")→($Dept$ d-3 travel-budget=?), based on the relation from($Dept,TR$)∈ R.

Based on the formalism of state-transition diagrams, we identified other possible forms of goal constraints, in light of the types of manipulations they (subgoaling rules) can apply to an SSM. These types of manipulations consider cases where both the RHS and the LHS of a goal constraint reference the same object, reference an object attribute that is categorical, reference an object attribute that is numeric, etc. Additionally, we have formally defined the syntactic and semantic traits that goal constraints must posses, for example: (1) a goal constraint can set only one elementary subgoal (add a new SSM object, set an attribute value of an existing SSM object, etc.), and (2) the LHS of a goal constraint cannot embed search control information, e.g., via intentional ordering of its pre-conditions.

Finally, there is one special goal constraint, termed *global goal constraint*, which embodies the termination conditions that every SSM must meet for problem solving to end. When conditions in the LHS hold in the SSM, the RHS returns a boolean value of True. A global goal constraints is specified as a first-order predicate formula:

$$\forall e_1 \ldots e_n \in E \; [\neg]\{r_i(e_1,e_2), a_k(e_i)=v\} \; [[\wedge,\vee,[\neg]]\{r(\ldots), a_k(\ldots)\}] \Rightarrow \text{TRUE}$$

Example 3:
$\forall TR$ state(TR)="done" $\vee$ state(TR)="rejected" $\Rightarrow$ TRUE – the processing of a travel request instance node, say tr-12, is complete when that instance simply reaches a state of "done" or "rejected".

Specifying S-Operators (*S-op*). Specified (non-global) goal constraints are the basis for specifying S-operators. Recall that S-operators are responsible for producing the results needed to satisfy subgoals in the SSM. Every S-operator can be used to satisfy only one specific type of subgoal, analogous to executing a single elementary processing step in a DFD. It either can acquire input data, or access and/or manipulate data instances in the application's (persistent) data stores (not the SSM). The results it returns are value(s) to which to bind the unbound node in a specific unsatisfied subgoal (or node-chain) already in the SSM. For example, the S-operators corresponding to the goal constraints in examples 1 and 2 above can be written respectively as:

- S-op($TR_{[\text{state="requested"}]} \rightarrow ?P$) ::= $\Rightarrow$ create-new(P) & ask(content(P))
  This S-operator creates a new object P and initializes its value using (or binds P to) user-provided input (a passengers list).
- S-op($TR_{[\text{state="ordered"}]} \rightarrow ?Dept_{[\text{travel-bdgt}]}$)   ::= $\Rightarrow$ travel-bdgt($Dept$)=travel-bdgt($Dept$)–approved-bdgt(TR)
  This S-operator simply updates the remaining departmental yearly travel budget.

Specifying Goal-Sequencing Rules (*C*). Based on the forms of subgoals specified for a target application, it is next necessary to specify goal-sequencing rules. Recall that every SSM node n_j is a tuple $(e \; i \; [a])_j$, where e denotes an entity type, i is an instance of e, and $[a]$ is an optional attribute of i. As such, n_j could be associated with several types of subgoals, each of which entails reliance on a different type of goal-sequencing rules. The following are two sample types of goal-sequencing rules:

- Subgoals of the form $(e \; i)_j \rightarrow ?(e)_k$ arise when an SSM node depicting an entity of type e_j is linked to nodes depicting entities not of type e_j. The kind of subgoaling rules needed here define order relations over subgoals that reference SSM nodes only by their entity identity. For example, suppose a travel request is linked in the SSM to an unbound passengers list, $TR \rightarrow ?P$, and to an unbound travel document set, $TR \rightarrow ?TDS$. A respective goal-sequencing rule could have the form $\{TR \rightarrow ?P > TR \rightarrow ?TDS\}$, meaning that a passengers list must be added to TR before a travel document set is produced

- Subgoals of the form $\{(e\ i\ a)_j\}\rightarrow?(e)_k$ arise when multiple SSM nodes depicting entities of the same type e_j appear in different subgoals, of which one subgoal is to be pursue next. Here, goal-sequencing rules look at attributes of e_j to be able to "break ties". For example, suppose two travel requests are awaiting CEO approval, where one has its "urgency" attribute positive. A respective goal-sequencing rule could have the form $\{TR_{[urgency=T]}\rightarrow?CeoD > TR_{[urgency=F]}\rightarrow?CeoD\}$, meaning that the urgent TR should be processed first.
- [1] offers a complete discussion of the various types of goal-sequencing rules.

Another type of goal-sequencing rules, termed *global goal-sequencing rules*, is needed for cases where the problem-space search must jump from one SSM subgraph to another. In principle, such cases could be analogized to situations where we interrupt the execution of some subprocess in a DFD and jump to execute another subprocess in a different part of the DFD. An example is when an inter-organizational application interrupts the processing of an "approved" travel request because the credit limit of the customer (firm) has been reached and some exception handling is necessary. Respectively, global goal-sequencing rules choose an SSM subgraph containing the subgoals among which one is to be selected for pursuit. Fig. 8 depicts a simple case illustrating the role of these rules. Suppose that node n_1 is the root of an SSM subgraph of current interest. Let us term this node the *focus node*. Now, assume that node-chain $n_1\rightarrow?n_3$ was just satisfied, and that node n_3 was found to be associated with the new subgoals $n_3\rightarrow?n_4$ and $n_3\rightarrow?n_5$. Global goal-sequencing rules are needed to determine whether n_1 is to remain the focus node so that subgoal $n_1\rightarrow?n_2$ would be pursued next, whether n_3 is to become the new focus node so that either $n_3\rightarrow?n_4$ or $n_3\rightarrow?n_5$ would be pursued next, or whether n_6 is to become the new focus node so that either $n_6\rightarrow?n_7$ or $n_6\rightarrow?n_8$ would be pursued next. Global goal-sequencing rules are specified formally as predicate logic formulas of the form:

$$\forall n_j \ldots\ldots\ldots \wedge condition_1 \wedge \ldots \wedge condition_n \Rightarrow \text{is-focus}(n_j)$$

In this sentence, the LHS states the conditions under which the RHS labels n_j as the focus node.

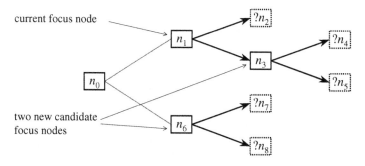

Fig. 8. Situation involving the use of global goal-sequencing rules

In summary, referring back to Section 1, where we briefly alluded to the main components of an ontology, it is easy to see that our formal specification of the four above elements (*D*, *G*, *S-op*, and *C*) constitutes much of the local ontology of an application. It is especially so due to the capturing of subgoaling rules and their specification in relation to their underlying data entity types.

5. Conclusion and Future Research

This paper presented an IS requirements specification method that enables making explicit the local ontology of an application, in support of semantic interoperability of distributed software applications as well as enterprise modeling and knowledge management.

Although our specification method starts with an ER model, just like data-oriented specification methods, it is different. Data-oriented methods proceed from an ER model to specify procedural DFDs for processes that manipulate data entities in the ER model, where the business rules underlying the processes depicted by these DFDs end up being implicit in the implemented software application. By contrast, our specification method proceeds to specify declaratively the subgoaling and goal-sequencing business rules governing these processes. At this point, a brief comment is warranted concerning so-called rule-based applications. Vendors of rule-based expert system tools, such as *Attar Software*,[4] argue that their tools permit capturing business rules and directly reasoning with these rules. However, note that even rule-based expert systems do not make explicit their local ontology [1]. In this sense, we saw how our method permits specifying subgoaling rules in terms pertaining to their underlying domain concepts (i.e., data entity types). These rules constitute a critical component of the local ontology of any IS application.

Relative to enterprise modeling and knowledge management, capturing declaratively the business rules underlying enterprise operations contributes to the creation of enterprise models and supports the goal of knowledge management. An *enterprise model* is a computational representation of the business rules constituting the core knowledge asset of an enterprise, and it provides the language for defining explicitly an enterprise in a form that is both descriptive and definitional. Using suitable meta-querying techniques [5], it is possible to interrogate an enterprise model in support of model-driven enterprise analysis and design. Take the case of travel-request processing, for example. An explicit enterprise model could answer questions like: who are the employees (titles) involved in approving a travel-request? and, who is in charge of updating the departmental travel budget whenever a travel request is ordered? It could also help to analyze the impact of changes on various parts of the enterprise (resource consumption, task attainment time, etc.), for instance: how would relaxation of some travel request approval policy affect the processing time of travel requests? Finally, it could also provide information for exploring alternative business process designs, for instance: assuming a new type of "urgent" travel requests, is a

---

[4] http://www.attar.com/ (April, 2002).

certain change in the approval process "consistent" with the process of handling normal travel requests?

While we have shown that the method proposed in this paper enables producing the local ontology of a target IS application as part of the standard IS requirements specification process, it is hard to tell at this point what are its true practical strengths and weaknesses. Like with every newly proposed method, these strengths and weaknesses can be revealed upon addressing several research issues of the kind summarized next. First, how much more or less effort does use of our method require in the specification of IS requirements (and the by-product creation of a local ontology), compared to the approaches currently used to create the local ontology of an IS application? Second, considering that our method currently uses only first-order predicate logic to specify subgoaling rules, is the scope of the method limited to only certain types of IS applications? Third, if so, what other kind of logic (e.g., situational logic) could extend the scope of our method to a much broader range of IS applications? Fourth, despite the fact our method permits expressing control (goal-sequencing) knowledge declaratively (something that lowers or even eliminates the need for procedural programming as well as simplifies testing and maintenance [1]), it remains to be seen whether (experienced) system developers are more comfortable (and productive) thinking about control knowledge in procedural terms. Finally, to what extent, if at all, could our method be rendered automatic?

References

1.   Benaroch, M.: Declarative Representation of Strategic Control Knowledge. Int. J. of Human-Computer Interaction. 55(6) (2001) 881-917
2.   Benaroch, M.: Knowledge Modeling Driven by Situation-Specific Models. Int. J. of Human-Computer Interaction. 49(2) (1998) 121-157
3.   Benaroch, M.: Goal-Driven Reasoning with ACE-SSM. IEEE Trans. on Knowledge and Data Engineering. 10(5) (1998) 706-726
4.   Conger, S.A.: The New Software Engineering. Wadsworth Publishing Co., Belmont California (1994)
5.   Fox, M.S., Gruning, M.: Enterprise Modeling. Artificial Intelligence Magazine Fall (1998) 109-121
6.   Gruber, T.R.: A Translation Approach to Portable Ontology Specifications. Knowledge Acquisition. 5(2) (1993) 199-220
7.   Guarino, N.: Formal Ontology and Information Systems. In: Guarino, N. (eds): Proceedings of the Int. Conf. on Formal Ontology in Info. Sys. (FOIS'98). IOS Press, Amsterdam (1998) 3-15
8.   Newell, A.: Unified Theories of Cognition. Harvard Press, Boston MA (1991)
9.   Schuster, C., Stuckenschmidt, H.: Building Shared Ontologies for Terminology Integration. In: Stumme, G., Maedche, A., Staab, S. (eds): Proceedings of the ONTO-2001 Workshop on Ontologies. CEUR-WS Online Publishing at http://CEUR-WS.org/Vol-48/ (2001)

10. Visser, U., Stuckenschmidt, H., Wache, H., Vögele, T.: Enabling technologies for interoperability. In: Visser, U., Pundt, H. (eds): Proceedings of the 14th Int. Symposium of Computer Science for Environmental Protection. TZI, University of Bremen, Germany, Bonn (2000) 35-46

11. Wache, H., Vögele, T., Visser, U., Stuckenschmidt, H., Schuster, G., Neumann, H., Hübner, S.: Ontology-based Integration of Information - A Survey of Existing Approaches. Proceedings of the Int. Conf. on Artificial Intelligence (IJCAI'01). Workshop: Ontologies and Information Sharing. Morgan Kaufmann Publishers, San Francisco (2001) 108-117

FOOM and OPM Methodologies – Experimental Comparison of User Comprehension

Judith Kabeli and Peretz Shoval

Dept. of Information Systems Engineering
Ben-Gurion University of the Negev, Beer-Sheva 84105 Israel
kabeli/shoval@bgumail.bgu.ac.il
Tel: +972-7-6472221; Fax: +972-7-6477527

Abstract. FOOM (Functional and Object Oriented Methodology) and OPM (Object-Processes Methodology) are methodologies for analysis and design of information systems that integrate the functional and object-oriented approaches. While the analysis specification of FOOM utilizes OO-DFDs (Data Flow Diagrams with object classes replacing "traditional" data-stores) and class diagrams, OPM defines a notational model that combines processes and classes in a unified diagrammatic notation – OPD (Object-Process Diagrams). We compare FOOM and OPM from the point of view of user comprehension. The comparison is based on a controlled experiment in which we measure: (a) comprehension of the analysis specifications; (b) time to complete the task of specification comprehension; and (c) user preference of models. Results of the comparison reveal significant differences between the methodologies, in favor of FOOM.

1. Introduction

FOOM is a methodology for analysis and design of information systems that combines the two essential software-engineering paradigms: the functional/data approach (or process-oriented) and the object-oriented (OO) approach [ShoKab01]. FOOM utilizes known methods and techniques such as DFDs (Data Flow Diagrams), and provides simple visual modeling and notations. It covers the structural and the behavior aspects of a system through the analysis and design phases, and provides a natural and smooth transition from one stage to the other. Object-Processes Methodology (OPM) is another methodology for analysis and design of information systems that combines the process and object approaches, and provides a unified notation for the structural and behavior aspects of a system [Dori01]. Since the two methodologies integrate the functional/process– and the object-oriented approaches, we found it interesting to compare them.

Methodologies can be evaluated and compared on various dimensions, e.g. quality of the analysis and design products, comprehensibility, ease of use, and model preference. This paper presents an experimental comparison of FOOM and OPM methodologies from the points of view of user comprehension of specifications. There are numerous studies that deal with experimental comparisons of development models/methods. Most such studies concentrated on comparing different data models,

A. Halevy and A. Gal (Eds.): NGITS 2002, LNCS 2382, pp. 107-122, 2002.
© Springer-Verlag Berlin Heidelberg 2002

such ER diagrams, normalization of relations, and object-oriented schemas. Some studies compared models/methods from a user perspective, attempting to find out which of the compared models or methods is easier to comprehend or apply. Other studies compared them from a designer perspective, attempting to determine which model/method yields more correct products, or requires less time to complete the analysis or design task, or which model/method is preferable by designers. Here are a few relevant examples.

Kim and March [KimMar95] compared EER (Extended Entity-Relationship) and NIAM (Nijssen Information Analysis Method) from the point of view of user comprehension. The authors prepared two equivalent specifications of a manufacturing company, one in each method. Comprehension was measured by counting the number of correct answers to questions concerning various modeling constructs. No significant difference in comprehension between the two models was found.

Shoval and Frumermann [ShoFru94] compared EER and OO Schemas from the perspective of user comprehension. Two groups of users were given equivalent EER and OO schema diagrams. Comprehension of schemas was based on a questionnaire consisting of statements concerning various constructs of the two data models. The authors found a significant difference in comprehension of ternary relationships in favor of the EER model, and no significant difference in comprehension of other constructs (e.g. binary relationships).

In a follow up study, Shoval and Shiran [ShoShi97] compared the same EER and the OO models from the point of view of quality, namely correctness of schema specification by designers. They also measured the time to complete the design tasks and the designers' preferences of the models. The subjects of this experiment were students of Information Systems. Subjects in two groups were given similar design tasks, each group using a different model. Performance was measured according to the number of correct/incorrect constructs created with each model. The authors found that EER model is better than the OO model in specifying unary and ternary relationships, with no significant differences in other constructs; that it takes less time to create EER schemas; and that the designers prefer modeling with EER more than with OO.

Peleg and Dori [PelDor00] compared two methodologies, OPM/T, a variant of OPM for real-time systems, and OMT/T, a similar variant of OMT [RBPEL91]. The comparison included both specification quality and comprehension. The subjects were divided into two groups. In the specification comprehension part, the subjects in each group received specifications of the same case study in one of those methodologies. They were asked to demonstrate comprehension using a questionnaire consisting of statements, which were classified according to different model constructs (similar to [ShoFro94]). The authors found that OPM/T specifications are significantly more comprehensible than OMT/T specifications.

In this paper we present results of a comparative experiment of comprehension of specifications, using FOOM and OPM. Sections 2 and 3 describe briefly FOOM and OPM methodologies, concentrating on the analysis stage, which is the main subject of this study. Section 4 describes the comparative experiment, Section 5 analyses the results, and Section 6 concludes and introduces further research topics.

2. Essential of FOOM Methodology

We provide only a brief description of FOOM, and demonstrate its analysis specifications with the *IFIP Conference* example [MMAS00]. For a more detailed description of FOOM see [ShoKab01].

FOOM is a methodology for the development of information systems that combines the functional approach and the OO approach. It can be viewed as an extension of ADISSA [Sho88], a functional-oriented analysis and design methodology. In FOOM, there is a clear distinction between the analysis and design phases. In the analysis phase, user requirements are presented in terms of two main products: an initial class diagram, and a hierarchical set of *OO-DFDs* (Object-Oriented Data Flow Diagrams). In the design phase the above products are used to create: a complete class diagram, the user-interface, the inputs and outputs, and a detailed behavior schema, which specifies the class-methods and application programs, expressed in pseudo-code and message diagrams. Here are some details on each of these phases.

2.1 The Analysis Phase

The analysis phase consists of two main activities: data modeling and functional modeling. The main products of this stage are a data model, in the form of an *initial class diagram*, and a functional model, in the form of *hierarchical OO-DFDs*.

The initial class diagram consists of "data" classes ("entity") classes, namely classes that are derived from the application requirements and contain "real world" data. (Other classes will be added at the design stage.) Each class includes various attribute types (e.g. atomic, multi-valued, tupels, keys, sets, and reference attributes). Association types between classes include "regular" (namely 1:1, 1:N and M:N) relationships, with proper cardinalities, generalization-specialization (inheritance) hierarchies, and aggregation-participation (is-part-of) links. The initial class diagram does not include methods; these will be added at the design phase. An example of an initial class diagram is shown in Figure 1. (Disregard the method names at the lower compartments of the classes; they do not belong to the initial class diagram.)

The hierarchical OO-DFDs specify the functional requirements of the system. Each OO-DFD consists of general (decomposable) or elementary functions, external entities – mostly user-entities, but also time and real-time entities, object-classes (instead of data-stores in "traditional" DFDs), and data flows among them. Two examples of OO-DFDs are shown in Figures 2-3: Figure 2 is the main (root) diagram, and Figure 3 details the *Papers Selection* function.

The analysis phase may start by creating an initial class diagram, followed by OO-DFDs, or vice versa. When the performing order starts with functional modeling, the analyst analyzes the user requirements and based on that creates a hierarchy of OO-DFDs, which, as said, include classes rather than "traditional" data-stores. Based on these OO-DFDs, the analyst can create an initial class diagram, which includes classes that already appear in the OO-DFDs. An alternative performing order, which may be more effective, is to first create an initial class diagram (from the description of user requirements), and then create the OO-DFDs, using the already defined classes. We plan to investigate the pros and cons of the alternative performing orders in experimental settings, hoping to be able to recommend on the preferred order. At any rate, the analysis activities must not be carried out in sequence. Rather, they should be performed in parallel or in iterations.

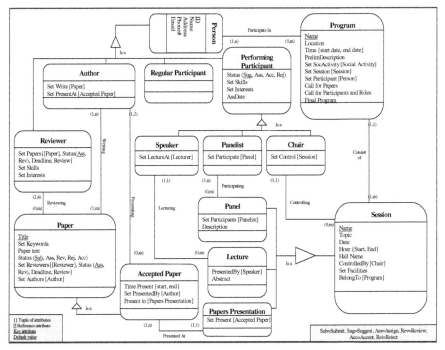

Fig. 1. Initial class diagram of *IFIP Conference*

2.2 The Design Phase

Since this paper concentrates on the evaluation of analysis specifications, we describe the design activities only briefly, without showing examples.

a. Definition of basic methods

Basic methods are attached to each data class in the initial class diagram. We distinguish between two types of basic methods: elementary methods and relationship/integrity methods. (Application-specific methods, for performing various user needs, will be added at next stages of design). Elementary methods include a) construct object, b) delete object, c) get object, and d) change attributes of object. Relationship/integrity methods are derived from structural relationships between classes. They are intended to perform referential integrity checks, depending on the relationship types between the classes and on cardinality constraints on those relationships. Generally, for each relationship between classes we can define an integrity method for operations of construct, delete, connect, disconnect and reconnect.

b. Top-level design of the application transactions

This stage is performed according to ADISSA methodology, where the application transactions are derived from DFDs (for more details see [Sho88]). According to ADISSA, a transaction is a process that supports a user of the system who performs a business function, and is triggered as a result of an event (like a "use case" in UML terminology). The application transactions are identifiable in the DFDs: a transaction consists of one or more chained elementary functions, and of classes and external-entities that are connected to those functions.

The products of this stage include transactions diagrams, which are extracted from the OO-DFDs, and top-level descriptions of the transactions. All application transactions will eventually belong to a "Transactions class", which is added to the initial class diagram. This virtual class will not contain objects – only transactions methods (as will be elaborated later on).

A top-level transaction description is provided in a structured language (e.g. pseudo-code), and it refers to all components of the transaction: every data-flow from or to an external entity is translated to an "Input from..." or "Output to..." line; every data-flow from or to a class is translated to a "Read from..." or "Write to..." line; every data flow between two functions translates to a "Move from... to..." line; and every function in the transaction translates into an "Execute function.." line. The process logic of the transaction is expressed by standard structured programming constructs. The analyst and the user, who presents the application requirements, determine the process logic of each transaction. This cannot be deducted "automatically" from the transaction diagrams alone, because a given diagram can be interpreted in different ways, and it is up to the user to determine the proper interpretation.

The top-level transaction descriptions will be used in further stages of design, namely Input/Output design, and Behavior design, to provide detailed descriptions of the application programs and the application-specific class methods.

c. Interface design – the Menus class

This stage is performed following the ADISSA methodology [Sho88, Sho90]. A menu-tree interface is derived in a semi algorithmic way from the hierarchy of OO-DFDs. Generally, a general function which is connected to a user-entity becomes a menu, and an elementary function which is connected to user-entity becomes a menu-item within the menu generate from its parent general function. Hence, there is a correspondence of the menus and their menu items, to the respective general functions and elementary functions in the OO-DFDs. All menus of the application belong to a "Menus class" which is added to the class diagram. The instances (objects) of the Menus class are the individual menus, and the attribute values of each object are the menu items. Note that, at run time, a user who interacts with the menu of the application system actually works with a certain menu object. He/she may select a menu item that will cause the presentation of another menu object (a sub-menu), or invoke a transaction, which is implemented as a method of the Transactions class (as will be detailed later).

d. Design of the inputs and outputs – the Forms and Reports classes

This stage is also performed according to ADISSA methodology and is based on the input and output lines appearing in each of the transaction descriptions. For each "Input from.." line, an input screen/form will be designed, and for each "Output to.." line an output screen/report will be designed. Depending on the process logic of each transaction, some or all of its input or output screens may be combined. Consequently, two new classes are added to the class diagram: "Forms class" for the inputs, and "Reports class" for the outputs. Obviously, the instances (objects) of each of these classes are the input screens and output screens/reports, respectively.

e. Design of the system behavior

In this stage, the top-level descriptions of the transactions are converted into detailed descriptions of the application programs and application-specific methods. A detailed description of a transaction may consist of various procedures, which can be handled as follows: A certain procedure may be identified as a *basic method* of some class. Another procedure may be defined as a new, *application-specific method*, to be attached to a proper class. Remaining procedures (which are not identified as basic methods or defined as application-specific methods) will be defined as a *Transactions class method*; this method is actually the "main" part of the transaction's program, which includes messages to other, application-specific or basic methods which are attached to proper classes.

The detailed description of a transaction is expressed in two complementing forms: Pseudo-code and Message Diagram. Pseudo-code is a structured description that details the process logic of the Transactions method as well as any other class method. The transition from a top-level description of a transaction to its detailed pseudo-code description is done as follows: Every "Input from..." and "Output to..." line in the top-level description is translated to a message calling an appropriate method of the Forms/Reports class; every "Read from..." or "Write to..." line is translated to a message calling a basic method of the appropriate class; every "Execute-Function..." line is translated to messages calling one or more basic methods or application-specific methods, or to procedures that become the "main" part of the Transactions method.

A Message Diagram shows the classes, methods and messages included in a transaction, in the order of their execution. This is actually a partial class diagram that shows only the classes involved in the transaction, the method (names and parameters) included in that transaction, and message links from calling to called classes. Message diagrams supplement the pseudo-code descriptions of transactions, but they are created only for non-trivial transactions.

To summarize, the products of the design phase include: a) a complete class diagram, including Data, Menus, Forms, Reports and Transactions classes, each with various attribute types and method names (and parameters), and various associations among the classes; b) detailed menu objects of the Menus class, each menu listing its items (selections); c) detailed form and report objects of the Forms and Reports classes, each detailing its titles and data fields; d) detailed transactions descriptions in pseudo-code; e) message diagrams, only for non-trivial transactions. At the implementation stage, the programmers will use the above design products to create the software with any common OO programming language.

3. Essentials of OPM Methodology

OPM (Dori01, DorGoo96) is a systems development method that combines the major system aspects - function, structure and behavior - within a single graphic and textual model, in which both objects and processes are represented without suppressing each other. This approach counters object-oriented systems development methods, notably UML, which require several models to completely specify a system. OPM is therefore not yet another OO analysis and design method, as it recognizes the fact that separating structure from behavior while engaging in system modeling, which results in the model multiplicity problem and, is counter-intuitive.

To avoid model multiplicity, OPM incorporates the static-structural and behavioral-procedural aspects of a system into a single, unifying graphic-textual model. In the OPM ontology, objects are viewed as persistent, state preserving things (entities) that interact with each other through processes - another type of things. Thing is a generalization of an object and a process. Processes are patterns of behavior that transform objects. Transformation is a generalization of effect, consumption and generation. Hence, transforming objects implies affecting them (i.e., changing their states), or generating new objects, or consuming existing objects.

OPM uses Object-Process Diagrams (OPDs) for the graphic specification. In OPM, objects and processes are connected by procedural links, which can be either enabling links or transformation links. These two different kinds of links are used to connect objects to processes, depending on the roles that these objects play in the process to which they are linked. Objects may serve as enablers - instruments or intelligent agents, which are involved in the process without changing their state. Objects may also be transformed (change their state, generated, consumed, or affected) as a result of a process acting on them.

An enabling link connects an enabler to the process that is enables. Enabler is an enabling object that needs to be present in order for the process to occur but it does not change as a result of the process occurrence. An enabling link can be an agent link or an instrument link. An agent link denotes that relative to the enabled process, the enabler is an intelligent agent - a human or an organizational unit that comprises humans, such as a department or an entire enterprise. An instrument link is an enabling link denoted by a white circle at the process end, which denotes that the enabler is an instrument - a non-human physical or informational object (machine, file, etc.) that must be present for the process to take place but is not affected by the process. The consumption link is a transformation link denoted as a unidirectional arrow from the consumed object to the consuming process.

OPM uses Object-Process Language (OPL) for the textual specification. Based on a constrained context-free grammar, a textual description in a natural-like language can be automatically extracted from the diagrammatic description in the OPD set.

Figures 4-7 present OPDs of the same *IFIP Conference* example that was used earlier. Figures 4-5 show part of OPM's object-class model. (Note that Figure 5 is an explosion of the object "Paper".) Figure 6 shows the main OPD (equivalent to FOOM's OO-DFD-0 in Figure 2), and Figure 7 explodes the "Papers Selection" process (which is equivalent to FOOM's OO-DFD-1 in Figure 3).

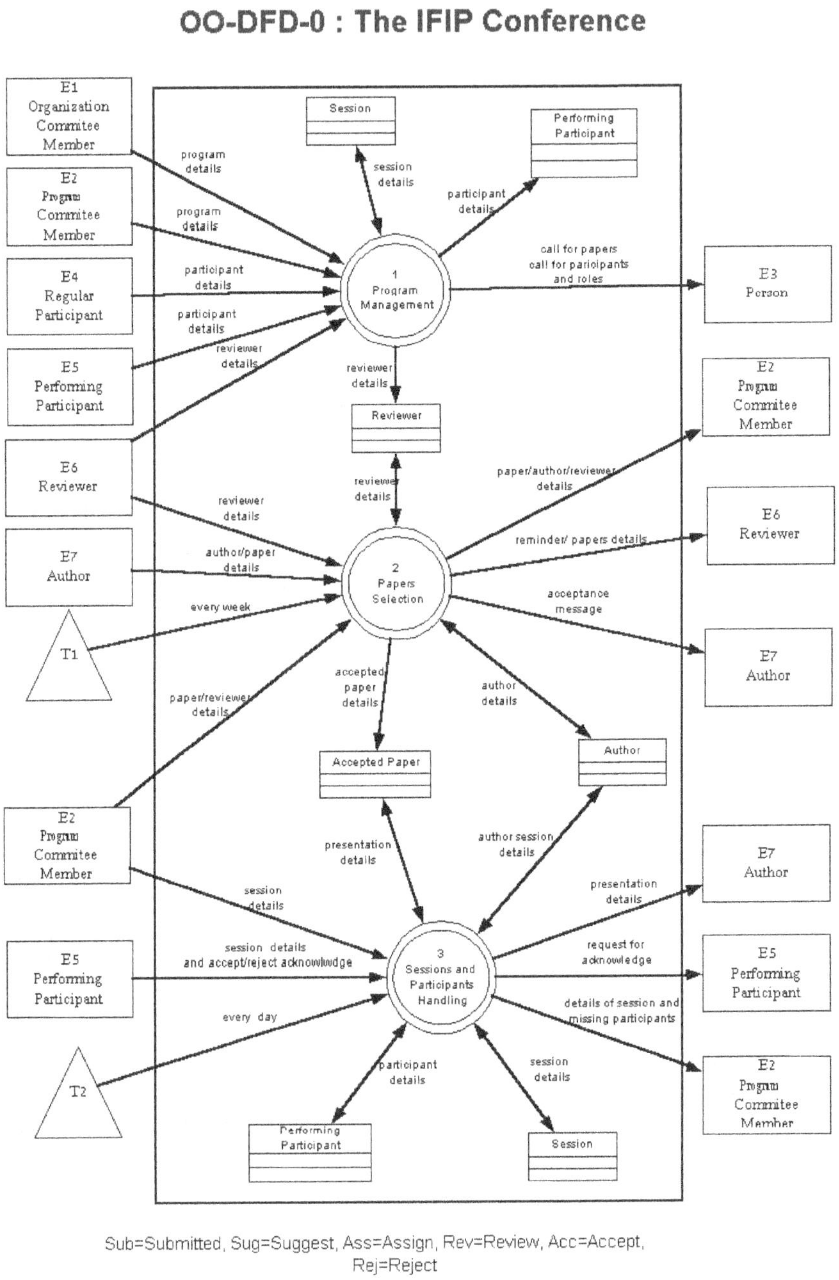

OO-DFD-0 : The IFIP Conference

Sub=Submitted, Sug=Suggest, Ass=Assign, Rev=Review, Acc=Accept, Rej=Reject

Fig. 2. OO-DFD-0 *IFIP Conference*

OO-DFD-2 : Papers Selection

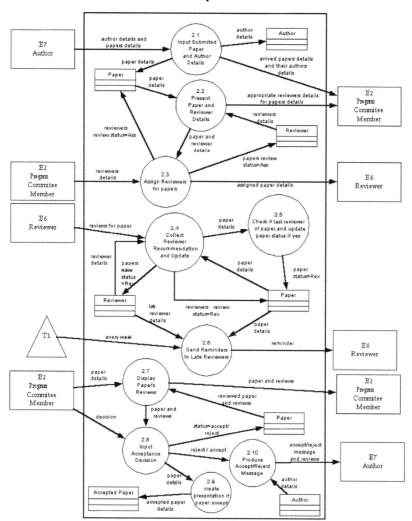

Fig. 3. OO-DFD-2 – *Papers Selection*

4. Experimental Comparison of FOOM and OPM

We compared FOOM and OPM from the point of view of user comprehension of analysis specifications of business-oriented information systems, by conducting a controlled experiment. Subjects were undergraduate students of Industrial Engineering and Management in their 4th year of studies. In their course "Information Systems Analysis", they studied the two methods, mainly to "read" and comprehend

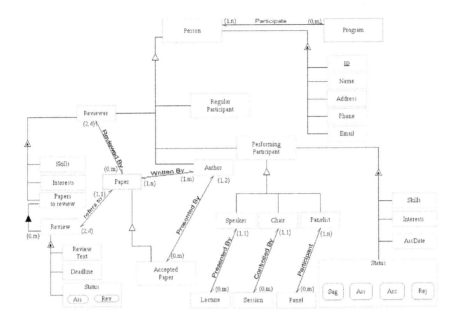

Fig. 4. OPD- class model- *IFIP Conference*

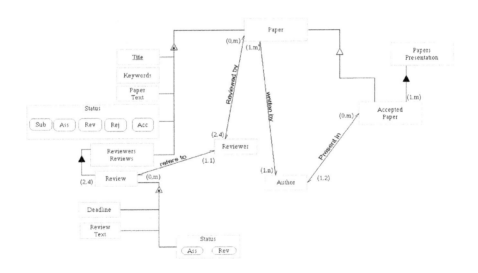

Fig. 5. Explosion of "Paper" Object

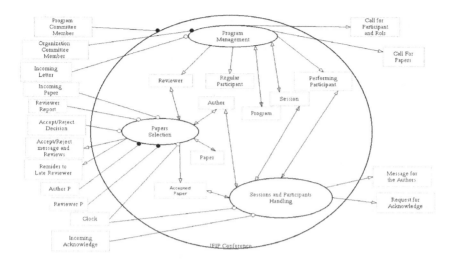

Fig. 6. Main OPD of *IFIP Conference*

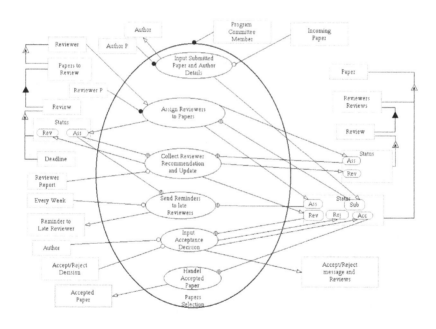

Fig. 7. Blowing of *Papers selection*

the products of specification. The research model is presented in Figure 8. For the experiment, we prepared printouts of two case studies: *IFIP Conference* [MMAS00] and *Greeting Cards* [DorGoo96]. For each case study we prepared equivalent specifications, namely a set of OO-DFDs and an initial class diagram for FOOM; and an equivalent set of OPDs (including an object model) for OPM. The subjects were divided randomly into two groups. Each subject, in each group, received a set of specifications in FOOM for one case study, and a set of specifications in OPM for the other case study, one set at a time (see Table 1). To avoid bias because of ordering effect, the subjects in each group were further divided randomly into two subgroups; in each subgroup they started to work with a different case study and model.

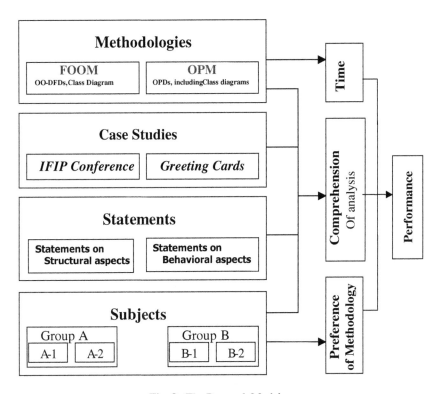

Fig. 8. The Research Model

Along with the specifications, each subject received a questionnaire consisting of 40 "true"/"false" statements about facts appearing in the diagrams. The subjects were asked to respond by marking "true" or "false" next to each statement, and to record the start and end time of each task (thus enabling to measure the time to complete the comprehension tasks). We classified the statements according to two categories: structure and behavior. The reason for this classification is that we wanted to be able to distinguish between comprehensibility of the two categories in each methodology. In order to avoid bias because of the order of statement in the questionnaire we prepared four different sets of questionnaires for each case, each with a different ordering of the (same) statements. At the end, each subject was asked to express preference of each methodology, using 1-7-point scales.

Comprehensibility of a model was measured according to the following categories: grade on structure category, grade on behavior category, overall grade, time to complete the comprehension task, and preference of method. We computed comprehensibility grades by counting the number of correct answers (whether 'true" or "false") given to the statements within each questionnaire. Then we computed the average grade per each category, per methodology and per case study, and then we tested the significance of differences of the average grades. In addition, we computed the average time to complete a task per methodology and case study, and based on that we tested the significance of time differences. Finally, we computed the average preference of model as expressed by the subjects at the end of the experiment.

Table 1. Experiment Design

Subjects	Subgroup A-1	Subgroup A-2	Subgroup B-1	Subgroup B-2
Number	30	30	33	33
1st Task	FOOM - *Greeting Cards*	OPM - *IFIP Conference*	OPM - *Greeting Cards*	FOOM - *IFIP Conference*
2nd Task	OPM - *IFIP Conference*	FOOM - *Greeting Cards*	FOOM - *IFIP Conference*	OPM - *Greeting Cards*

5. Results

Table 2 presents a summary of all effects between the factors (namely methodologies, case studies and task order), according to two dependent variables - overall grade and time - using 3-way ANOVA/MANOVA. The values of the three factors are: OPM and FOOM methodologies, CARDS and IFIP case studies, and 1st and 2nd order of tasks. The results show *significant differences* in the main effects (1, 2, 3 in Table 2), and *insignificant difference* in all their interactions (12, 13, 23, 123).

The result for the methodology main effect (1-Method) shows that FOOM is much more comprehended than OPM - users of FOOM achieved higher overall grades and it took them less time to complete the task. The result for the case study main effect (2-Case) shows a significant difference: the *Greeting Cards* case study turned out to be easier than the *IFIP Conference* case study, as its overall grade of comprehension was higher, and it took them less time to complete this task. Because of the difference in the case studies, we decided to compare the methodologies for each case study separately - as will be shown below. The result for the task order main effect (3-Task) shows a considerable difference: subjects spent more time on the 1st task (no matter which is the case study or methodology), and obtained marginally higher grades on comprehension of this task. This result seems to be reasonable.

Table 3 presents the results of the methodology comparison for each case study separately. We can see significant differences in favor of FOOM in each case study, and on both criteria of comprehension and time. Namely, in each case study subjects achieved higher overall grades, and it took them less time to complete the tasks with FOOM, compared to OPM. (Table 3 does not show the TASK effect and its interactions, because there was not a significant difference.)

Table 4 shows the mean grades of comprehension for the structure and behavior categories separately. The results reveal that in the more complex case study (*IFIP Conference*), FOOM gained a significant advantage over OPM in the behavior category, and an insignificant advantage in structure category. In the simpler case study (*Greeting Cards*) FOOM gained insignificant advantages over OPM in both structure and behavior categories. Hence, at any rate there were not significance differences in the structure category. This can be explained by the fact that the objects model of OPM is not much different from the class diagram of FOOM. Therewith, the grade on the behavior category was significantly higher when using FOOM with the more complex case study (*IFIP Conference*). This implies that while in simple systems there may not be a meaningful difference in comprehension, in more complex system FOOM is more comprehensible.

The last line of Table 4 shows subjects' preference of methodology, using 1-7 point scale. We see a significant preference of FOOM (mean grade 4.734) versus OPM (mean grade 4).

Table 2. Results of 3-Way ANOVA

Factor No.	Factor Name	Values of Factor	F	p-level ($\alpha=0.05$)	Mean of	
					Overall Grade (%)	Time (min.)
1	Method	OPM	11.43	**0.000029**	68.413	73.358
		FOOM			71.452	60.054
2	Case	CARDS	27.60	**0.000000**	73.743	58.976
		IFIP			66.122	74.435
3	Order of Task	1st	5.346	**0.006004**	70.328	72.394
		2nd			69.537	61.018
12	Interaction		1.147	0.234654		
13	Interaction		0.123	0.884464		
23	Interaction		1.055	0.351353		
123	Interaction		0.842	0.433656		

Table 3. Results per Case Study

Case	Category	Methodology	Mean Grade	F	p-level ($\alpha=0.05$)
Greeting Cards	Overall Grade (%)	OPM	72.8	3.297	**0.0438**
		FOOM	74.42		
	Time (min.)	OPM	63.12		
		FOOM	53.87		
IFIP Conference	Overall Grade (%)	OPM	63.83	9.43	**0.000275**
		FOOM	68.26		
	Time (min.)	OPM	84.0		
		FOOM	65.76		

Table 4. Results of Structure and Behavior Categories

Case	Category	Methodology	Mean Grade	F	p-level ($\alpha=0.05$)
Greeting Cards	Structure	OPM	73.48	1.176	0.282
		FOOM	77.5		
	Behavior	OPM	72.5	0.061	0.806
		FOOM	73.09		
IFIP Conference	Structure	OPM	63.09	0.365	0.548
		FOOM	65.15		
	Behavior	OPM	64.23	4.84	**0.032**
		FOOM	69.93		
Preference of Method (7-Point scale)		OPM	4.000	-2.15 (paired t-test)	**0.0368**
		FOOM	4.734		

6. Summary and Further Research

We found that overall; the analysis specifications of FOOM are significantly more comprehensible than those of OPM, that it takes less time to complete the comprehension task with FOOM, and that users prefer the specifications of FOOM. While there are no significance differences in comprehension of the structure category, in both case studies, we found that comprehension of the behavior category of FOOM is significantly better when used for a more complex case study (*IFIP Conference*).

The experiment presented in this paper has several limitations. For one, we concentrate on the domain of business-oriented information systems, but not on other domains (e.g. real time systems). Another limitation is that the authors, who developed FOOM, were the same people who taught and tested the methodologies, which might have affected the experimental outcomes. On the other hand, OPM was taught for a longer time than FOOM – four 3-hour meetings compared to two 3-hour meetings.

In further research, we plan to conduct two more experimental evaluations of FOOM. One experiment will examine the quality of specifications when performing the analysis stage in different orders, as explained in Section 3.1. Recall that one possibility is to start with data modeling (namely creating first an initial class diagram), and then to perform function analysis (namely creating the OO-DFDs). Another possibility is to start with functional analysis, and then continue with data modeling. In another experiment, we plan to compare FOOM with OPM from the point of view of analysts and designers. Subjects will be given tasks to analyze and design systems with the two methodologies, in order to measure quality (namely correctness) of the products.

References

[DorGoo96]   Dori D. and Goodman M. (1996), "From Object-Process analysis to Object-Process design", Annals of Software Engineering 2 pp. 25-50.

[Dori01]   Dori D. (2001), "Object-Process Methodology applied to modeling credit card transactions", Journal of Database Management, Vol. 12, No 1, pp. 4-14.

[KimMar95]   Kim Y.G. and March S.T. (1995), "Comparing data modeling formalisms for representing and validating information requirements". Communications of the ACM, Vol. 38, no. 6, pp. 103-115.

[MMAS00]   Mathiasssen L., Munk-Madsen A., Axel Nielsen P. and Stage J. (2000), Object Oriented Analysis and Design, Marko Publishing ApS, Aalborg, Denmark.

[PelDor00]   Peleg M. and Dori D. (2000), "The model multiplicity problem: experimenting with real-time specification methods", IEEE Transaction on Software Engineering, Vol. 26, No. 6., pp. 1-18.

[RBPEL91]   Rumbaugh J., Balaha M., Premerlani W., Eddy F., and Lorenson W. (1991), Object-Oriented modeling and design. Englewood cliffs, N.J.: Prentice-Hall.

[Sho88]   Shoval P. (1988), "ADISSA: architectural design of information systems based on structured analysis", Information System, Vol. 13 (2), pp. 193-210.

[ShoFru94]   Shoval P. and Frumermann I. (1994), "OO and EER conceptual schemas: a comparison of user comprehension", Journal of Database Management, Vol. 5, No. 4 pp. 28-38.

[ShoKab01]   Shoval P. and Kabeli J. (2001), "FOOM: functional- and object-oriented analysis and design of information systems - an integrated methodology", Journal of Database Management, Vol. 12, No.1, pp. 15-25.

[ShoShi97]   Shoval P. and Shiran S. (1997), "Entity-Relationship and Object-Oriented data modeling - an experimental comparison of design quality", Data & Knowledge Engineering, Vol. 21, pp. 297-315.

The Natural Language Modeling Procedure

Peter Bollen

Department of Management Sciences, University of Maastricht, P.O. Box 616
6200 MD Maastricht, The Netherlands
p.bollen@mw.unimaas.nl

Abstract. In this paper we define an information modeling procedure for the application of the modeling constructs from the Natural Language Modeling (NLM) methodology. The information modeling procedure that is presented in this paper contains a number of semantic bridges that specify when a specific user-input is required and what transformations must be applied in order to create an information model for a specific Universe of Discourse.

1 Introduction

An information modeling methodology is a combination of a set of information modeling constructs (in general defined as the meta model for that methodology) and an accompanying (set of) procedure(s) that 'prescribe' how the modeling constructs should be applied in practice. In this paper a *methodology* for *natural language modeling* (NLM) will be given. The information modeling constructs in NLM are based upon the axiom that all verbalizable information (reports, web-pages, note-books, traffic signs and so forth) can be translated into natural language sentences (natural language axiom) [16]. Taking this axiom as a starting point in information modeling will constrain the feasible modeling constructs to those constructs that enable analysts to model natural language sentences. It also means that it is *not* a real or abstract world that is subject to modeling, but that it is the *communication about* such a real or abstract world.

1.1 Related Work

The modeling constructs of Natural Language Modeling (NLM) are rooted in the *binary model* [1], the *object-role model* [5], *NIAM* [22] and *Fact oriented information modeling* [17]. The modeling constructs for the data perspective in NLM and its ancestor methodologies differ from (extended) Entity-Relationship ((E)E-R) approaches [4, 16, 20] in the way in which *facts* and *population constraint types* can be encoded. The most striking difference is in the absence of a modeling procedure in most (E)E-R approaches. A survey of recent (extended) E-R literature shows that in [19] the MOODD method is documented in which a restricted subset of English (RSL) can be used to express user requirements. However, the RSL specifies the possible outcomes of the requirements gathering process, but does not give explicit guidance for the analyst on how these outcomes are obtained in the requirements gathering process.

A. Halevy and A. Gal (Eds.): NGITS 2002, LNCS 2382, pp. 123-146, 2002.

The information modeling procedure for the NLM modeling constructs can be considered a further extension and specification of the *conceptual schema design procedure* [6]. In the NLM modeling procedure we will exactly specify *when* a *specific type* of user input is required. These user inputs can be considered *semantic bridges* between the 'real-world' that is subject to modeling and the 'model-world' that consists of projections of such a real-world in terms of the modeling constructs in the methodology that is used. The availability of such a procedure, furthermore, becomes a necessity for software processes that should qualify at least at level 3 of the *Capability Maturity Model* [18].

2   An Overview of the NLM Modeling Constructs

NLM is a substantially improved and extended version of N-ary NIAM [17]. The basic modeling constructs for the information perspective in NLM are *fact types, roles, naming conventions* and *constraints*. The fact types in NLM are N-ary which means that they can have any length. The fact type in figure 1 for example is a N-ary fact type for which N equals 4. A *binary* fact type in NLM, therefore is no more than a special case of the *N-ary*.

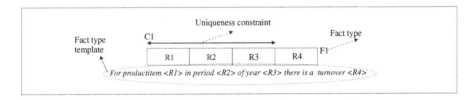

Fig. 1. Fact type (template) in NLM (example 1)

The semantics of a fact type in NLM can be captured in its fact type template. For example: *For productitem <R1> in period <R2> of year <R3> there is a turnover <R4>* is the template that belongs to fact type F1 in figure 1.

Definition 1. An *intension* is the meaning or the definition of a concept in a real or abstract world.

Let X be a concept. Let DX be the definition of the concept X
It now holds that: $Int(X) = \forall y[DX(y)]$

We can for example give the definition of the concept *Client*: *A client is a person that has bought at least one item in the past from ABC or is in the process of buying a product now.* The names of things or instances to which this (definition of) a concept applies within a *specific* application subject area at a *specific* point in time is called the *extension*.

Definition 2. The *extension* of a concept is the set of names of things or instances to which the *definition of the concept* or its *intension* applies.

Let X be a concept. Let DX be the definition of the concept X.
Let A be the set of names of things or instances to which definition DX applies
It now holds that : $Ext(X) = A$

In our example fact type template in figure 1, role *R1* is played by an instance of the intension '*product item*', role *R2* is played by an instance of the intension '*period*', role *R3* is played by an instance of the intension '*year*' and role *R4* is played by an instance of the intension '*turnover*'. Other business rules that govern that application subject area can be modeled in NLM as (population) constraints. If each instance of a fact type is determined by the values for a subset of the roles within that fact type then NLM will add *a uniqueness constraint* defined on those roles in the NLM information model. A *uniqueness constraint* is represented by a double-arrowed straight line over the roles on which it is defined (see figure 1). The business rule in example 1 that states: *that for a product item in a specific period in a specific year there can exist at most one turnover* can be modeled in NLM as the uniqueness constraint C1 in figure 1. For an illustration of additional constraint types we refer to [17, p.109-121].

3   The Basic Information Model Design Procedure in NLM

In this section and sections 4 and 5 we will define the procedure that specifies how a NLM information model for a given Universe of Discourse (UoD) can be created. The starting point for every information modeling project will be a (set of) *real-life user example(s)* that represent a specific 'external' user view on the subject area. We note that the application of 'real-life' user examples is not restricted to 'as-is' situations but also applies to projected 'real-life' examples of a 'to-be' or 'reengineered' application domain. The only requirement is that a user example must contain verbalizable information.

Definition 3. A user example is an informational document. An informational document can have several manifestations. It can be paper-based, it can be a web-page, a note-book, it can even be a formatted conversation. An informational document should contain *verbalizable* information.

3.1   The Verbalization Transformation

In NLM the information modeling constructs are applied in the analysis of the structure of natural language sentences (as laid down in the natural language axiom). This means that we must translate 'real-life' examples that are not in the format of 'natural language sentences' into *natural language sentences*. The first step in this modeling procedure, therefore is the 'visual-to-auditory' transformation [15] that will 'standardize' each *verbalizable* example into natural language sentences. During this transformation the user is asked to verbalize the content of a verbalizable 'real-life' user document that **not** necessarily should contain written natural language sentences. The result of this verbalization is a set of (verbalized) sentence instances. In figure 2 the *information flow diagram* is given for the *verbalization* transformation. When the *verbalization* transformation is executed the following sequence of actions should take place. Firstly, a knowledgeable user is asked to read aloud the content of a *representative* part of a document, sentence by sentence, as if he/she were talking to a colleague (information flow *3* in figure 2). While the knowledgeable user is reading (information flow *6* in figure 2) the analyst is listening to the user (information flow *4* in figure 2), subsequently the analyst will shade the verbalized parts in the original example (information flows *2* and *7* in figure 2) and add *every* new sentence onto the output document (information flow *5* in figure 2).

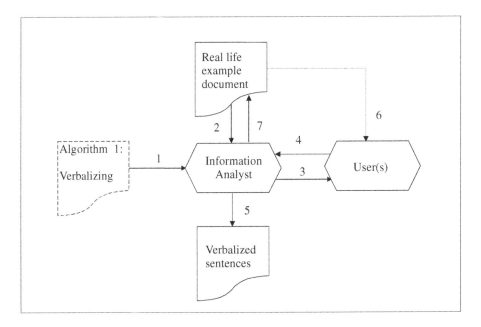

Fig. 2. The verbalization transformation

If all the *representative* information is read aloud, it is checked with the user that each sentence on the output document can be traced back to a shaded pattern on the input document by reconstructing (the representative part of) the original example. If it is not possible to reconstruct the original example then these steps have to be performed again until the reconstruction of the original example(s) is possible.

Initial check on naming conventions. In the *verbalization* transformation, the user is asked to verbalize the content of a *real-life example*. Whilst verbalizing, the user will reference the relevant *concepts* and *entities* in his/her UoD by using names. In the *NLM* methodology the concept of *naming convention* is crucial for bridging the gap between the *business domain* (or *knowledge domain*) and the *formal structure* with regard to the information perspective. In the NLM information modeling methodology we will exactly determine what name classes are of interest and we will enforce the domain users to select those 'candidate' name class(es) for the naming convention for a specific intension within the application subject area that can be considered a reference type in the selected portion of the real world that consists of the union of instances of the intension.

Definition 4. A naming convention is called a *reference type* for a selected portion of the real world if every element in the selected portion of the real world can be referenced by exactly one name from the name class in the naming convention and that one name from such a name class references at most one element in that selected portion of the real world.

> *Let IS be an naming convention*
> *T: elements or concepts in a selected portion of the real world*
> *N: All names from a given name class .* $IS = \{(t,a) | t \in T \wedge a \in N\}$
>
> $$\left(\forall_{(c,t),(d,v) \in IS} \left[c = d \Leftrightarrow t = v \right] \right) \Leftrightarrow \text{(IS is a reference type)}$$

The analyst should check whether **all** names that are uttered by the user for referencing elements in that selected portion of the real world belong to a name class that is of the reference type. If this is **not** the case then a different name class must be selected. Finding an appropriate naming convention for a given intension in cooperation with a user can be considered *a semantic bridge* that is embodied in the choice of the proper name class by the user for a specific *intension*.

Example 2:

Consider the 'real-life' example in figure 3.

ABC COMPANY INVOICE		345	Client: 123145	
Item	**Description**	**price**	**quantity**	**subtotal**
Ab102	*Hose*	*$ 12,--*	*2*	*$ 24,--*
Cd879	*Pipe*	*$210,50*	*1*	*$ 210,50*
				Invoice total: *$ 234,50*

Fig. 3. 'Real-life' document ABC invoice (example 2)

The ABC company creates an invoice for each client order. A *client* is identified by a *client code* among the union of clients of the ABC company. An *item* is identified by an *item code* among the union of items that are contained in the assortment of the ABC company. A *description* and a *unit price* exist for each item. An *amount (of money)* is identified by a *decimal number*. Furthermore, it is explicitly recorded how many units of a specific item are ordered by a *client*. Such a product *quantity* is identified by a a *natural number*. Finally, a subtotal is derived for each item in the invoice by multiplying the (unit) price for that item by the quantity that is ordered. A specific *invoice* is identified by a combination of a *client* and a *ranknumber*.

The analyst has to check that every verbalized sentence is self-contained. For example: The two sentences: *There exists an invoice 345 for client 123145* and *On that invoice the total amount is $ 234,50* must be replaced by the following sentence: *The invoice 345 for client 123145 totals $ 234,50*. Furthermore, if the user has verbalized the following sentence: *The item hose has a unit price of $ 12,--*, the analyst should ask the user following questions: *Does the name "Hose" refer to exactly one item among the union of items in ABC's assortment ?* and *Does the name $12,--refer to exactly one price among the union of prices ?* It should be noted that in many cases the initial verbalization is very *compact*. In these cases a *formal check* on the naming convention will take place during the *classification and qualification* transformation.

Definition 5. Verbalization is the process of transforming *user examples* into *natural language* sentences.

The document *verbalized sentences* exclusively contains natural language sentences. (A part of) the result of the verbalization transformation applied on the invoice example in figure 3 is given in figure 4.

> The item Ab102 has the description hose
> The item Ab102 has a unit price of $ 12,--
> The invoice 345 of client 123145 has a total of $ 234,50
> . . . .

Fig. 4. Example document verbalized sentences

We will now give the algorithm for the transformation *verbalization*.

Algorithm 1. Verbalization

```
BEGIN VERBALIZATION (UoD_i, G) {UoD_i is the universe of
discourse that contains 1 or more 'real-life'user
examples. G is the group of users of the 'real-
life'examples in UoD_i}
WHILE still significant parts of user examples are not
       shaded
DO     let knowledgeable user (g∈G) verbalize the next
       unshaded part from the significant¹ part of the
       UoD. The analyst will shade this part on the real-
       life example and he/she will add the verbalized
       sentences on the document verbalized sentences.
ENDWHILE
Replace dependent sentences by self-contained sentences.
{Reconstruction check}
```

---

¹ A significant part of a Universe of Discourse in this step of the information modeling methodology should be considered a part of that UoD that contains all possible variation in sentence types.

```
Let the analyst recreate the original example documents
by translating the verbalized sentences document onto the
corresponding parts on the original document.
    IF the recreated document is identical with the shaded
part of the verbalized document
    THEN {no information loss has occurred}
    ELSE{information loss has occurred,
        VERBALIZATION(UoDⱼ,G)
{Have the user verbalize the example again, thereby using
a different naming convention and/or verbalizations that
refer to bigger parts on the example document}
    ENDIF
END
```

The *verbalization* transformation is essential for the implementation of the modeling foundation of *NLM* (the natural language axiom in section 1). The *verbalization* transformation is the *unification* transformation that uses *all* appearances of *declarative verbalizable* information as an input and will converge it into natural language sentences as an output.

3.2   The Grouping Transformation

The transformation *grouping* is the process of sorting sentences from the document *verbalized sentences* according to what they have in common into a number of (sentence) groups. The document verbalized sentences should contain a *significant* set of sentences. If a resulting sentence group only has *one* sentence instance on the significant part of the example document the user should verbalize a second sentence of the same type (eventually from a different example for the same UoD) until all possible variability is reflected within the sentence groups.

Definition 6. Grouping is the process that divides *verbalized sentences* into groups of the same type.

A grouping GR is a partition of a set of sentences.

$$GR: \quad \mathfrak{Z}^{WORDCON} \text{ -----> } \prod_{i=1}^{M} \mathfrak{Z}_i^{WORDCON}$$

Where $\forall_i$ $\mathfrak{Z}^{WORDCON}$ is the powerset of WORDCON

Grouping is the mapping of N sentences into M ($\leq$ N) groups of sentences by some *similarity criterion*. We note that in principle a set of N sentences can be grouped in different ways. The resulting information models for these groupings are (semantically) equivalent, in the sense of [17, p.216].

Example 3:

Verbalized sentences:
The ABC company had a turnover for item ab 102 of $ 345 in week 34 of year 1997.
The ABC company had a profit for item ab 102 of $ 45 in week 34 of year 1997.

The ABC company had a turnover for item ab 103 of $ 745 in week 35 of year 1996.
The ABC company had a profit for the item ab 103 of $ 75 in week 35 of year 1996.

Result of transformation grouping by user 1:
<u>Group 1:</u>

The ABC company had a turnover for item ab 102 of $ 345 in week 34 of year 1997.
The ABC company had a turnover for item ab 103 of $ 745 in week 35 of year 1996.

<u>Group 2:</u>

The ABC company had a profit for the item ab 102 of $ 45 in week 34 of year 1997.
The ABC company had a profit for the item ab 103 of $ 75 in week 35 of year 1996.

We will now give the *grouping* transformation algorithm for a given UoD.

Algorithm 2. Grouping {VS is the document verbalized sentences which contains the results of the verbalization transformation applied on UoD_i}

BEGIN GROUPING(UoD_i,G,VS)

Divide the sentences into groups of the same type
    FOR all sentences groups in which the number of
       sentences= 1
    DO let knowledgeable user ($g \in G$) verbalize a second
        piece of information belonging to that sentence
        group from the existing example or a second
        example document of the same type. This second
        piece of information together with the first
        sentence from this sentence group should contain
        all variability within the sentence group.
        The analyst will shade this part on the real-life
        example and he/she will add the verbalized
        sentences on the document verbalized sentences. If
        such a second sentence does not exist, remove the
        singleton group from VS.
    ENDFOR
{completeness check} Each sentence in the resulting
verbalized sentences document should belong to a sentence
group. Each sentence group should at least have two
sentences on the document verbalized sentences.
END

3.3   The Classification and Qualification Transformation

Colleagues know the background of their co-workers and the language they use refers to a *shared world*. An example of such an implicit communication between colleagues is: *35467 is due for 23-97* (example 4). Suppose another sentence is communicated between two colleagues in this subject area: *35469 is due for 25-97.*

We can now group these sentences as follows:

Group 1:   *35467 is due for 23-97*
                            35469 is due for 25-97

For the colleagues in the *logistics and supply* department of a company these sentences have a definite meaning but it can be very hard for an *outside* person (who works for the same company) to find out what the communication is about. Because a conceptual schema should reflect the 'organizational' semantics of the *complete* application subject area we have to ask the user that has verbalized the sentences to inject 'additional semantics' in such a way that the resulting sentences can be understood by a colleague from another department within the same company. The result of this 'semantic injection' would yield sentences like: *The supply order with order number 35467 is due for week 23 of the year 1997* **and** *The supply order with order number 35469 is due for week 25 of the year 1997.* This is the reason that we need a transformation that transforms of the sentence groups on the document *grouped sentences* into a *semantic rich format* that specifies exactly what the communication is about (e.g. what concepts are involved and how these concepts are defined) and what naming conventions are used to identify instances of these concepts. We will call this transformation the *classicification and qualification* transformation. Firstly the variable and fixed parts for each sentence group will be determined (the *classification* subtransformation). Secondly the intension of the concepts that play the roles will be determined and a naming convention will be established, e.g. it will be made explicit to what *name class* the individual names, that reference those concepts, belong (the *qualification* subtransformation).

The classification sub-transformation. In the classification tranformation we will investigate *each* sentence group at a time. We will depict those parts of a sentence group from example 2 that are fixed and the parts that are variable :

Example 2(ctd.): *Sentence Group1=:{ The item Ab102 has a unit price of $ 12,--,*
                    The item Cd879 has a unit price of $ 210,50}
            Variable parts sentence Group1=:{ The item Ab102 has a unit price
                of $ 12,--, The item Cd879 has a unit price of $ 210,50}
            Fixed parts sentence Group1=:{ The item Ab102 has a unit price of
                $ 12,--, The item Cd879 has a unit price of $ 210,50}

We will call the names in the sentences that are variable within a significant set of sentences of the sentence group: *individual names.* The remaining positions in the sentence groups contain text parts that are fixed for every sentence (instance) of the sentence group. In the remainder of this paper we will call the *variable* parts in a sentence group *roles* and we will call the *fixed* parts in a sentence group *verb parts* in the accompanying fact type template. We will now be able to specify a sentence group by replacing the sentence positions for the roles by a *role name*. This leads to the following sentence group template for sentence group 1: *The item <r1>has a unit price of <R2>*. An equivalent graphical notation for a sentence group for this example is shown in figure 5.

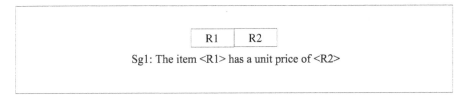

Fig. 5. Graphical notation sentence group for (a part of) example 2

In the graphical notation we will denote each role by a box that contains the role name. The sentence group template(s) will be placed under the 'role-boxes' and each template will contain at least one reference to *each* 'role box'.

The qualification sub-transformation. Now we have classified the sentence group elements into *variable* and *fixed* parts we can start deriving the additional semantics for the Universe of Discourse by establishing additional semantic bridges with the user. Firstly, the *type* of concept or thing (defined as *intension*) and its *definition* to which the *individual names* in a role of the sentence group refer, will be recorded. For every *role* in a sentence group we will determine its intension from a sample extension of that concept by posing the *what* question:

*To what **type of thing or concept** refer the individual names in this role ?*

For each *intension* that is distinguished by the user in the answers to the *what* question, a definition should be recorded in the *application concept repository (ACR)*. Every definition of an intension should be expressed in terms of general known concepts and/or intensions that are already defined in the *application concept repository*. Dependent upon the way in which the initial user verbalization has taken place, a specific intension might *not* be contained in the sentence group (e.g. the example in the grouping transformation in which an 'inter-colleague' level of verbalization exists). In those cases we will add the intension to the sentence group by putting the intension in front of the role names in the sentence group template.

Example 2(ctd.):
Sentence group:_The item ab102 has a unit price of the amount $ 12,--_
The item cd879 has a unit price of the amount $ 210,50

Sentence group template: *The item <R1> has a unit price of the amount <R2>*

Intension(ab102, cd879):= Item;
Intension ($12,--, $ 210,50):= Amount

Asking the user to define the intension in terms of other 'known' intensions leads to the *application concept repository* (ACR) in figure 6. We remark that the ACR should be based upon the ontology of the integrated application subject area, and it is therefore, defined on a business level.

Intension Synonym	definition
Item	a product that is contained in ABC's assortment
Client Customer	a person that has ordered or that is about to order an item at ABC
Invoice	a document that specifies the payments for an order
Amount	a specific quantity of money in dollars
Product quantity	a specific quantity of items

Fig. 6. Initial application concept repository for example 2

Secondly, we will *formally* establish the naming convention for the intensions that have been defined in the UoD in this sub-transformation. We will ask the user the *how* question one time for *every* intension that has been distinguished. In some situations this question serves as a quality check on the initial naming convention that has been performed during the *verbalization* transformation in which the user initially has verbalized the 'real-life' example.

> **How** *? (or **by what names**) are instances of a given intension in the application repository within this UoD identified ?*

This question tries to determine if a *name class* can be specified that configures a *reference type naming convention* for the selected portion of the real world that consists of the *union* of instances of the intension. In the example of the *The item <R1> has a unit price of the amount <R2>* sentence group the following two *how* questions can be posed:

Question 1: *How ? (or* by *what names) are instances of an item in the ABC invoice UoD identified ?*

Question 2: *How ? (or by what names) are instances of an amount in the ABC invoice UoD identified ?*

The answer to question 1 is that an *item* is identified by a name from the *item code* name class and the answer to question 2 is that an *amount* is identified by a name from the *decimal number* name class. The answer to these 'how' questions is another 'semantic injection' to the existing sentence groups. We will model these additional semantics as a sentence group that is 'connected' to the appropriate intension. In this example the naming convention sentence group for the intension person is *:<R3> is a name from the **item code** name class that can be used to identify an item within the union of items in ABC's assortment* and for the intension Amount it is: *<R7> is a name from the **decimal number** name class that can be used to identify a specific amount of money in dollars within the union of money amounts*. It should be noted that the selected portion of the real world in which the names from the name class can be considered to be of the reference type should be explicitly mentioned in the fact type template. In figure 7 we have illustrated how all extensions of the role *R1* that are played by the intension *item* at any time must be a subset of the instances of the name class *item code* (subset constraint C1) and how all extensions of role R2 played by the intension *amount* at any time must be a subset of the instances of the name class *decimal number* (subset constraint C6).

We have now shown that in principle we can pose *two* questions for *every* role in a sentence group. The answer to the *what* question will lead to the identification of a specific application *intension* for that *role*. The answer to the *how* question leads to the detection of a specific *name class* and is encoded as *a naming convention* sentence group plus the appropriate referencing constraint..

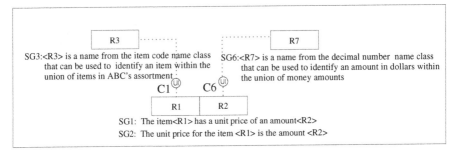

Fig. 7. Application of naming convention fact types in NLM

Until now we have assumed that the name of the name class that can be used to identify instances of the intension is different than the name of the intension. However, it is possible that an intension of an individual name coincides with the name class. Consider the following verbalized sentences from example 2 (that constitute one sentence group):

> *The invoice 345 for client 123145 totals $ 234,50*
> *The invoice 345 for client 578995 totals $ 125,00*
> *The invoice 348 for client 578995 totals $ 25,75*

The above sentence group has three variable parts (denoted by an <u>underscore</u>):

> *The invoice 345 for client 123145 totals $ 234.50*
> *The invoice 345 for client 578995 totals $ 125.00*
> *The invoice 348 for client 578995 totals $ 25.75*

The intensions for the respective role extensions are the following:

> Intension(*345,348*):= *number*
> Intension(*123145, 578995*):= *client*
> Intension (*$ 234.50, $125.00, $ 25.75*):= *amount in dollars*

If we would now ask the *how* question for every intension that was discovered, we yield:

> Name class (*number*):=*number*
> Name class (*client*):=*person name*
> Name class (*amount in dollars*):=*number*

In this example we see that for the 'first' role in the sentence group the name class that can be used to identify instances of the intension is *identical* to the intension itself. This means that there does **not** exist an intension for this role other than the name class itself. In this case we do not define a naming convention fact type. Instead we will record the name class in the position of the intension name in the sentence group. We can now conclude that for each *role* in a sentence group we must record the *intension* of the individual names that play that role in the sentence group and the *naming convention sentence group* for that intension **or** we must record the *name class* to which the individual names that play that role in the sentence group belong.

Complex naming conventions. In some subject areas users have introduced naming conventions that are *complex*, e.g. that consist of names that have an *internal* structure. The qualification of every role in such a sentence group, therefore, will *not* necessarily lead to the detection of all *intensions* that have extensions that consists of value combination of two or more roles in a sentence group. Thus, in some sentence groups the *intensions* are *not* linked to exactly *one* role. We will illustrate this once again in example 2.

Example 2(ctd.):
Sentence group: *The invoice 345 for client 123145 totals $ 234,50*
                                   The invoice 345 for client 578995 totals $ 125,00
                                   The invoice 348 for client 578995 totals $ 25,75
Sentence group template: *The invoice <R4> for client <R5> totals <R6>*
Qualified Sentence group template: *The invoice having rank number <R4> for*
                                   client <R5> totals the amount in dollars <R6>

We discover a fourth intension or name class in this qualified sentence group: *invoice*. If we once again ask the question : *by what naming convention is an instance of an invoice depicted ?*, it will turn out that this is a complex identification structure, consisting of combinations of individual names in roles <R4> and <R5>. We will create a third naming convention sentence group between the brackets of the communicated fact type:

The invoice [identified by rank number <R4> for client <R5>] totals the amount in dollars of <R6>

This means that in those sentence groups that contain at least one *complex* intension we will have to incorporate the naming convention sentence group, in the communicated sentence group itself. In case such a complex intension is not contained in the initial verbalization by the user we will have to trace the existence of such a 'complex' intension by systematically confronting the user with all possible role combinations (of a sentence group) and ask the user whether such a role combination can be considered as a potential naming convention for a potential 'complex' intension. The classification and qualification transformation should enforce the analyst and the user(s) to specify all intensions that have a complex identification structure. Consequently, the naming convention template for these complex intensions will be added to 'flat' sentence group in which they appear.

Intension	synonym	naming convention
Item		item code
Client	Customer	client code
Invoice		ranknumber ,client
Amount		decimal number
Product quantity		natural number

Fig. 8. Excerpt ACR including naming conventions for example 2

We will now give the algorithm for the classification and qualification transformation for a specific sentence group.

Algorithm 3. Classification and Qualification {SG_k is a specific sentence group on the document grouped sentences that is the result of the transformation grouping}
BEGIN CLASSIFICATION and QUALIFICATION(UoD_j ,G, SG_k)
FOR all sentence groups
DO   List all sentences in the sentence group.
      Mark the common parts throughout all the sentence
      instances in the group.Insert a role code[2] for
      every variable part.
      FOR all roles in the sentence group
      DO Determine the intension of a role in a
         sentence group by posing the what question
         (answer: Ix).
         Pose the How question for Ix: (answer Nx)
         IF Nx=Ix THEN Ix is a name class
                     ELSE Ix is an intension,
Let the user define the intension and record this
definition in the ACR. Determine the naming convention
fact type[3] that connects Nx to Ix.
         ENDIF
      ENDFOR
Check on complex intensions with the users[4]
      FOR each complex intension
      DO Determine identification structure for CI in terms
of the roles of the 'flat' structure.Add the na-ming
convention sentence group for the complex inten-sion in
brackets into the sentence group
      ENDFOR
ENDFOR
{consistency check} For each sentence group on the final
version of the document 'grouped sentences', exactly one
(non-naming convention) fact type should exist in the
document 'classified and qualified sentence groups'
END

---

[2] Such a role code must be a *reference type* identification structure within a project or a group of projects.

[3] In the template of the naming convention fact type the 'selected portion of the real world' in which the naming convention is of the *reference type* should be included.

[4] Consider a fact type consisting of roles R_1, ..., R_N. For each combination of j ($2 \leq j \leq N$) roles try to determine an intension, that is identified by a **complex identification structure.** As soon as all roles are contained in a (complex) identification structure, we can stop this algorithm. We will now replace the complex identification structure by creating one role for each intension having such a complex identification structure. The resulting fact type template will be called the **complex** fact type template as opposed to the **flat** fact type template.

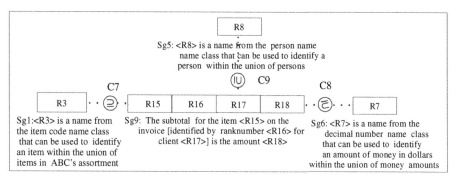

Fig. 9. Result of classification/qualification transformation of example 2

3.4   The Atomization Transformation

In the *ANSI/SPARC three-schema architecture* [21] different *external schemata* on the same *conceptual schema* can be defined. A conceptual schema according to the *ANSI/SPARC three-schema architecture* should enable all workers in the enterprise to access all *corporate* facts. The definitions in a conceptual schema, therefore, should not favour one external schema over another. The sentence groups in the conceptual schema in this architecture are considered to be *atomic elements* of which the compounds in the external schemata are created.

Definition 7. An *elementary* or *atomic sentence group* is a sentence group of which the sentence instances can not be split up into two or more sentences without losing information and can not be contained in another atomic sentence group referring to the same Universe of Discourse. An elementary sentence group is also called semantic irreducible [5].

Let $\{FFT_{ij}\}$ be the set of sentence group templates defined on a Universe of Discourse UoD_k and a user group G. Where FFT_{ij} refers to sentence group template i for sentence group j in this UoD.

Let the sentence α be an instance of a sentence group template FFT_{im} for sentence group FT_M ($\subset \{FFT_{ij}\}$) referring to the universe of discourse UoD_k.

The sentence α is atomic $\Leftrightarrow$

$$(\neg \exists \; \beta 1,.. \; \beta N \; \blacklozenge^6 \; \{FFTij\} \setminus FFTim \; [\; \alpha \Rightarrow^{m(G)^5} \beta 1,.. \; \beta N \;]) \quad \vee$$

$$(\exists \; \beta 1,.. \; \beta N \; \blacklozenge \; \{FFTij\} \setminus FFTm \; [\; \alpha \Rightarrow^{m(G)} \beta 1,.. \; \beta N \; \wedge \; \beta 1,.. \; \beta N \; \neg \Rightarrow^{m(G)} \alpha])$$

---

[5] $\alpha \Rightarrow^{m(G)} \beta 1,.. \; \beta N$ is defined as : The existence of sentences $\beta 1,.. \; \beta N$ is implied by
where   sentence α according to user group G in the given *universe of discourse*.

[6] Where $[a \; \blacklozenge \; A]$ is defined as: *a* is an instance of *A*.

We will now give the algorithm for the *atomization* transformation for a given UoD and a user group G.

Algorithm 4. Atomization {F is the set of fact types that results form the application of algorithm 3: classification and qualification}
BEGIN   ATOMIZATION({SG_i},G)

Consider exclusively the complex fact type structures as defined in algorithm 3
 take a fact type template (ftt) from the first fact type f ($\in$ F)
 WHILE not last fact type template from F AND
       arity(fft) > 2
 DO Take following sentence as a first sentence
     instance of this fact type template (Let the arity
     of the fact type template = N): $a_1 b_1$ .. N_1
{ Comment: we define the set of different role combinations consisting of j roles within the fact type
template ftt as follows: $RCOMBSI(j) := \{C_{j1}, \cdots C_{jk}, \cdots C_{j\binom{N}{j}}\}$

   WHILE j # N-2
         DO   k:=1
             WHILE k # $\binom{N}{j}$

         DO   Create a new sentence instance of the fact
               type template ftt_i: si2

               si2 should have different names in all
               roles except the roles in c_{jk}.

               Check with the user in user group G
               whether a combination of sentences si1 and
                si2 is allowed
               IF such a combination is not allowed
               THEN the fact type f of fact template ftt
                   sg_i is not atomic. Ask the user to
                   split the fact type sg_i into 2 or
                   more fact types $sg_{i,1}$, $sg_{i,2}$ ····
                   $sg_{i,p}$ such that the shading of
                   instances of these new sentence
                   groups on the original examples used
                   in the verbalization are equal to
                   the shaded part for the corresponding
                   instances of the non-atomic sentence
                   group sg_i

$$\{ SG_j \} := \{ SG_j \}/sg_i \cup \{ sg_{i,1}, \ .. \ sg_{i,p} \}$$

```
        ELSE k:=k+1
        ENDIF
        ENDWHILE
        j:=j+1
ENDWHILE
take next fact type template from F
ENDWHILE
{reference check}
Check that each fact type on the (input) document
'classified and qualified sentence group' refers to at
least one fact type on the output document 'atomized
sentence groups'.
END
```

We remark that even in the case in which there exists *exactly one* external view on the corporate information base we still need to atomize the sentence groups that are contained in the document *sentence group templates* simply because an *elementary* fact should be *stored at most* one time in the *application information base* in order to avoid update anomalies. The atomization process results in a conceptual schema for which algorithms can be defined that group these atomic fact types into relation types in an optimal normal form (ONF) [6, p.109]. The mapping in [17, p. 254-267] typically generates tables in fifth normal form (5NF). For an elaboration on atomization we refer to [8, 17].

4   The NLM Methodology: The Procedure for Integrating Basic Information Sub-models

We will now give a number of equivalence transformations that are required in order to be able to integrate information models that are created in a a number of different analyst/user interactions. This is generally kown as *schema integration* [2]. Many schema integration approaches are based on the (E)E-R approach for conceptual modeling [2, 7, 10, 11, 13]. In [7] the schema integration process is divided into *schema comparison*, *schema conforming* and *schema merging*. In [11] schema-level conflicts are classified into (*relationship) naming*, *structural*, *identifier*, *cardinality* and *domain* conflicts. [10] in addition, proposes to resolve *conflicts on synonyms and homonyms*, *merge entities by generalization* and *merge entities by suptype relationships*.

4.1   Conflicts on Naming, Synonyms, and Homonyms

In NLM schemas we can encounter naming conflicts on two levels: names for *intensions* and names for the *verbs* in the fact types. To resolve the first conflict we need *primary naming convention postulation*. In principle it is possible that more than one reference type naming convention is used for a specific intension in the different sub-schemas. In an integrated UoD however it is essential to have *exactly one* primary naming convention for each intension.

Definition 8. Primary naming convention postulation is the process of selecting one naming convention for every intension for (a) given integrated UoD (s).

After this negotiation process [14], the primary naming conventions for the intensions in the application subject area must be known together with their synonyms that can be incorporated into the conceptual information model, by means of *synonym fact types*, e.g. *The employee with employee ID <r1> has social security number number <r2>*. Furthermore, for all intensions that are contained in the first UoD *and* the second UoD and that have identical naming convention fact types, it should be checked whether these naming conventions still can be considered having a *reference type identification structure* in the integrated UoD.

Example 4:

UoD 1: *affiliate A: Employee with employee id[7] <R1> lives on Adress <R2>*

UoD 2: *affiliate B: Employee with employee id <R1> lives on Adress <R2>*.

In example 4 the conceptualization into an enterprise wide conceptual schema forces users in the integrated UoD to determine a *new* naming convention for *employees*. In such a case it is likely to create a complex identification structure in which the extension of the first role consists of names from the name class *employee ID* and the extension of the second role of the names from the name class *affiliate code* (e.g. A or B). An alternative naming convention that is of the reference type for the integrated UoD in example 4 is an *employee ID* that identifies employees within the integrated application subject area. The advantage of selecting the former naming convention is that the company can capitalize on the existing naming conventions.

Concerning the possibility of homonyms for application intensions, provisions have been made in the application concept repository in which different definitions for an intension are prohibited. With regard to the names in the verbs we remark that when we integrate two fact types from two sub-UoD's having different fact type templates in which the same intensions are involved (in the same roles) we need to determine whether they belong to the same group of fact type templates (for a given fact type) or whether they can be considered to represent two *different* fact types. In order to facilitate such a comparison we suggest that the main concepts that are contained in the verb-parts of the fact type templates should be defined in the Application Concept Repository (ACR). In such a way a common business ontology is preserved.

---

[7] It is assumed that the instances of the name class *employee ID* are (potentially) overlapping within the union of UoD1 and UoD2: The name class employee ID is of the reference type within UoD1 and within UoD2, but it is **not** of the reference type within the integrated UoD.

4.2   Specialization and Generalization Relationships

The second integration transformation is the *generalization/specialization* transformation. The reason for applying this transformation is that it can not be expected that all users have complete domain knowledge on the integrated enterprise subject area. For some user groups the intensions *person* and *student* can be considered synonyms because the extensions of both intensions will always contain the same instances. Whenever the subject area is extended (which is the case when UoD's are integrated) there will be a possibility that the extensions of some intensions in the integrated model are overlapping or are contained in one another. For example the following intensions *person, student, traveller, customer, dutch citizen* can refer to overlapping or inclusive classes of "physical persons" depending upon the scope of analysis [9]. In case the extension of an intension is an inclusive class of the extension of another intension we will call the former a *subtype* of the latter. Furthermore, it is possible that the extensions of two intensions that always exclude each other or that partially overlap can be generalized into an 'overlapping' intension in an integrated UoD whose extension is defined as the *union* of the extensions of the intensions in the different UoD's. We will call such an intension in the integrated UoD a *supertype*.

Definition 9. Generalization/specialization is the process of determining supertypes and subtypes for instances of the intensions in the integrated basic information model.

Example5:

UoD 1:	*Tennis player <R1> lives on address <R2>*
UoD 2:	*Employee <R3> lives on address <R4>*
Integrated UoD:	*Person <R5> lives on address <R6>*
	Tennis player <R7>is a person.
	Employee <R8>is a person

This transformation is called: **generalization**

In example 5 we have defined the intension *Person* as a supertype of the intensions *Tennis player* and *Employee*. It should be noted that the generalization transformation can only be applied when there exists a naming convention for the derived *supertype* that is of the *reference type* [3] in the UoD .

Example 6:

UoD 1:	*Person <R1> lives on address <R2>*
UoD 2:	*Student <R3> lives on address <R4>*
Integrated UoD:	*Person <R5> lives on address <R6>*
	Person <R7> is a student

This transformation is called: **specialization**

We will define the intension *Student* as a subtype of the intension *Person* in the integrated UoD of example 6.

4.3   Identifier, Cardinality, and Domain Conflict

The integration of sub-schemas in NLM is defined on a basic information model level. This means that identifier (or key) conflicts and cardinality conflicts [11, p.158] will not occur. It is assumed that in a 'first-pass' requirements analysis the population constraints will be derived directly in the integrated UoD. Furthermore, the attribute domain conflicts are not relevant in NLM because the only fact encoding construct is the fact type .

```
Algorithm 5. Integration of basic information models {BIM₁
and BIM₂ are two basic information models that refer to
sub-UoD's of UoD}
BEGIN Basic information model integration
(BIM₁,BIM₂,G₁,G₂.)
          Let BIM₁:= { {FTTij} | j∈{1,...,K}}
          Let BIM₂:= { {FTTij} | j∈{1,...,M}}
          where K and M are the number of fact types in
          BIM₁,BIM₂, respectively.
          check the naming convention fact types
          for these intensions in  all the fact types
          that have an  overlapping intension.
          harmonize the naming convention with the
          relevant user groups.
          FOR each intension
          DO  IF the identification structure within the
                  integrated universe of discourse is not
                  a reference type
              THEN create a new identification structure
                  for that intension for the integrated
                  UoD having a reference type structure.
              ENDIF
              Determine what group of intensions can be
              considered synonyms, specializations or
              generalizations.
          ENDFOR
{ontological equivalence check}
Every fact type that can be expressed in each sub-model
should be expressed in the integrated model. Every fact
type that can be expressed in the integrated model should
be expressed in at least one submodel.
END
```

5   The Population Constraint Modeling Procedure in NLM

Once a basic information model is created for a specific UoD, the analyst can elicit additional business rules from the domain user(s) by systematically confronting him/her (them) with new (combinations of) domain examples. The domain user only needs to confirm or reject the possibility that such a (combination of) examples can exist. It is possible to create an algorithm for each population constraint type in NLM. In this section we will give an illustration of such an algorithm for the group of *uniqueness constraints*. Uniqueness constraints will constrain the occurence of two or more fact instances in which a subset of the roles have *identical* name combinations.

Lemma 1. For each elementary (or atomic) fact type f with arity N assuming a 'one to one' naming convention[8], one of the following rules apply:

1) No uniqueness constraint exists.
2) There is at least *one* uniqueness constraint defined on exactly N-1 roles of fact type f.

It is assumed that the basic information model consists of *atomic* fact types. This assumption has been embedded in algorithm 6. It is however, possible to, create an algorithm in which the possibility of uniqueness constraints that cover less than N-1 roles is considered. Such an extended algorithm can serve as a quality check on the outcome of (the atomization) algorithm 4.

```
Algorithm 6. Uniqueness constraints derivation
BEGIN UNIQUENESS(IBIM ,UoD ,G ) {IBIM is basic information
model that refers to an integrated UoD}
WHILE not last fact type
DO take a random sentence instance from a complex fact
   type template for this fact type from the example
   UoD: (a₁,...., aₙ): FTj∈ IBIM
   Take the first role from this fact type (m:=1)
   WHILE not last role in fact type
      DO  Create an example sentence where the instance
          of role m is altered. Determine whether the
          combination of this sentence with the first
          sentence is allowed
          IF the existence of such a sentence is allowed
             together with (a₁,.... aₙ)
          THEN  add this sentence to the uniqueness
                significant population
          ELSE  define a uniqueness constraint UC on
                roles {1,...,N}\m
          ENDIF
      Go to the next role in fact type (m:=m+1)
   ENDWHILE
         Take next fact type
ENDWHILE
{N-1 law check}.Apply the N-1 law in Lemma 1 on each fact
type
END
```

---

[8] We will use the **complex** fact types for the derivation of uniqueness constraints according to the definition in algorithm 3

After the uniqueness constraint derivation procedure has been applied the analyst can add the uniqueness constraint to the application's basic information model (see figure 10).

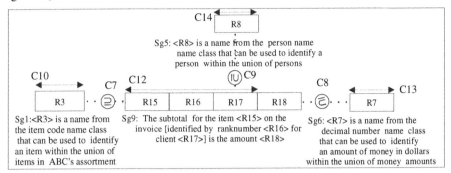

Fig. 10. Basic information model for example 2 with uniqueness constraint(s)

6   Conclusion

We can conclude that the NLM information modeling procedure explicitly shows the separation of concerns between the analyst and the user in the process of information modeling by providing the *semantic bridges* for this analyst-user dialogue. The semantic bridges from the natural language modeling methodology in the information perspective can be summarized as follows:

semantic bridge 1): Capturing the general domain knowledge (or sentence groups) (algorithms 1 and 2).
semantic bridge 2): Capturing the intension of the individual names (algorithm 3)
semantic bridge 3): Capturing the naming conventions (algorithms 1 and 3)
semantic bridge 4): Capturing the right level of atomization (algorithms 1 and 4)
semantic bridge 5): Arbitrating on the primary naming conventions for the integrated UoD (algorithm 5)
semantic bridge 6): Capturing domain generalizations and specializations for the integrated UoD (algorithm 5).
Semantic bridge7): Capturing additional business rules that can be encoded as population constraints (algorithm 6 and others).

Although a number of transformations in the NLM information modeling methodology at first sight have a 'trivial' appearance, the consistent application of the information modeling procedure in this article in practice has proven to improve the 'quality' levels of the resulting information models, because even the experencied analyst can always 'fall back' on the procedure in those situations in which the application subject area becomes too complex. The biggest advantage, however, is that unexperienced information analyst will be able to create information models that have the same quality level as the models created by experienced analysts. In a project in which the NLM methodology is applied for conceptual modeling the division into sub-projects and the order in which these sub-projects are executed does not have an impact on the final modeling results. The NLM modeling methodology therefore is fully scalable in terms of the complexity of the subject area and the availability of analyst capacity. Another advantage of the application of the NLM information modeling methodology is in the full accountability of the modeling results in which the user inputs and the analyst modeling transformations are precisely defined. The concept of 'total quality management' as advocated in the capability maturity model is an essential part of the transformation algorithms in the NLM information modeling procedure.

References

1. Abrial, J.: Data Semantics. In: Klimbie, J. , Koffeman, K. (eds.): Data Base Management, North Holland, Amsterdam (1974) 1-59
2. Beynon-Davies, P., Bonde, L., McPhee, D., Jones, C. : A Collaborative Schema Integration System. The journal of collaborative computing **6** (1997) 1-18
3. Bollen, P.: Using the OO paradigm for conceptual modeling: the need for a methodology. In: proc. ISoneworld 2002, Las Vegas, USA, (2002)
4. Chen, P.: The entity-relationship model: Towards a unified view of data. ACM Transactions on Database systems **1** (1) (1976) 9-36
5. Falkenberg, E.: Significations: the key to unify data base management. Information Systems **2** (1976) 19-28
6. Halpin, T., Orlowska, M.: Fact-oriented Modelling for Data Analysis. Journal of Information Systems **2** (1992) 97-118.
7. Johannesson, P.: Supporting schema integration by linguistic instruments. Data & Knowledge Engineering **21** (1997) 165-182.
8. Kent,W.: Data and reality, North-Holland,Amsterdam (1978)
9. Kung, C.: Object subclass hierarchy in SQL: a simple approach. Communications of the ACM **33** (7) (1990) 117-125.
10. Kwan, I., Fong, J.: Schema integration methodology and its verification by use of information capacity. Information Systems **24** (1999) 355-376
11. Lim, E., Chiang, R.: The integration of relationship instances from heterogeneous databases. Decision Support Systems **29** (2000) 153-167
12. Markowitz, V., Shoshani, A.: Representing extended entity-relationshp structures in relational databases: A modular approach. ACM Transactions on Database Systems **17** (3) (1992): 423-464
13. McBrien, P., Poulovassilis, A.: A formalisation of semantic schema integration. Information Systems **23** (5) 307-334
14 Meersman, R.: Some methodology and representation problems for the semantics of prosaic application domains. In Z. Reis and M. Zemanskosal (eds.): Methodologies for intelligent systems (1994) 39-45.
15. Nijssen ,G.: On experience with Large-Scale Teaching and Use of fact-based Conceptual Schema's in Industry   and University. In R. Meersman and T.B. Steel   Jr. (eds.): Proceedings of IFIP conference on Data Semantics (DS-1), Elsevier North-Holland (1986)189-204.
16. Nijssen,G.: An Axiom and Architecture for Information Systems. In: Falkenberg, E., Lindgreen,P. (eds.): Information System Concepts : An Indepth analysis, North-Holland, Amsterdam (1989) 157-175
17. Nijssen, G., Halpin, T.: Conceptual schema and relational database design: A fact based approach, Prentice-Hall, Englewood Cliffs (1989).

18. Paulk, M., B. Curtis, M.B. Chrissis and C.V. Weber.: Capability Maturity Model for Software, Version 1.1, Software Engineering Institute, Carnegie Mellon University, Pittsburgh, USA (1993)
19. Silva, M., Carlson, C.R.: MOODD, a method for object-oriented database design. Data & Knowledge Engineering 17 (1995) 159-181
20. Teory, T., Yang, D., Fry, J.:A logical design methodology for relational databases using the extended E-R model. ACM Computing Surveys, 18(2) (1986):197-222
21. Tsichritzis, D. , Klug, A.: The ANSI/X3/SPARC DBMS framework. Information Systems 3 (1978) 173-191.
22. Verheijen,G., van Bekkum J.: NIAM: An Information Analysis Method. In: Verrijn-Stuart,A., Olle T., Sol H., (eds.): proceedings CRIS- 1, North-Holland Amsterdam (1982) 537-590.

Conversation about Software Requirements with Prototypes and Scenarios

David Bahn[1], J. David Naumann[2], and Shawn Curley[2]

[1] Metropolitan State University, 730 Hennepin Avenue,
Minneapolis, Minnesota USA 55403
`David.Bahn@metrostate.edu`
[2] Carlson School of Management, University of Minnesota, 321
19th Avenue South, Minneapolis, Minnesota USA 55455
`{dnaumann, scurley}@csom.umn.edu`

Abstract. Determining the functional requirements for new software is a significant problem because it is dependent upon effective conversation between software designers and users. Prototypes and scenarios are two key techniques that have been advocated to improve the specification and communication of software requirements. This paper describes experimental research examining the utilization of prototypes and scenarios during designer-user conversation to determine and validate software requirements. This study is among the first to empirically test the effectiveness of employing scenarios in requirements determination. The results indicate that scenarios can affect user feedback in conversation about software requirements. The results also suggest that software designers should present users with a combination of software prototypes alongside abstract, diagrammatic models when discussing software requirements.

1   Introduction

One of the most widely noted reasons for software development failure is the lack of success that most organizations have in clearly defining the goals and requirements for new software systems [17]. Requirements determination is the more formal term sometimes used to describe this critical fact-finding activity that is an essential prerequisite component of software development [23]. Communication between software designers and users has been described as a fundamental element of requirements determination and successful software development [7,18].

One significant approach taken to improving requirements communication has been to improve the techniques used by software designers as they conduct requirements determination activities with users. One school of thought known as Participatory Design has espoused the overall need for enhancing user involvement in software design. In this vein, advocates of Participatory Design have proposed a number of elicitation techniques to improve the capacity of users and designers to communicate about software requirements with each other. These techniques generally tend to fall into one of two approaches:

- Improvements to the representations of software that are prepared by software designers for review by users
- Techniques for directing the way that users review representations of software

A. Halevy and A. Gal (Eds.): NGITS 2002, LNCS 2382, pp. 147-157, 2002.

In a more general sense the distinction between these two approaches is that one addresses the form of requirements representations being reviewed during the requirements determination process whereas the other approach addresses the way in which requirements representations are utilized during requirements determination. This paper describes an experimental study that investigated the relative efficacy of each approach to improving requirements communication. Two particular techniques, prototypes and scenarios, were tested to assess their efficacy in stimulating user feedback during conversation about software requirements.

2   Conceptual Framework

2.1   Prototypes and Prototyping

A Prototype is a working model of an intended software system that is constructed in order to facilitate learning about software requirements [14]. In general, the process of prototyping involves the creation of working models of software in order to enhance the articulation of requirements through a simulated experience of software use. Prototyping is a software development process that consists of four steps [15]:

- Identifying the user's most elementary requirements
- Developing a working prototype according to those 'primitive' requirements
- Implementation and trial use of the prototype by users
- Revision and enhancement of the prototype by designers in response to user feedback

Prototyping is iterative: the cycle of trial use of the prototype by users followed by further revision and enhancement by designers is repeated until the users (or designers) declare that the prototype adequately satisfies the requirements for the intended software.

As an iterative methodology for software requirements determination, prototyping emphasizes an evolutionary approach to discovering user requirements [8]. An underlying assumption of prototyping is that users must experience what it is like to interact with intended software in order to articulate what they really want that software to do [9]. This contrasts strongly with the traditional *Construction* approach to software development that emphasizes the creation of static and complete specifications of software requirements that are to be composed with near-architectural precision [8].

As a dynamic and evolving model of software requirements, a prototype is purported to have several advantages over the static and architecturally oriented requirements models that are espoused by traditional structured approaches to software development. One advantage is that, in response to user feedback, a prototype can be modified almost immediately [3] and thus help sustain user involvement and interest in the IRD process [19]. Another advantage of a prototype is that it affords "trial and error" learning by users during requirements determination and validation [21, p. 62]. A third purported advantage is that developing several prototypes in parallel enables user experimentation with a number of candidate software solutions [12].

2.2   Scenarios

Scenarios are narrative descriptions of one or more business transactions that "explicitly envision and document typical and significant user activities" that are to be supported by an intended software system and that support "reasoning about situations of use, even before those situations are actually created" [4, p.29]. Scenarios can be employed by a software designer during requirements communication in order to engender a more careful user evaluation of software requirements. The concept of a scenario has been linked with stories and episodes [10], even though a scenario could simply be just a description of a sequence of activities that constitute a business transaction.   Scenarios can direct the user's attention towards some features of the intended software (to the exclusion or diminishment of attention towards others) and therefore serve as a tool by which a software designer can direct the user's review of a particular requirements representation during requirements conversation.   Kyng [11] has postulated two distinct categories of scenarios:

Work situation descriptions   descriptions of current user task performance and
                                        instrumental interaction with a software system
Use scenarios   descriptions of future use of an envisioned
                                        software system.

   Work situation descriptions have been hypothesized to engender perceptual 'breakdowns' that assist a designer in learning about the user's task domain.   Use scenarios have been thought to engender perceptual breakdowns by users that are generative not only of new ideas about the intended software but also of ways in which that software might shape future manifestations of the relevant business tasks [2].

   Scenarios have typically been seen as a tool to be employed in conjunction with working software prototypes [16].   Recent research has suggested that scenarios and prototypes operate symbiotically in stimulating user feedback and user involvement in requirements validation [20].

3   Description of the Study

3.1   Research Model and Propositions

The general research model viewed prototypes and scenarios as each being an instance of more universal approaches to improving the communication of software requirements between designers and users.   Prototypes were seen as an instance of one of several forms of representations of software requirements that are prepared by designers for review by users.   These forms could include abstract design specifications (process and data models), paper-based depictions of prototypes (i.e. mock-ups) or fully interactive software prototypes.   Scenarios were considered as an instance of one of several methods for directing the way that users review representations of software requirements.   These methods could include a standard, loosely guided review of software requirements, structured interviewing techniques, scenarios, or others.

There are prescriptions in the literature for a particular technique like scenarios to be used in conjunction with a specific form of requirements specifications [11]. These prescriptions imply that there is a potential interaction between the form of the requirements representation and the method of directing the user's review of requirements. The research model therefore included investigation of an interaction effect between prototypes and scenarios.

The research model envisioned the requirements determination activity that precedes software development as a conversational process that takes places interactively between designer and user, rather than as a static exercise by designers discover a (perhaps mythical) 'correct' set of requirements, waiting to be elicited out of the user's head. Furthermore, this conversational process was not seen as taking place as completely unstructured communication. It was viewed as communication taking place around the joint review of a representation of software requirements about which the designer and user had to achieve some common reference and understanding. This goal of common reference and understanding in conversation is known in the research literature of socio-linguistics as "grounding" [6]. Grounding in conversation is the basis for the dyadic construction of "Joint projects" between conversational participants [5]. The joint projects that are the output of this interactive conversational process were conceptualized in the research model as user feedback in response to the presentation of the requirements. The general research model and research propositions (GP1, GP2, & GP3) are depicted in Figure 1 and Table 1 below.

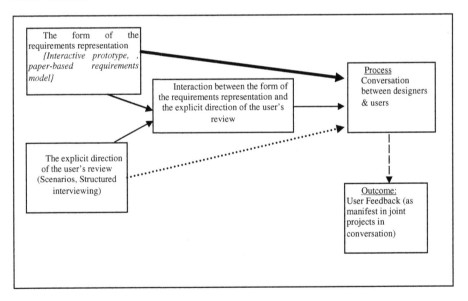

Fig. 1. The general research model: Potential determinants of user feedback during software requirements determination

Table 1. Research Propositions

Proposition	Proposition Statement
GP1:	The form of the requirements representation is the primary determinant of user feedback in requirements conversation.
GP2:	The designer's explicit direction of the user's review of the requirements representation is the primary determinant of user feedback in requirements conversation.
GP3:	An interaction between the form of the requirements representation and the designer's explicit direction of the user's review of the requirements representation is the primary determinant of user feedback in requirements conversation.

3.2   Pilot Study and Output Measures

A pilot study was conducted to investigate the impact of different forms of requirements representations upon user feedback. Subjects were presented with different forms of requirements representations, both paper-based (abstract process & data models along with mock-ups of intended screens and reports) and interactive software prototypes.

User feedback was measured primarily in terms of different kinds of user critique of the requirements representation under review. 'User critique' refers to change suggestions made by a user in response to the presentation of the designer's understanding of user requirements as embodied in the requirements representation. For example, a software prototype presented for user review and a scenario presented by the designer that envisions use of an intended software system are both of manifestations of the designer's comprehension of user requirements. When a user critiques this presentation by the designer and makes a suggestion for changing the intended software, the user is expressing new requirements for the software that have not been previously determined. In the language of ethnography, an expression of user critique could be considered the achievement of a successful "breakdown" of understanding that reveals new knowledge [1]. Among the various types of joint projects that may comprise designer-user conversation, an expression of user critique that is (a) in response to either of these presentations and that that (b) is acknowledged by the designer is the least ambiguous instance of a joint project that clarifies user requirements.

In the pilot study and subsequent research, user critique was classified according to a taxonomy developed by Mayhew, Worsley and Dearnley [13]. This taxonomy of user critique (see Table 2 below) posited a hierarchy of three levels of change requests expressed by users in response to the intended software system design as embodied in the software requirements.

Since changes to an intended software system increase in cost as the software project progresses from design to implementation, a classification based on impact of a change request upon an intended software design would reflect differentiation in the usefulness of various instances of elicited user feedback. To put this differently, Cosmetic changes are typically easy to make to new software even after it has been constructed. However, Global change suggestions that are not elicited from users during requirements determination can result in very costly modifications to new software. Hence, from the normative economic standpoint of promoting cost efficiency in software engineering projects, Global change suggestions appear to be generally more valuable to elicit than change suggestions that are Cosmetic (or even Local) in scope.

Table 2. Three levels of user critique as feedback during requirements communication

Type of critique	Definition
Cosmetic changes	Proposed modifications of the system requirements that are "trivial" and that cause "no additional repercussions" to it. Included within this category are modifications to a screen layout or report format that merely involve the reordering, re-formatting or movement of data elements.
Local changes	Proposed modifications of the system requirements that have a relatively local impact on the software such as the addition or deletion of data elements, regrouping of data elements as they appear on a screen layout, report format, or even over a sequence of screens.
Global changes	Proposed modifications of the system requirements that will have a significant effect on other components of the system that are not being immediately reviewed by the user. These may include modifications to data elements that are used to index and uniquely identify data records (i.e. key fields), creation of data querying facilities that transcend functional boundaries within the software system, and creation of additional system components.

The results of the pilot study indicated that subjects reviewing an interactive prototype expressed less Global critique than subjects reviewing either abstract requirements specifications (process & data models) or mock-ups of intended screens and reports[1]. Subjects reviewing abstract requirements specifications expressed less Cosmetic critique than those reviewing either interactive prototypes or mock-ups. The results of the initial research indicated that when a user reviews and interacts with a prototype, expression of Global critique becomes inhibited. Closer qualitative analysis of the pilot study protocols indicated that the review of a prototype appeared to focus the user on either Cosmetic critique of the prototype's user interface or on open-ended Cosmetic critique of the functional interaction with the prototype. It also appeared that users reviewing a software prototype become bound to a script of interaction with it, thus inhibiting their recollection of the business domain and their expansion of the topic of conversation from cosmetic features of the prototype into software functions that are Global in scope.

3.3   Experimental Study

To better investigate the research model, a set of laboratory experiments was conducted to examine the review of software requirements. In the experimental

---

[1]   These results were statistically significant, but since the subject pool for this pilot study lacked experimental power these results are not reported here.

exercise, pairs of subjects playing the role of software and user jointly reviewed and discussed requirements representations for a new software system for on-line grocery shopping. This particular domain was selected because it involved a task that would be familiar to all subjects.

As an outcome of this simulation of requirements validation, user critique was collected and analyzed. Thirty-three subject pairs were randomly assigned to one of the four experimental treatments that contrasted prototype review with the review of mock-ups, and a loosely guided review of software requirements with an explicitly scenario-based review of requirements. These treatments are summarized in Table 3.

Table 3. The experimental conditions that were investigated

Form of Requirements Representation --→		
Direction	Mock-ups	Software Prototype
Loosely guided review of requirements representation	**Experimental condition 1:** Subjects reviewed the content of the grocery shopping software's screens and reports on paper. The review was loosely directed.	**Experimental condition 3:** Subjects reviewed the grocery shopping software. The review was loosely directed.
Scenario-based review of requirements representation with explicit descriptions of shopping transactions	**Experimental condition 2:** Subjects reviewed the content of the grocery shopping software's screens and reports on paper. The review was directed through scenarios that described user interaction with the software to execute shopping transactions	**Experimental condition 4:** Subjects reviewed the grocery shopping software. The review was directed through scenarios that described user interaction with the software to execute shopping transactions

Subjects were business professionals attending graduate and extension classes on systems analysis for software development. The subjects were divided into two groups according to their level of experience with software, high or low. Subjects with a high level of software development experience were assigned to play the role of software designer. Those with a low degree of experience (typically less than 1-2 years experience) were assigned to play the role of user.

Subsequent to the experiment, subject feedback forms from each exercise were entered into a computer database. Each instance of feedback was classified by a pair of coders into one of the categories stated below in Table 4. This coding taxonomy was an extension of the classification of feedback utilized in the pilot study. The extended taxonomy helped to refine the categorization of user feedback expressed during the requirements dialogue.

Table 4. Categories of user feedback

Abbreviation	Type	Description
G	Global	Global critique
L	Local	Local critique
C	Cosmetic	Cosmetic critique
E	Externality	Critique directed at the business operations, rather than at the functions of the software
A	Approval	Subject indicates approval, rather than disapproval of a particular feature of the intended software
N	Not Applicable	Subject feedback does not fall into one of the categories above

3.4   Experimental Results

In assessing the total amount of user critique that was substantively related to the requirements specifications (i.e. Global, Local and Cosmetic), a contrast of the scenario-based review of requirements (experimental conditions 2 & 4) with the loosely guided review (experimental conditions 1 & 3) showed significant differences in the amount of feedback expressed. Surprisingly, while scenario-guided review of software requirements had an effect, it was a dampening one. Subjects engaged in a scenario-based review of requirements expressed significantly less feedback than subjects engaged in a loosely guided review. Furthermore, when the expression of Local and Cosmetic user critique was considered independently of Global critique, the results were more pronounced. Table 5 below presents the contrast of the mean number of instances of user critique between scenario-guided and loosely guided review of requirements).

Table 5. Tests of Between-Subjects Effects (Scenario vs. Loosely guided review)

	Mean number of instances of User Feedback:		
	Global, Local & feedback	*Local & Cosmetic*	*Global*
Loosely guided review	26.438	21.375	5.063
Scenario— based review	20.529	15.765	4.764
P =	.019 **	.010 **	.862

In respect to testing the distinction between conditions of prototype review versus conditions of mock-up review, no significant differences were found.   Similarly, no significant effect was observed respect to a possible interaction between scenario-based review of requirements and prototype review (proposition 3 above).   In respect to all other categories of user feedback, no significant differences were observed between treatments.

4   Discussion of Findings

4.1   Assessment of Experimental Results: Scenarios

In general, in as much as scenarios have been described as having a positive effect on user feedback, it was surprising to see that the scenario-guided review of requirements resulted in fewer instances of substantive user feedback.   However, two issues are important to consider.   First, the diminishment of user feedback for scenario-guided reviews took place within the Local and Cosmetic categories of user critique, whereas Global critique remained constant between treatments.   Secondly, the scenarios used in the experimental portrayed instrumental shopping transactions that users would execute with the intended software, rather than being broad situations encompassing some intended future vision of software in the business domain.   In that respect, the scenarios tested here more closely resemble what Kyng [11] described as *work situation descriptions* rather than being *use scenarios* that imaginatively project future uses of a software system.

Accordingly, the results indicate that while scenarios may be of benefit to user feedback during software requirements determination, the effect of scenarios may be more complex than has hitherto been assumed.   In some instances scenarios may circumscribe user feedback, particularly when that feedback is more pertinent to instrumental interaction with an intended software system (i.e. Local and Cosmetic critique).   In effect, scenarios that are work situation descriptions may serve to better focus the user on what will be accomplished with the intended software and therefore result in a somewhat more efficient communication between designer and user.

4.2   Assessment of Experimental Results: Prototypes

Ostensibly, the lack of significant differences in user feedback between the experimental conditions of prototype review versus mock-up review would seem to preclude any conclusions.   However, if the experimental results are contrasted with the results of the pilot study, an interesting question emerges.   In the pilot study subjects reviewing both abstract requirements specifications and mock-ups appeared to express more Global critique feedback that those engaged in prototype review. This indicated that a comparable contrast between mock-ups and prototypes in the experimental study should have yielded significant differences in user feedback (at least in respect to Global critique).

The answer to this question may lie in a subtle change that took place in the mock-up review treatment between the initial pilot study and the full experimental study.   In the pilot study, subjects in the mock-up review treatment were presented with a stack of graphical depictions of the screens and reports from the prototype, but were also presented with some abstract requirements specifications (data and process models) at the very end of the requirements specifications. In the experimental study, in order to tighten up experimental controls, subjects in the mock-up review treatments were only presented with graphical paper-based depictions of the screens and reports from the prototype, but did not review any abstract requirements specifications. This would seem to indicate that the review of abstract specifications during requirements determination did engender user feedback that is more focused on the larger functional issues of the intended software (i.e. Global critique). In contrast, the review of prototypes or the review of only paper-based content of software prototypes (i.e. mock-ups) appeared to be equally less effective in eliciting such feedback.

4.3   Overall Implications

This study provides experimental corroboration to the proposition that the way in which a user is directed to review software requirements can affect user feedback in designer-user conversation. In particular, the experimental results support the notion that scenarios, a popularly advocated means for improving designer-user communication about software requirements, can have an effect upon the expression of user feedback during requirements determination.

The results of this experimental study suggest some support for the notion that, in the context of a controlled contrast, prototypes and mock-ups are essentially equivalent in their respective capabilities to stimulate user feedback. Despite the understandable desire for users to interact with and 'try out' a software prototype during requirements determination, prototypes can be quite a bit more expensive to build than mock-ups. Mock-ups contain the content of the software prototype and do not provide instrumental interaction but appear to be a more cost-efficient means of eliciting the same degree of user feedback during communication about an intended software system. Moreover, given how critical it is to elicit all types of user feedback and critique during requirements communication, the essential equivalence of prototypes and mock-ups strongly suggests that the additional review and discussion of some abstract requirements specifications (data and process models) is highly advisable.

References

1.   Agar, M.H.: Speaking of ethnography. Sage Publications, Beverly Hills, CA. (1983)
2.   Benyon-Davies, P. & Holmes, S.: Design Breakdowns, Scenarios and Rapid Application Development. International Workshop on Representations in Interactive Software Development, London. (1997)
3.   Boar, B.: Application prototyping. Wiley, New York (1984)
4.   Carroll, J.: Making Use: A Design Representation. Communications of the ACM, 37:12, pp 29-35 (1994)
5.   Clark, H.: Using Language. Cambridge University Press, New York (1996)

6. Clark, H. & Brennan, S.: Grounding in Communication. In Resnick, L. Levine, J. & Teasley, S. (eds.): Socially Shared Cognition. American Psychological Association, Washington, D.C. (1991)
7. Cole-Gomolski, B.: Users loathe to share their know-how. Computerworld, November 17, 1997, p. 6 (1997)
8. Dahlbom, B. & Mathiassen, L.: Computers in Context: The Philosophy and Practice of Systems Design. Blackwell Publishers, Cambridge, Mass. (1993)
9. Jorgensen, A.H.: On the Psychology of Prototyping. In Budde, R., Kuhlenkamp, K., Mathiassen, L. & Zullighoven, H. (eds.): Approaches to Prototyping, pp. 278-289. Springer-Verlag, Berlin (1983)
10. Kuutti, K.: Work Processes: Scenarios as a Preliminary Vocabulary. In Carroll, J. (ed.): Scenario-Based Design: envisioning work and technology in systems development, pp. 19-36. John Wiley, New York (1995)
11. Kyng , M.: Making representations work. Communications of the ACM, 38:5, pp 46-55 (1995)
12. Lichter, H., Schneider-Hufschmidt, M. & Zullighoven, H.: Prototyping in Industrial Software projects - bridging the gap between theory and Practice. IEEE Transactions in Software Engineering, 30:11, pp. 825-832 (1994)
13. Mayhew, P., Worsley, C. & Dearnley, P.: Control of Software Prototyping Process: Change Classification Approach. Information & Software Technology, 31:2, pp. 59-66, (1989).
14. Mayhew, P. & Dearnley, P.: Organization and Management of Systems Prototyping. Information & Software Technology, 32:4, pp. 245-252, (1990)
15. Naumann, J. & Jenkins, A.: Prototyping: The new Paradigm for Systems Development. MIS Quarterly, 6:3, pp. 29-43 (1982).
16. Nielsen, J.: "Scenarios in Discount Usability Engineering." In Carroll, J. (ed.): Scenario-Based Design: envisioning work and technology in systems development, pp. 59-84. John Wiley, New York (1995)
17. Standish Group: "The CHAOS Report". Standish Group White paper. The Standish Group, Dennis, MA. http://www.standishgroup.com/sample_research/chaos_1994_1.php (1994)
18. Tan, M.: Using Communication Theory for Systems Design: A model for eliciting information requirements. In Avison, D., Kendall, J.E., and DeGross, J.J (eds.): Human, Organizational and Social Implications of Information Systems. Elsevier Science Publishers, B.V., North Holland (1993)
19. Wanninger, L. & Dickson, G.: Phased Systems Design, Development, and Implementation: Process and Technology. Proceedings of the IFIP WG 8.2 Workshop (1992)
20. Weidenhaupt, K., Pohl, K. Jarke. M. & Haumer, P.: Scenarios in System Development: Current Practice. IEEE Software, March/April 1998, pp. 34-45 (1998)
21. Wetherbe, J.C.: Executive Information Requirements: Getting it Right. MIS Quarterly, 15:1, pp. 51-65 (1991)
22. Whitten, J. & Bentley, L.: Systems Analysis and Design Methods, 4th ed. Irwin/ McGraw-Hill. (1998)
23. Whitten, J., Bentley, L., & Barlow, V.: Systems Analysis and Design Methods, 3rd ed. Irwin/McGraw-Hill (1994)

The Situation Manager Component of Amit – Active Middleware Technology

Asaf Adi, David Botzer, and Opher Etzion

IBM Research Laboratory in Haifa, Israel
(Asaf/Botzer/Opher)@il.ibm.com

Abstract. Reactive applications are applications that include a substantial processing that is triggered by events. This paper describes an application development tool that resolves a major problem in this area: the gap that exists between events that are reported by various channels, and the *reactive situations* that are the cases to which the system should react. These situations are composition of events or other situations (e.g. "when at least four events of the same type occurred") or content filtering on events (e.g. "only events that relates to IBM stocks") or both ("when at least four purchases of more than 50,000 shares have been performed on IBM stocks in a single week"). The paper describes the generic application development tool that is being developed within Amit (active middleware technologies) project in HRL, describes its language and features and demonstrate some of its capabilities using examples.

1. Introduction

1.1. The Problem

Many applications are reactive in the sense that they respond to the detection of events. These applications exist in many domains, and are very useful for e-business applications (stock market, business opportunities, sales alerts etc.). While the event types are known, the exact timing and content of the event instances are usually not known prior to their occurrence. Many tools in different areas have been built to detect events, and to couple their detection with appropriate actions. These tools exist in products that implement active databases capabilities, event management systems, the "publish/subscribe" protocol, real-time systems and similar products.

Current tools enable the application to respond to a single event. A major problem in many reactive applications is the gap between the events that are supplied by the event source, and the situations to which the clients are required to react. In order to bridge this gap, the client must monitor all the relevant events, and apply an ad hoc decision process in order to decide if the conditions for reactions have been met. Some examples of situations that need to be handled are:

- The client wishes to receive an alert if at least two (out of the four) stocks: IBM, Oracle, Sun, Microsoft are up 5 percents since the beginning of the trading day.

A. Halevy and A. Gal (Eds.): NGITS 2002, LNCS 2382, pp. 158-168, 2002.
© Springer-Verlag Berlin Heidelberg 2002

- The client wishes to activate an automatic "buy or sell" program if, for any stock that belongs to a predefined list of stocks that are traded in two stock markets, there is a difference of more than 5 percent between the values of the same stock in different stock markets, where the time difference of the reported values is less than 5 minutes ("arbitrage").

In current implementations the clients need to store and process all the stock quotes from the different markets and decide when to issue the alert (in the first case), or when to operate the "buy or sell" program (in the second case).   This may be impossible in some cases, such as "thin" clients without significant storage and processing capabilities. Even if it is possible, the solution that requires a client to process single events may result in a substantial overhead (ad-hoc programming efforts, communication traffic is significantly increased, redundant storage).

The required functionality is to enable each client to detect customized situations without the need to be aware of the occurrence of the basic events.

1.2. Related Work

Several academic proposals of composite events (specially for active databases) allow some functionality of looking at an event that is composed of several events. Some of the models are: Snoop[1], Naos[2], Sentinel [3], ODE [4], Trigs[5] and several others (e.g. [6]).

While these proposals support some functions of compositions, they do not provide a complete solution, because all models assume that additional filtering is possible after the event has been detected. Thus the provided solutions are inadequate for many cases. None of the above mentioned models can express the two examples mentioned above without additional filtering.

Additional tools that require active capabilities are system network management tools. These tools identify network faults and send some types of alerts to an event console. These systems often flood the event console with large quantities of alerts. The system operator, who watches the event console, must look through overabundance of data before he can identify the real problem and take a corrective action.

These event correlation systems filter network-messages and correlate network data to determine if a network problem occurred. Commercial event correlation solutions include VERITAS NerveCenter [7], HP OpenView [8] and SMARTS InCharge [9]. Note that in these tools the ability to define situations is limited to strict patterns and to various sources.

Event correlations of network management systems are designed to handle only network events. Their expressive power is limited to the network management domain and they do not aim at providing a general (domain independent) solution that supports the fundamentals of a situation definition we described earlier.

Nebula by Lynmore[10] is a tool that can also provide limited event composition capabilities.

Our relative benefits with respect to these products are:

- richer event language.
- flexibility in the language semantics (the "decision variables" exemplified above).
- higher level abstractions (situations, context).
- sophisticated filtering of events.
- a tool assisting in the debug, design and control, provided by the diagnostics systems of the rule analyzer.

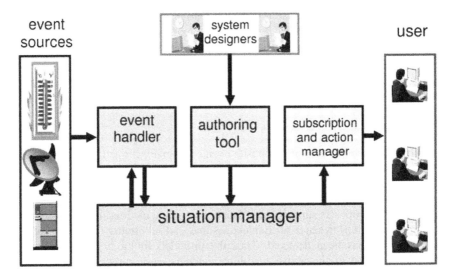

Fig. 1. Amit – Situation Manager Architecture

2. The Situation Manager Architecture

The architecture consists of the following components:

2.1. Event Sources

Events can be reported in two ways:
- "push" - the event report is being initiated by the source.
- "pull" - the source is polled or queried periodically about the events that occurred during a certain period.

The "push" style of event reporting is typical for applications that require real-time reactions.

Example: enabling any user to subscribe on events of the types:
- A user entered the system.
- A user left the system
- A user changed its status (e.g. from available to not available).

2.2. Event Adapters

Event adapters are programs that convert the reported events to a standard format.

2.3. The Meta-data – Definitions

The meta-data defines situations and actions. It is defined as XML propositions; the meta-meta-data is defined as DTD.

2.4. Amit – The Situation Manager

This is the system's engine. Its goal is to detect the desired situations.

The situation manager receives two types of input:
- The meta-data, which is a collection of parsed XML propositions that guide the situation manager.
- The event instances that are being submitted from the sources using the event adapters.

The situation manager employs composition operators and content filtering on the row events, and detect situations. Each detected situation is detected as an event, a feature that enables the definition of nested situations.

2.5. Subscription and Action Management

This component uses the meta-data definitions to decide what to do when the situation is detected. This information has two components:
- Who are the subscribers of this situation?
- What action should be taken for each subscriber (e.g. real-time alert notification, Email message, putting a message on a message queue...)?

3. The Situation Language

A situation is a reactive entity that receives events as an input, combines composition filtering with content filtering, and detects situations as an output. This section presents the composition types (3.1), and discusses the unique features of simultaneous content and composition filtering (3.2) which is mainly a performance issues, and the unique functionality issue of lifespan management (3.3) and fine-tuning of the detection process (3.4).

3.1. The Composition Types

Figure 2 shows the composition types for this language. Following is a short description of the different composition types. A situation instance is detected only if there is an open lifespan for this situation. The concept of lifespan is explained in Section 3.3.

- all (e1,..,en) : occurs when an instance of each event has been detected.
- before (e1,..,en): occurs when an instance of each event has been detected, such that detection-time (e1) < detection-time (e2) <....< detection-time (en).

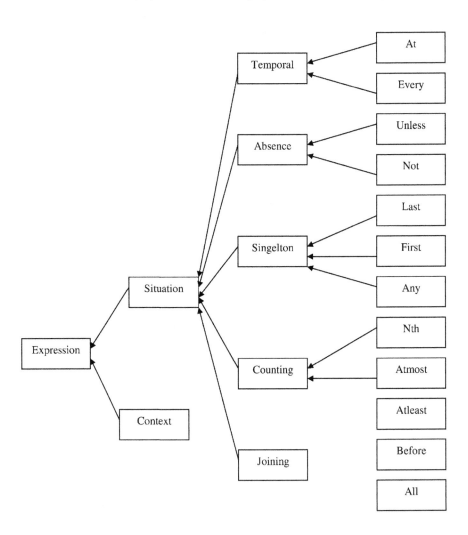

Fig. 2. Situation Types

- atleast (N, e1,..en): occurs when at least N instances of the specified events (optionally unique from each event) are detected.
- nth (N, e1,..en): occurs when the Nth instance of the specified events (optionally unique from each event) is detected.
- atmost (N,e1,..,en) : occurs when the number of instances of the specified events (optionally unique from each event) detected at the lifespan termination time is < = N.
- any (e1,..en): occurs when any instance of the specified event occurs.
- first (e1,..en): occurs once during a lifespan, returning the first selected instance.
- last (e1,..en): occurs at the termination of a lifespan, returning the last instance (if any).
- not (e1,..en) : occurs at the termination of a lifespan if there is no instance of any of the specified event within the lifespan.
- unless (e1, e2): occurs at the termination of a lifespan if there is an instance of e1 and there is no instance of e2 within the lifespan.
- every (T): occurs every T time-units since the start of the lifespan.
- at (e,T, MULT): occurs T time-units after the occurrence of an instance of e. MULT is a decision-variable that determines what to do in case that another instance of e occurs between detection-time (e0) and detection-time (e0) + T, where e0 is the previous instance of e (see the initiator's discussion in the Section 3.3).

3.2. The Combination of Content and Composition Filtering

All the tools that followed the ECA (Event-Condition-Action) approach took the two-phased approach of:
- phase I: composition filtering (the "event" phase)
- phase II: content filtering (the "condition" phase) on the result of the first phase.

In our solution, phase I combines the composition filtering with content filtering capabilities, while phase II is optional. This approach enables to construct **more efficient** reactive applications relative to those, which are being developed by current tools.

The two-phase approach may be inefficient when the number of detected situations is much smaller relative to the number of the combinations that are produced in phase I. Furthermore, the number of combinations produced in phase I can be exponential.

We claim that the ability to combine composition and content filtering is a unique property, and that it improves the performance in the general case, and enables the detection of situations that are not practically feasible in other solutions, in extreme cases.

The example in Table 1 demonstrates this capability: Let e1 be an event with the argument x, and e2 be an event with the argument y. Let the situation s be defined as **the first instance of before (e1, e2) such that e1.x > e2.y.**
Let the event history be the following:

Table 1. A scenario that demonstrates composition and content filtering.

Time	Event type	Event instance id	Argument
1	e1	e11	X = 5
2	e2	e21	Y = 7
3	e2	e22	Y = 4
4	e1	e12	X = 12
5	e1	e13	X = 4
6	e2	e23	Y =11
7	e2	e24	Y = 10
8	e2	e25	Y = 8
9	e2	e26	Y = 7
10	e2	e27	Y = 12

In the two-phase approach the following compositions are created:
(e11,e21), (e11, e22), (e11, e23), (e11, e24), (e11,e25),(e11,e26), (e11,e27)
(e12, e23), (e12, e24), (e12, e25), (e12, e26), (e12, e27)
(e13, e23), (e13, e24), (e13, e25), (e13, e26), (e13, e27) - 17 compositions.

All these combinations are required, because in phase I we cannot rule out any combination that may be the first combination to satisfy the content filtering.

The second phase will select the combination (e11, e22), which is the only one that satisfies the condition. In our approach both phases are unified, and when this combination is found (it is the second combination) there is no need to look for the rest (15 more combinations!).

In the general case the number of combinations may be exponential, and the sought combination typically can be found, without creating a substantial part of the combinations.

3.3. Lifespan Management

A lifespan is a time interval during which situation detection is relevant. A lifespan is bounded by two events called *initiator* and *terminator*. An occurrence of an initiator event initiates the lifespan and an occurrence of a terminator event terminates the lifespan. A situation may have more than one open lifespan simultaneously if two initiator events occur before a terminator event, depending on the initiator duplicates policy.

An initiator is an event that initiates a lifespan. The initiator event is either an occurrence of event that satisfies the conditions for initiation, or the system startup. A situation may have more than one initiator.

A unique feature of the situation manager is a dynamic and local decision about multiple occurrences of initiators. The system designer can decide what should the *duplicates policy* be in the level of a single initiator of a lifespan. The possible values are add | ignore | override| replace.

- ◆ add: any additional instance starts a separate lifespan for the same situation, while the existing instances remain active.
- ◆ ignore: any additional instance of the initiator event is ignored until the terminator will be detected (this is the default).
- ◆ replace: any additional instance starts a separate lifespan, and the original lifespan will be terminated.
- ◆ override: the new instance starts a separate lifespan, and the original lifespan is discarded without detection of delayed and deferred situations (situations that are reported only at the end of the lifespan).

A terminator is an event that closes a lifespan of a situation. A situation may have more than one terminator. A terminator can close the first, the last or each lifespan of the situation. On lifespan termination delayed and deferred situations are detected.

While the concept of lifespan exists in other tools, it has some unique properties in our model:

- The duplicates policy provides system design flexibility. This is required from the assumption that the situation manager is a generic tool, and different applications have different needs.
- When multiple lifespans of the same situation are open, a terminator instance may close the first, last or all the lifespans.
- Initiator and terminator may be conditioned, i.e. the occurrence of the initiator and terminator event affects the lifespans only if a condition is satisfied. The condition may be different for different situations.
- The lifespan may have an expiration time. If the lifespan expires then there is an optional decision whether to execute situation detections that is done when the lifespan terminates.
- A lifespan may be initiated by different initiators.

3.4. Fine Tuning of the Detection Process

The detection process is defined as the *process of detecting that a situation has occurred.*
In case there are multiple candidates of matching compositions, our model has the unique flexibility to fine tune the detection process. We use the example illustrated in Table 2 in demonstrating the different options.
The lifespan starts at time stamp = 0 and is terminates at time stamp = 7.

Table 2. An example of fine-tuning of detection decisions.

Time stamp	Event-type	Instance-id
1	e1	e11
2	e1	e12
3	e2	e21
4	e2	e22
5	e1	e13
6	e2	e23

The unique features of the detection process are:

- The ability to decide when to compose the situation (immediately or on termination). Example: the first instance of the situation **before (e1, e2)** is detected in time stamp = 3, (e11, e21) if the situation is detected immediately, while if the composition is detected at termination, then all the situation instances are detected in time stamp = 7.

- The ability to use quantifiers for each operand (in other models there is a concept of "consumption modes" which is global for all operands, and covers only part of these combinations).

The quantifiers are **first, last, each.** example: the situation **before (first e1, each e2)** yields the situations (e11, e21), (e11, e22), (e11, e23) if we assume that we can reuse the event instance e11 for multiple situations.

- The ability to decide if an event instance that participates in the detection can be reused. If not, this event is consumed. This decision may be different for each operand and may be conditioned. Example: in the previous example
- **before (first e1, each e2)**, we assumed that the event instance e11 can be reused as the first instance of e1. If we choose the option of using each instance only once, the detected situations are: (e11, e21), (e12, e22), (e13, e23).
- The ability to decide what should be done with the "skipped" instances: are they considered for further compositions or not? Example: in the previous **before (first e1, each e2)**, the detected situations are (e11, e21), (e13, e23), if the skipped instances are ignored, and each instance can be used only once (e12 is ignored, thus e22 has no match)
- The ability to use threshold conditions for the inclusion of events in the composition process.

4. An Example

The following example is taken from the stock market domain. The example is intended to demonstrate some of the situation managers' capabilities. This is a part of an application that helps a trade supervisor to detect situations that may require reactions.

4.1. Basic Events

Event	Arguments	Explanation
trade-start		start of the trading day
trade-end		end of the trading day
Buy	customer, stock, quantity	a buying transaction
Sell	customer, stock, quantity	a selling transaction

4.2. Situations

The situations are defined in a pseudo-code language.

- **Heavy-stock-demand**
  atleast 3 events of buy of the same stock within the same day such that for each event, buy.quantity > 100,000.

- **Heavy-customer-activity**
  atleast 3 events of sell or buy by the same customer within the same day, such that the quantity of the buy or sell in each event > 100,000.

- **Stock-Collapse**
  atleast 5 events of sell of the same stock within 2 hours period.

- **Customer-sell-after-buy**
  There is an event of buy followed by an event of sell, for the same customer and the same stock within the same day.

- **Speculative customer**
  For a customer there are atleast 5 situations of "Customer-sell-after-buy" within the same day (this is a nested situation, because it is based on another situation).

5. Conclusions

The situation manager described in this paper is a generic application development tool that enables fast development of reactive applications. It is currently being developed in the framework of two IBM products: Tivoli Event Console, and Lotus' Sametime. The situation manager has some unique features that have been discussed in this paper. Its meta-data is based on XML as a standard means of communication.

The main benefit of such an application development tool is that it simplifies the development process of reactive applications and in certain cases generates more efficient solutions with respect to other tools. Such an application development tool is an enabler to many types of e-business applications, which require automatic alerts, and actions to complex situations.

References

1. S.Chakravarthy & D. Mishra - Snoop: an expressive event specification language for active databases. Data & Knowledge Engineering, 13(3), Oct 1994.
2. C. Collet, T. Coupaye, T. Svenson - NAOS - Efficient and modular reactive capabilities in an object-oriented database system. In Proceedings. VLDB'94..
3. S. Gatziu, K. Dittrich - Detecting composite events in active database systems using Petri Nets. Proceedings IEEE RIDE'94.
4. N.H. Gehani, H.V. Jagadish, O. Shmueli - Composite event model specification in active databases: model and implementation. Proceedings VLDB'92.

5   G. Kappel, S. Rausch-Schott, W. Retschitzegger - A Tour on the TriGS active database system - architecture and implementation. Proceedings ACM SAC'98.

6.   D. Zimmer, R. Unland, A. Meckenstock - A General model for event specification in active database management systems. In Proceeding 5th DOOD, 1997.

7.   "VERITAS NerveCenter^tm" VERITAS Software.
     http://eval.veritas.com/webfiles/docs/ NCOverview.pdf

8.   K. R. Sheers - HP OpenView Event Correlation Services. HP Journal. Oct 1996.

9.   Nebula white paper: http://www.linmor.com/library/white_pa/nms_wp.html

10. S. Yemini et al.- High Speed and Robust Event Correlation. IEEE Communications Magazine, May 1996.

Author Index

Lecture Notes in Computer Science

For information about Vols. 1–2287
please contact your bookseller or Springer-Verlag

Vol. 2323: À. Frohner (Ed.), Object-Oriented Technology. Proceedings, 2001. IX, 225 pages. 2002.

Vol. 2324: T. Field, P.G. Harrison, J. Bradley, U. Harder (Eds.), Computer Performance Evaluation. Proceedings, 2002. XI, 349 pages. 2002.

Vol 2326: D. Grigoras, A. Nicolau, B. Toursel, B. Folliot (Eds.), Advanced Environments, Tools, and Applications for Cluster Computing. Proceedings, 2001. XIII, 321 pages. 2002.

Vol. 2327: H.P. Zima, K. Joe, M. Sato, Y. Seo, M. Shimasaki (Eds.), High Performance Computing. Proceedings, 2002. XV, 564 pages. 2002.

Vol. 2328: R. Wyrzykowski, J. Dongarra, M. Paprzycki, J. Waśniewski (Eds.), Parallel Processing and Applied Mathematics. Proceedings, 2001. XIX, 915 pages. 2002.

Vol. 2329: P.M.A. Sloot, C.J.K. Tan, J.J. Dongarra, A.G. Hoekstra (Eds.), Computational Science – ICCS 2002. Proceedings, Part I. XLI, 1095 pages. 2002.

Vol. 2330: P.M.A. Sloot, C.J.K. Tan, J.J. Dongarra, A.G. Hoekstra (Eds.), Computational Science – ICCS 2002. Proceedings, Part II. XLI, 1115 pages. 2002.

Vol. 2331: P.M.A. Sloot, C.J.K. Tan, J.J. Dongarra, A.G. Hoekstra (Eds.), Computational Science – ICCS 2002. Proceedings, Part III. XLI, 1227 pages. 2002.

Vol. 2332: L. Knudsen (Ed.), Advances in Cryptology – EUROCRYPT 2002. Proceedings, 2002. XII, 547 pages. 2002.

Vol. 2334: G. Carle, M. Zitterbart (Eds.), Protocols for High Speed Networks. Proceedings, 2002. X, 267 pages. 2002.

Vol. 2335: M. Butler, L. Petre, K. Sere (Eds.), Integrated Formal Methods. Proceedings, 2002. X, 401 pages. 2002.

Vol. 2336: M.-S. Chen, P.S. Yu, B. Liu (Eds.), Advances in Knowledge Discovery and Data Mining. Proceedings, 2002. XIII, 568 pages. 2002. (Subseries LNAI).

Vol. 2337: W.J. Cook, A.S. Schulz (Eds.), Integer Programming and Combinatorial Optimization. Proceedings, 2002. XI, 487 pages. 2002.

Vol. 2338: R. Cohen, B. Spencer (Eds.), Advances in Artificial Intelligence. Proceedings, 2002. X, 197 pages. 2002. (Subseries LNAI).

Vol. 2340: N. Jonoska, N.C. Seeman (Eds.), DNA Computing. Proceedings, 2001. XI, 392 pages. 2002.

Vol. 2342: I. Horrocks, J. Hendler (Eds.), The Semantic Web – ISCW 2002. Proceedings, 2002. XVI, 476 pages. 2002.

Vol. 2345: E. Gregori, M. Conti, A.T. Campbell, G. Omidyar, M. Zukerman (Eds.), NETWORKING 2002. Proceedings, 2002. XXVI, 1256 pages. 2002.

Vol. 2346: H. Unger, T. Böhme, A. Mikler (Eds.), Innovative Internet Computing Systems. Proceedings, 2002. VIII, 251 pages. 2002.

Vol. 2347: P. De Bra, P. Brusilovsky, R. Conejo (Eds.), Adaptive Hypermedia and Adaptive Web-Based Systems. Proceedings, 2002. XV, 615 pages. 2002.

Vol. 2348: A. Banks Pidduck, J. Mylopoulos, C.C. Woo, M. Tamer Ozsu (Eds.), Advanced Information Systems Engineering. Proceedings, 2002. XIV, 799 pages. 2002.

Vol. 2349: J. Kontio, R. Conradi (Eds.), Software Quality – ECSQ 2002. Proceedings, 2002. XIV, 363 pages. 2002.

Vol. 2350: A. Heyden, G. Sparr, M. Nielsen, P. Johansen (Eds.), Computer Vision – ECCV 2002. Proceedings, Part I. XXVIII, 817 pages. 2002.

Vol. 2351: A. Heyden, G. Sparr, M. Nielsen, P. Johansen (Eds.), Computer Vision – ECCV 2002. Proceedings, Part II. XXVIII, 903 pages. 2002.

Vol. 2352: A. Heyden, G. Sparr, M. Nielsen, P. Johansen (Eds.), Computer Vision – ECCV 2002. Proceedings, Part III. XXVIII, 919 pages. 2002.

Vol. 2353: A. Heyden, G. Sparr, M. Nielsen, P. Johansen (Eds.), Computer Vision – ECCV 2002. Proceedings, Part IV. XXVIII, 841 pages. 2002.

Vol. 2358: T. Hendtlass, M. Ali (Eds.), Developments in Applied Artificial Intelligence. Proceedings, 2002 XIII, 833 pages. 2002. (Subseries LNAI).

Vol. 2359: M. Tistarelli, J. Bigun, A.K. Jain (Eds.), Biometric Authentication. Proceedings, 2002. XII, 373 pages. 2002.

Vol. 2360: J. Esparza, C. Lakos (Eds.), Application and Theory of Petri Nets 2002. Proceedings, 2002. X, 445 pages. 2002.

Vol. 2361: J. Blieberger, A. Strohmeier (Eds.), Reliable Software Technologies – Ada-Europe 2002. Proceedings, 2002 XIII, 367 pages. 2002.

Vol. 2363: S.A. Cerri, G. Gouardères, F. Paraguaçu (Eds.), Intelligent Tutoring Systems. Proceedings, 2002. XXVIII, 1016 pages. 2002.

Vol. 2364: F. Roli, J. Kittler (Eds.), Multiple Classifier Systems. Proceedings, 2002. XI, 337 pages. 2002.

Vol. 2366: M.-S. Hacid, Z.W. Raś, D.A. Zighed, Y. Kodratoff (Eds.), Foundations of Intelligent Systems. Proceedings, 2002. XII, 614 pages. 2002. (Subseries LNAI).

Vol. 2367: J. Fagerholm, J. Haataja, J. Järvinen, M. Lyly. P. Råback, V. Savolainen (Eds.), Applied Parallel Computing. Proceedings, 2002. XIV, 612 pages. 2002.

Vol. 2368: M. Penttonen, E. Meineche Schmidt (Eds.), Algorithm Theory – SWAT 2002. Proceedings, 2002. XIV, 450 pages. 2002.

Vol. 2370: J. Bishop (Ed.), Component Deployment. Proceedings, 2002. XII, 269 pages. 2002.

Vol. 2374: B. Magnusson (Ed.), ECOOP 2002 – Object-Oriented Programming. XI, 637 pages. 2002.

Vol. 2382: A. Halevy, A. Gal (Eds.), Next Generation Information Technologies and Systems. Proceedings, 2002. VIII, 169 pages. 2002.

Vol. 2385: J. Calmet, B. Benhamou, O. Caprotti, L. Henocque, V. Sorge (Eds.), Artificial Intelligence, Automated Reasoning, and Symbolic Computation. Proceedings, 2002. XI, 343 pages. 2002. (Subseries LNAI).

Vol. 2386: E.A. Boiten, B. Möller (Eds.), Mathematics of Program Construction. Proceedings, 2002. X, 263 pages. 2002.

Vol. 2389: E. Ranchhod, N.J. Mamede (Eds.), Advances in Natural Language Processing. Proceedings, 2002. XII, 275 pages. 2002. (Subseries LNAI).